W9-AXS-131

Performance Notes by Greg P. Herriges

ISBN 1-4234-0777-6

HAL•LEONARD®
CORPORATION

7777 W. BLUEMOUND RD. P.O. BOX 13819 MILWAUKEE, WI 53213

Visit Hal Leonard Online at
www.halleonard.com

Table of Contents

Introduction

*W*elcome to *Acoustic Guitar Songs for Dummies*! Everything you need to play some of the greatest and most popular acoustic songs in rock, pop, and folk music is here, including note-for-note transcriptions of the songs, and performance notes that will help you through them — without the need for a music degree to understand the terms.

About This Book

The music in this book is in standard notation and *tablature* (also known as *tab*) — which is a diagram of the guitar strings with numbers that tell you what *frets* to play. I assume you know a little something about reading tab or music, but there's a guitar notation legend in the back that will help translate all those strange symbols and hieroglyphs that are the written language of guitar. I assume that you know a little bit about the guitar itself — like how to hold it, where the neck and frets are, how to tune it, basic chord strumming, and how to look cool while doing it. If you need a refresher course on guitar basics, please check out *Guitar For Dummies*, 2nd Edition by Mark Phillips and Jon Chappell (Wiley).

Also included in the back is a chart of common chords, so (for my own sake) I don't have to list them for every song. This is handy, because where a line of tablature gives you fret numbers, a chord diagram shows you the visual *shape* of the chord and which fingers to use.

New concepts are introduced as they appear, and referred back to when necessary. So you can skip around the book and pick out your favorite songs first, without missing out on essential information.

Here are some common guitar terms you'll see discussed throughout the book:

- **Barre chords** (chords in which one finger holds down two or more strings at once)
- **Open strings** (strings played in **open position**, without a finger on the fretboard)
- **Riffs** (repeating bits of music that are noteworthy enough to mention) and **licks** (common lead guitar tricks)
- **Strumming** (using a guitar pick to "fling" across the strings, often in a pattern of **downstrokes** — strumming down toward the earth — and **upstrokes** toward the sky)

Icons

In the margins of this book are several little icons that will help make your life easier:

A reason to stop and review advice that can prevent damage to your fingers, ears, or ego.

Optional bits, like solos, that may be too challenging for many guitarists, but are discussed anyway for the learned and/or ambitious "champion" players among you. In these discussions I'll have to throw lots of strange terms at you, all of which can be found in the guitar notation legend.

Details (like tunings and special techniques) that you need to know, and will probably need again in the future.

Notes about specific terms and concepts that are relevant but confusing to the layperson; sometimes it's just something I notice that's especially cool.

Shortcuts and suggested ways to get through some of the difficult bits without tangling your fingers.

Performance Notes

About a Girl (page 27)

Kurt Cobain and Nirvana led the *grunge* movement that booted glossy 1980s glam-rock and dance-pop off the charts with a more "real" look and sound. Even before Cobain's untimely death in 1994, Nirvana had blazed the trail for all modern rock musicians to follow. The cheeky band once called itself "a cross between Black Sabbath and the Bay City Rollers," but their punk-ish ballad "About a Girl" has a taste of '60s British Invasion pop à la the Kinks or the Beatles. This version is from *Unplugged in New York* (1994).

Alternate tuning

This song is in an alternative standard "rock tuning" used by great guitarists who like to make life difficult for guitar teachers. Each string is tuned down a half step lower than standard, making it easier to bend strings and belt out high vocals. Open strings, low to high, are E♭–A♭–D♭–G♭–B♭–E♭, but you don't need to tune down unless you plan to play with the recording.

Strumming

You'll be *strumming* through most of this song, which means that your picking hand is in constant motion, but not hitting the strings every time. Try holding down the first chord of the song (E5) and just strumming across the strings, "down–up–down–up–down–up–down–up." Keep repeating until you're in a steady rhythm, then try a new pattern: *miss* the strings on the first upstroke, so you're going "down, down–up–down–up–down–up" for every measure. That's the main strum pattern.

Muting

Those little Xs in the tab aren't Roman numerals — they show where certain strings are muted so they don't sound. The first E5 chord is played like an E minor, but the finger you use on the D string touches the G string next door, just enough to mute it. The same sort of thing happens on the G chord.

Barre chords

The chorus has some chords (C♯ and C) that would be best played with a barre. Just use your first finger on the A string, and lay your ring finger flat over the D, G, and B strings, all on the same fret. Likewise on the A chord, lay one finger over all three strings.

The guitar solo has some more barres, but first there's a *hammer-on* from fret 5 to 7 on the A string. Pick the first note but not the second; instead, just "hammer" your left-hand finger down to make the note sound. The rest of the solo is a lot of sliding around with one finger barring across the same strings as before. Repeat in variation, and have fun with it!

D.C. al Coda, short for ***Da Capo al Coda***, means "from head to tail," but has nothing to do with animal measurement. When you see it, go back to the beginning (or "head"), play (with ***no repeats***) until you see ***To Coda*** ⊕, skip to ⊕ Coda, and play to the end.

Across the Universe (page 31)

This spiritual ballad from the Beatles was played and sung by John Lennon and released on the *Let It Be* album (recorded 1969). You'll notice that it's in "rock tuning," as discussed in the song "About a Girl" (refer back for the notes if you like). Why is it tuned down? Because Lennon's original recording of the song was slowed down in production to accommodate the chorus vocals in the background!

Hybrid picking

Most of "Across the Universe" is strummed with a pick, except for the first measure, which is picked *hybrid* (with pick and fingers). The most efficient way to play it is to pluck the upper notes with index and middle fingers while the pick hits the open D string, but any combo of pick and digits will do — as long as you're able to jump into strumming at the F♯m in the next measure. Technically speaking, what you're doing in measure 1 is descending the D major scale in *dyads* (two-note chords).

The rest of the song is just chords and a pick. The main strum pattern is simply "down, down, down, down–up," repeated. You'll be hitting some barre chords (F♯m and Gm) in addition to the tasteful bottom-of-the-neck variety. (Refer to the chart of common chords if necessary.)

Time warp

Notice the alternating measures of 5/4, 4/4, and 2/4 in the verse? This is referred to as *alternating time signatures*, and it's really just the music transcriber's way of dealing with extra beats that can't fit into the 4/4 box. The 5/4 measure gives the singer an extra beat to breathe, and the 2/4–4/4 measures allow for a pause before the chorus. (You'll see more of the Beatles' time warping in "Blackbird.")

D.S. ("Dal Segno") *al Coda* means "from the sign to the tail." In musician's English, it means stop, go back and look for the sign 𝄋. Play from there to **To Coda** ⊕, skip to ⊕ **Coda**, and play to the end. On this song there are two codas, played in sequence.

Angie (page 36)

The Rolling Stones' #1 single from their 1973 *Goats Head Soup* album was a rare acoustic ballad for the legendary rock 'n' roll band. Guitarist Keith Richards lets his "inner balladeer" shine on this one.

Harmonics

The opening note of "Angie" is the perfect intro to the string overtones known as *harmonics* or "chimes." *Lightly* touch the A string on fret 12 — right over the twelfth fret bar, *not* between the frets as if you're playing a "regular" note. (Don't push down on the string!) Pick the string, and you should get a bell-like tone that rings out after you remove your finger. Harmonics like this can be played on all strings, most easily at frets 12, 7, and 5.

Chords

This is one of those songs that is best learned by finding all the chord positions first, then figuring out all the picking and fills. With that in mind, note the cool position of the E7 chord: an open low string and some very close notes on top. The Gsus4 and Fsus4 are *partial* barre chords, both played with your first finger laid across the B and E strings. This is how Keith plays barre chords throughout the tune, allowing him to ignore what guitar teachers always tell us about keeping the thumb on the back of the neck at all times.

Playing in the verse and interlude is casual and varied. Some fills are *improvised* (played off the cuff), and some recur like clockwork. The most important bit comes after the line "Angie"

— a bluesy riff made up of *double stops* (two-note chords played on adjacent strings). You only need two fingers to play it, barring each pair of strings.

Strumming in the chorus and bridge is in a straight-ahead pattern; the best way to play it is "down, down, down, down–up." When you strum those partial barres, be sure to mute the low E and A strings so they don't muddy up your chords.

Annie's Song (page 42)

This timeless love song from John Denver is destined to live on forever in wedding ceremonies — and for good reason! The lyrical, harplike guitar complements the poetic theme of undying love. In fact, it contains the same harmonic themes as some of the classical wedding standards by Pachelbel and Bach! "Annie's Song" was first a Gold single from the 1974 album *Back Home Again*.

Fingerpickin' good

Ready for some fingerpicking? Good. "Annie's Song" could be covered by an incredibly fast and accurate pick, but fingers are what's called for. Most of the song consists of *arpeggios* (chords played one note at a time), so our strategy is to use the thumb for each bass note, and the next three fingers, one at a time, to *arpeggiate* the chords. Try this on the G chord in the first measure of the verse: thumb, index, middle, ring, middle. Let your fingers follow each other like waves on a "sleepy blue ocean," and repeat until you have it steady. Then try the chord changes, one at a time.

The one-finger-per-string approach works for the verse, but may be a challenge in the intro (unless you're a classical guitar maestro). Use any combo of fingers that works for you — thumb, index, and middle are fine.

Partial chords

You can navigate the verse chord changes with a little more ease by fretting only the parts of the chords that you need — in other words, just play the bass note and the top three notes of each chord, instead of the full textbook versions.

Instead of the standard D chord fingering, use the secret *For Dummies* alternative: put your middle finger on fret 3 of the B string, and a first-finger barre on fret 2 across the three bottom strings. That puts you in position to play the F♯m/C♯ that comes next, and the Bm barre chord that follows.

The end of the verse is just a variation of the intro, played with the one-finger-per-string technique; just pluck the top note along with the bass note this time, classical-style.

Behind Blue Eyes (page 46)

Behind the blue eyes and smashed electric guitars of the Who's Pete Townshend, there lurks a masterful balladeer with acoustic guitar chops that go on forever. "Behind Blue Eyes" was a single from the groundbreaking album *Who's Next* (1971). Equal amounts of delicacy and angst make up this two-sided tune.

Picking

The meat of this song consists of *arpeggios* galore, using a straight up-the-chord-and-down-the-chord approach. (Remember, arpeggios are chords played one note at a time.) Generally, use downstrokes when you're ascending the chord (playing from low to high, pitchwise) and upstrokes when descending — but this is flexible. In Townshend fashion, the pattern is rarely played the same twice, and little chord bursts are thrown in for dramatic effect. As always, the best advice is to learn the chords first, then the picking and frills.

Strumming

The chorus has a basic strum pattern: down, down, down–up — but this is varied as well. Just remember to keep the groove with your right hand, constantly moving "down–up–down–up–down–up–down–up" but missing the strings strategically; in other words, play imaginary strums when the strings aren't played.

The chorus ending builds up to a quick flourish of strumming — down–up–down–up (within the space of half a beat!) — with a quick snap of the wrist to set up the next verse and the middle section.

The guitar solos are clearly not for acoustic, so either break out your Les Paul or play the chords from the middle verse, including a Bm barre chord, in a powerful "down, up–down" pattern (muting the chords wherever your see a rest). Then comes the climactic power-chord section (with more of those strumming flourishes), and it's back to picking arpeggios for the outro.

Best of My Love (page 52)

An acoustic collection wouldn't be complete without a nice, relaxed California country-rock ballad. This #1 hit from the Eagles' 1974 album *On the Border* is tastefully strummed by guitarist Glenn Frey.

Inversions

The first C chord has a G note on the bottom (instead of the usual C), making it an *inversion* — a chord with a bass note that is different from its title. Here it makes the chord sound extra full, and it's a big word that you can use to impress your jazz-musician friends.

This is a vocal tune first, and straight-ahead strumming supports the vocals. The hooky intro and verse pattern is based on two chord shapes — C and F — that complement each other nicely, alternating open and fretted notes with each change. The basic strum pattern is "down–up–down–up (pause) up–down–up." As in all strumming, keep "strumming the air" through the pause, so the rhythm is consistent.

Barre chords

You'll be traveling up the neck a bit to play the barre chords in this song. The Em7 is played with your first finger over fret 7, and the following Dm7 is the same thing two frets down. Watch for a quick jump down to F/G at the pause. This is best played as a full barre, with the index finger over all six strings and the ring finger covering the low G note. Similarly in the second verse, hit a full G7 barre and *arpeggiate* (there's that word again) tastefully.

On the chorus, notice how Frey plays a C chord on the first "whoa," and opens it up to a Cmaj7 the second time through. Tasty! The bridge contains more tasteful minor and major 7th chords, and the rest of the tune is a piece of cake.

Blackbird (page 58)

Throw away your guitar pick! It's time for some fingerpickin' (grinnin' is optional) on a Beatles classic, originally performed solo by Paul McCartney on *The White Album* (recorded in 1968), with some very unique fingerstyle techniques.

Alternating time signatures: Let's do the time warp again

Don't be intimidated by the fact that this song starts out with a new beat count for every measure. The Beatles often did this sort of thing, not just to confuse music teachers, but to accommodate vocal lines that fell outside the 4/4 box. No one ever sat down and said, "I think I'll write a song with a measure of 3/4, then 4/4, then 2/4." It's a natural thing, and it's better felt than analyzed.

Picking or strumming?

You can pick this with thumb, index, and middle, or just thumb and index fingers, depending on which ones cooperate. What you see right away in the second measure is a kind of neo-banjo picking style, in which the index finger *strums* two notes at a time (down–up) between thumb-picked notes. (You'll see something similar, called *Travis picking*, in "Dust in the Wind.")

Chords

Chords are played with a constant open G note inside them, so make sure your fretting fingers don't trample on it while you switch chords. And yes, there is a lot of chord movement, but it's all very logical and finger-friendly, roughly following the outlines of a G major scale. What's more, you only ever need to fret two notes at one time — and there are no barre chords!

I've already discussed *D.S. al Coda* and other secret Italian phrases (see "About a Girl"), but double codas and signs? **D.S. al Coda 1** means the same as usual, but **To Coda 1 ⊕** will be your next prompt. But wait, there's more! Play from ⊕ **Coda 1** to **D.S.S. al Coda 2**, find the double sign (✶✶), play until **To Coda 2 ⊕**, and skip to ⊕ **Coda 2**. Now you can play to the end. If all these shortcuts didn't exist, one song would last about 50 pages.

Crazy Little Thing Called Love (page 63)

The acoustic guitar isn't all about weepy love songs or pickin' and grinnin'. Queen's #1 hit "Crazy Little Thing Called Love" (from the 1980 album *The Game*) proves it with a swinging strum pattern in the style of early rock 'n' roll.

Swing it!

When you play with a *shuffle* (or *swing*) *feel*, a pair of eighth notes turns into something completely different (see the tempo indicator at the start of the song). But don't sweat the notation; just think of it as playing more like a heartbeat. Unless you're a robot, your heart doesn't beat in straight eighth notes; it has a long beat and a short beat. When you strum or pick with a shuffle feel, the downstroke is usually longer than the upstroke. It's a natural feel that is big in rock 'n' roll and blues, but used universally.

Strumming

Get into strumming mode, and let your hand play an imaginary strum whenever you don't hit the strings. The intro pattern is played "down–up–down–up, up–down–up," missing one down-stroke on purpose. The chords are just a D, and a D with your pinky added on fret 3.

Chords are mostly in open position, except for B♭ and F barre chords in the bridge. Then comes a fun break that's easier than it might look. Disregarding the crazy time signatures (7/8 and 5/8), you can count to four all the way through this descending *chromatic* run. (Chromatic notes are one half step, or one fret, away from each other.) Then you play the following E note *staccato* (short), by lifting your finger off the string — but not off the fretboard — after each time you pick. Next comes a "walk" down the C major scale, back into the verse.

"Crazy Little Thing Called Love" has two codas, but one *segno* (✶). **D.S. al Coda 1** and **D.S. al Coda 2** both send you to the same place, but you still have to look for separate directions for coda 1 and coda 2.

While your friend with a telecaster (and ideally, a pompadour) plays the solo, see if you can follow the accompanying chords. The solo ends just like the bridge, and the rest of the song is a cool breeze, daddy-o.

Drive (page 67)

Do acoustic guitars and turntable scratches mix? Incubus proved that under the right circumstances in the right song, they belong together. "Drive," off their 1999 CD *Make Yourself*, combines acoustic sounds and a modern groove with a lyrical melody and inspiring words — modern rock at its finest, played by guitarist Mike Einziger.

Pick 'n' strum

This has a combo pick-and-strum pattern, a little different from what you've seen elsewhere. It involves picking a bass note and a middle chord tone, then strumming the top of the chord ("down, up" or "down, down–up"). The pattern varies a bit from one chord to the next. Unlike most strum patterns, your hand doesn't have to be in constant motion playing "ghost strums," but it helps to think of it as if you're alternate picking sixteenth notes. Stop the strings wherever you see rests; slapping your hand down to mute them actually helps keep you in the groove.

Half-open chords

The nice, open sound of the chords is a result of open strings that are played within them. For example, the Em would normally be barred on the seventh fret, but with the open G and E string it sounds more transparent. Open strings abound throughout this tune, making it important to keep your fretting fingers out of their way. Some position shifting is necessary: after playing the first Em chord, shift so that your middle finger is on fret 7, and the rest of your fingers line up to create the Em9. Continue finding the best ways to navigate the chords throughout the tune.

Let your friend with an electric guitar, overdrive, and a Leslie speaker cabinet take the solo, while you play through the verse pattern. The rest of the song is more of the same tasteful, half-open pickin' 'n' strummin'.

Dust in the Wind (page 73)

Question: Is "Dust in the Wind" the ultimate progressive rock ballad or the perfect introduction to country-style fingerpicking?
Answer: Yes and yes!

In the 1970s, Kansas was one of few American bands to take the path of British prog-rockers like Yes and Emerson, Lake and Palmer. Known for classically-based arrangements, introspective lyrics, and songs of epic length, they also got quite lyrical in tunes like this, penned by guitarist/songwriter Kerry Livgren for the 1977 album *Point of Know Return*.

Travis picking 101

Not only is this a beautiful tune, it also gives the pickin' fingers a chance to show their stuff. What you'll be doing here is *Travis picking*, a style named after the country and western legend Merle Travis (who was never a member of Kansas). Merle discovered a bouncy way to play two or more parts on the guitar at the same time. Travis picking might sound like acrobatics — and sometimes it is — but not in "Dust in the Wind," which is more song than flash.

First, get your picking hand into the Travis groove. Put your left hand in a C chord (the first chord of the song) and leave it there. Now try playing just the bass part from the first measure with your right-hand thumb; bounce it between the A (5th) and D (4th) strings. When you've got this down, start adding your fingers. Your middle finger plays the B (2nd) string; your index finger plays the G (3rd string). Play the first half of measure 1, over and over, until your neighbors start complaining.

Picking notation

See the picking notation under the staff? Remember these secret Italian codes: *p* (*pulgar*) = thumb; *m* (*medio*) = middle finger; and *i* (*indice*) = index. Notice that your thumb and middle finger pluck together at the start of each two-beat phrase.

Now you can move your other hand! In the intro you're sticking with two basic chord positions, C and Am, and only the notes on the B string move. It's just a matter of picking up and setting down the right fingers at the right time on that string, until the verse. Then the chord positions move around, and the picking pattern stays pretty much the same all through the song but changes strings accordingly. Sometimes your picking thumb has to jump a string, as on the G chord in the verse. Take it very slowly at first, and work it up to speed when you have all the chord changes down.

Fly to the Angels *(page 78)*

An acoustic/electric anthem from the school of glam rock, "Fly to the Angels" was single number two from Slaughter's first album, *Stick It to Ya*, in 1990. Coming into the hard-rock scene just as 1980s-style glam was dying out, the band's music had a Led Zeppelin-esque sophistication that kept it on the charts through the grunge revolution of the early '90s. This song features the pickin' and riffin' of singer/guitarist Mark Slaughter and lead guitarist Tim Kelly.

Another tuning

"Rock tuning" didn't rock enough for Slaughter — they tuned everything down a *whole* step lower than standard. The notes, low to high, are D–G–C–F–A–D. Tuning down adds extra crunch and low end to riffy tunes like this one. You don't have to tune down to learn the tune, though.

The intro descends the neck over the open A string. Fret the licks just before the verse with two fingers, sliding from one position to the next. The verse progression is a common one, but with uncommon open strings within the chords. Find the chords first; start with ring, middle, and index fingers on frets 3, 2, and 1, and move down from there.

The pre-chorus and chorus

The pre-chorus straightens out the same chords, and the chorus adds some very fun riffs, doubled on electric guitar and bass. On those quarter-step *bends*, make sure you only bend the string slightly after you pick it.

The powerful interlude is a variation on the chorus, now played with descending *dyads* (two-note chords) with open strings added for extra thickness. There's a lot of riffing happening in between; the best advice is to try and play everything evenly, alternate picking (down–up–down–up) wherever possible. On the first ending, do your usual quarter-step bend, but pull it off to the open string — just let it go without picking again. This happens again later.

All these parts repeat with breakdowns here and there, and the ending is the intro repeated. A rock anthem if ever there was one!

Free Fallin' *(page 85)*

Tom Petty tastefully strums the acoustic guitar on this #1 hit from his unbelievably huge 1989 album, *Full Moon Fever*. Co-written by another household name, musician/producer (and fellow Traveling Wilbury) Jeff Lynne, the song combines a simple acoustic riff with off-beat lyrics and lush backing vocals — the makings of a mega-hit.

The capo

You already learned one meaning of *capo* (see "About a Girl"), but the "Capo I" shown at the beginning of the music has nothing to do with D.C.s and codas. It refers to the bar device you clamp on the fretboard to raise the pitch of all the strings. Put it on the first fret, and the "head" (of the fretboard) is I. The capo can be bought at any music store or, in desperate times, made from a pencil and a rubber band!

Capo chords

When you put on a capo, reality changes. The fret after the capo becomes fret 1, and it's best to think of all chords accordingly. On the sheet music, the chord symbols in parentheses (E) are in capo reality, and the ones listed above them reside in the parallel universe you just left behind.

Here's the suggested general strum pattern for the verse: "down, up–down, down, up–down, down, down–up / down, down, down, up–down, down, down–up." The hand should bounce as if you're playing sixteenth notes, to keep the rhythm. Learn it, then forget about strokes and beats and just feel it!

Bonus material

In the interlude, the electric guitar part is included. Play with all downstrokes, and *palm mute* — rest the edge of your picking hand right where the strings end at the guitar bridge. Now play these *power chords*, sliding between them as shown.

Use your ring finger to fret on the E chord, so you can easily slide up to the next chord on fret 5.

I'd Love to Change the World (page 90)

The legendary guitarist Alvin Lee has worn many musical hats, most notably as the frontman for the prolific British blues-rock band Ten Years After. Their 1971 album *A Space in Time* featured their biggest hit, "I'd Love to Change the World," a sort of anti-establishment hippie anthem for the Vietnam era.

Our favorite word

This song is built largely on chord *arpeggios* (chords played one note at a time!) with *chromatic* passing tones. It's always best to learn the chord shapes first, then get into the picking.

Starting on the Em chord, use your middle and ring fingers on fret 2. That makes it easy to do the following chromatic run, one finger per fret. (Chromatic notes are just as you see — one fret, or half step, away from each other.) Then you get chromatic on the A string. After the B7, you're in position to start over.

Power chords

A chord labeled with a 5 after it, as in the verse, is known as a *power chord* (or simply a "five" chord), and it owes that distinction to the fact that it's neither major nor minor. It only contains two notes, the 1st and the 5th (and higher octaves of both), and is missing the all-important 3rd — the note that determines the mood: major or minor, happy or sad. Without that note, you get a "powerful" sound.

The verse gets into rhythmic strumming and "dead notes" — for all the Xs in the tab, lay your fretting hand over the strings and strum for a percussive "chick-a-chick."

Iris (page 95)

The Goo Goo Dolls were first a punkish alternative rock band, but their less-punkish alternative ballads made them a household name. Their sixth album, *Dizzy up the Girl* (1998), produced the breakthrough hit "Iris," also included on the *City of Angels* soundtrack for extra-added success. Singer/guitarist Johnny Rzeznik strums and croons on this swaying, melancholy tune in a very alternative tuning.

Goo tuning

This song is in a very "open" tuning that allows for a wall of upper *drone* strings. Tune your low E string down to B, A down to D (leave the D string as-is), G down to D, B up to D, and high E down to — you guessed it, D. Make sure you don't strum too hard, or the very floppy low strings will sound sharp and embarrass you in front of whomever you're serenading.

Do the math

What's with the time signatures? Don't fret — just feel it, but notice that most of the tune is in a "six" feel (12/8), and it straightens out to "four" (8/8) during instrumental sections.

Those open D strings ring out hypnotically throughout this tune. Aside from the intro and interlude, you only need one finger to play this song! Except for muting purposes, one finger moves while open strings ring. On the verse, hit the moving low notes and then *sweep pick* the three D notes, all with upstrokes.

Mutes

In the chorus, mute the second-lowest string (which we would normally call the A string) while you strum. You can do this with the edge of your fretting finger, just touching the mute string while it frets the string next door.

The stops in the interlude are played like: "down–up–down–up (mute), down–up–down–up (mute), down, down," and so on. Mute by laying your picking hand on the strings while releasing pressure on the frets.

Landslide *(page 104)*

The first incarnation of Fleetwood Mac formed in 1967, but the band didn't reach the height of popularity until the mid-'70s, beginning with the release of the 1975 album *Fleetwood Mac*. "Landslide" was one of many confessional ballads dealing with the band's turbulent inner relationships. Guitarist Lindsay Buckingham *Travis picks* this song written and sung (for him) by Stevie Nicks.

More travis picking

Refer to "Dust in the Wind" for the lowdown on this very cool, banjo-like fingerpicking style. The technique is exactly the same, and can easily be applied to "Landslide."

Tune for the capo

Refer back to "Free Fallin'" and you'll know what "Capo III" means. Sometimes, putting on or taking off a capo makes the strings go out of tune (especially when the capo is on higher frets). Remember to check your tuning, and adjust if necessary, whenever you attach or remove the capo.

If you already know "Dust in the Wind," you have a head start. Learn these chord positions first, then the pickin'. Repeat the first two measures until you have it down in a steady rhythm.

In the chorus, all you need to fret the G chord is your ring finger on fret 3 (or literally, 6). That leaves your other digits prepared to nail the upcoming D with an F# bass note. Don't miss the first appearance of the high E string on the next chord! Play the verse pattern through the guitar solo, and note the little pause toward the end of the song.

The song is in the key of C (in relation to the capo), but it ends cleverly on an Am chord — what we call an *unresolved* ending, leaving us wanting more!

Layla *(page 111)*

"See if you can spot this one," said Eric Clapton, before launching into this acoustic rendition of a classic 1970 hit from his days with Derek and the Dominos. This "shuffle" version, from Clapton's 1992 *Unplugged* album, is quite different from the original. It has a swinging groove and some formidable blues-inspired acoustic solos, played off the cuff by "Slowhand."

Shuffle feel

"Layla" is played here with a *shuffle*, or *swing feel*, in which eighth notes are not really eighth notes. Confused? Refer to "Crazy Little Thing Called Love" for a full briefing on swingin'.

The song has two sections — verse and chorus — and all other parts are based on the same patterns or variations of them. The intro, same as the chorus, starts with a *hammer-on* from open A to fret 3, then *power chords*. The same pattern keeps playing under the intro solo.

The verse is full of 7th and minor 7th chords, most of them barres. Strum in a casual pattern, roughly "down, down, down–up–down–up," until the straight-ahead C–D move. Don't sweat the fast chord switching; those chords are *parallel* — each pair is just a different position on the same fret (or open).

Solos

All the solos in this song are optional. You're not expected to navigate the fretboard like EC, but just in case . . .

The intro solo and main solo are in D minor, with a lot of position shifting, *hammer-ons* and *pull-offs*, *vibrato*, and *slides*. Clapton plays in groups of *triplets*, dividing one beat into three (and subdividing) — but don't think about it mathematically; it's really just part of the shuffle feel.

The main solo is all over the neck, starting with those cool quarter-step bends; push both strings *upward* after you pick them. Then comes a classic blues lick courtesy of Robert Johnson; pick a pair of notes *(double stops)* and quickly slide them up a fret while you keep picking. Repeat in groups of three. Improvised blues-isms continue throughout the solo and at song's end — consult the notation legend and the spirit of Mr. Johnson for guidance.

Leaving on a Jet Plane *(page 118)*

I already explored the balladeering of John Denver with "Annie's Song." Here's another example, as covered by folk music legends Peter, Paul & Mary — back in the days when Denver was a relatively unknown songwriter! "Leaving on a Jet Plane" was on Peter, Paul & Mary's 1967 release, *Album 1700,* and has been covered by many other artists since then.

More shuffling around

It's swing time again! "Leaving on a Jet Plane" is played with a *shuffle feel*, à la "Crazy Little Thing Called Love" and "Layla." Refer to those songs for the lowdown on shuffling.

With the shuffle feel, your strumming pattern is: "down, down–up, up–down–up." Remember that to stay in the groove, your hand should be in constant up–and–down motion like a metronome, but "missing" the strings at selective times.

Supportive strumming

Peter, Paul & Mary are a vocal group above all else, and your job here is to support those vocals with this strum pattern, which never changes in this song. (If your hand won't stop strumming the pattern, consult a specialist.) That said, the chords are not all run-of-the-mill. In the intro and verse, you're just moving one chord shape back and forth over an open A string to create jazzy voicings. Watch for occasional barre chords throughout the song (see "About a Girl" for an intro to those).

A groovy twist toward the end of the chorus: E, Esus4, and D chords — really just moving variations on a D chord shape, all played over A in the bass. To play this without a bass player, just let the open A string ring out under the chords for that whole measure.

The song is officially in the key of A, but it ends cleverly on an E chord — what we call an *unresolved* ending, very much in the spirit of the lyrics! ("I don't know when I'll be back again.")

Love of a Lifetime (page 125)

Underneath the hairspray and behind the power chords, there were sensitive songsmiths. Another band that prospered at the end of the "glam rock" era and lived on to tell about it, FireHouse are not members of the firefighters' union, but makers of rock ballads like "Love of a Lifetime," a Top 10 hit from their self-titled debut album in 1990. Guitarist Bill Leverty juggles acoustic and electric.

It's "rock tuning" again! All strings are tuned down half a step, but you can play it in standard. (See "About a Girl" for more explanation on the tuning.)

The song has three basic sections: verse, pre-chorus, and chorus. Most of the acoustic playing is based on those good old chord *arpeggios*, best played with an economy picking style. Take the first G5 chord: pick "up the chord" with downstrokes, but play the top note and all descending notes with upstrokes.

Make a quick review of chords. Notice that the Em chord is played at fret 7, and you jump back down to the bottom of the neck for the Dsus2. There are convenient pauses in the picking pattern that allow you to hit an open string and rearrange your fingers for the next chord during the pause.

Composite arrangement

In the pre-chorus, the acoustic and electric parts are combined, giving you the electric notes at the end of each measure in case you want to combine the parts. Strum down for every change in the pre-chorus, then pick the single notes. A little position shifting is necessary between the parts.

In the chorus, what you see on the page are the electric guitar *power chords*. The acoustic picks in the same style as the verse, but you could also strum the chords for extra momentum, especially if you're playing by the campfire.

The key change

Break out the lighters! After the guitar solo comes a *key change*, the true mark of a rock anthem. Now you're in the key of A, and all chords are *transposed* up one step, or the distance of two frets. Finally, you reach the *ritard* (slow down!) and resolution to wrap it all up. Just listen to those screams.

Maggie May (page 132)

The unmistakable grit of Rod Stewart's voice, mixed with a signature acoustic sound, make for this classic ballad. His breakthrough #1 hit from the #1 album *Every Picture Tells a Story* (1971), "Maggie May" was co-written by Stewart and Martin Quittenton, who shares guitar duties with Ron Wood.

Intro to the intro

The opening is an optional mini-tune from the album version, not part of the "Maggie May" you hear on the radio. If you choose to, play it with your fingers, classical-style. Two- and three-note *pull-offs* abound.

In the intro to the song proper, you shift chords on top of an open D string *drone*, in the style of British folk music. Heads up for a quick chord change going into the verse: Bm and G are both barre chords, played *staccato* (short). Lift your fretting hand off the fretboard (but not off the strings) to stop the ringing after you hit each chord, for a punctuating "bump, bump."

Strumming

The main strum pattern in the verse couldn't be more straight-ahead: "down, down, down–up–down." Notice that the second and third times through the verse, the chord fingerings are slightly different, as shown in fill 1 and fill 2, the boxes at the bottom of the page — the differences are slight, so if you miss the fills, just carry on and don't look back.

Solos

Try the guitar solos if you like — they're electric, but could easily transfer to acoustic if you've got a rhythm player. Otherwise, play the chords shown with the main strum pattern. The solos are played in the D major *pentatonic scale*, with lots of *slurs*, *slides*, and *bends*. (Tip: when you bend lower strings like this, *pull* the string down toward the floor for extra leverage.)

Same deal with the mandolin solo. (The chords are roughly the same as in the song intro.) This is an example of *tremolo picking*, in which you pick single notes in a constant "down–up–down–up" motion. On the outro, play the chords shown with the main strum pattern, or keep up the mando pickin'.

Night Moves *(page 141)*

Nothing like some good old Midwest American rock 'n' roll. Ann Arbor, Michigan native Bob Seger reminisced about good old Midwestern teenage lust on the title track from his 1976 album *Night Moves*, a Top 10 hit in 1977. Seger and Pete Carr were the acoustic strummers in the Silver Bullet Band.

Capo 1

Capo 1? That's right. Clamp the capo on fret 1, effectively moving everything up one fret. Refer to "Free Fallin'" to learn the difference between the guitar capo and the cranium.

"Night Moves" is built around a three-part structure (verse, chorus, and bridge), but with a middle verse section that breaks down to just voice and guitar in *free time* (no counting!). In the main pattern, strums alternate rhythmically with muted strings — play the chord, then slap your hand down, but not too hard, for a pattern something like "down–up–X–up–down –up–X–up–," and so on. Play steadily but casually (the pattern isn't necessarily the same each time).

Notice that the C chord is a thick *inversion* — see "Best of My Love" for a full explanation.

Strumming

The strumming opens up on the chorus, played more spaciously with chords on the *off beats*. Things stay straight-ahead until just before the free-time verse, introduced by country-style *hammer-ons*. Then it's straight chord strums to mark the changes, each strummed with a graceful "fling."

The main strum pattern comes in with another country-style lick: a hammer-on from the open A string to fret 2, followed by a quick upstroke on the open D. From then on it's heavy strumming through to the climactic chord progression that ends the song. Thank you, Michigan!

Norwegian Wood (This Bird Has Flown) *(page 150)*

An English pop band plays Indian sitar in a song about Norwegian lumber. That's what I call eclectic! You won't be learning the sitar here, but you will get familiar with John Lennon's rhythmic strumming on this groundbreaking hit from the Beatles' 1965 album, *Rubber Soul*.

Capo II

I bring back the *capo*, not to make your life difficult, but because it's an essential part of this song. Put it on fret 2, and that becomes your frame of reference for guitar reality. (See "Free Fallin'" for more on the capo.)

The *6/8 time signature* has a kind of natural shuffle to it. There are six beats to every measure, and an eighth note gets one beat. In "Norwegian Wood," it lends a kind of Celtic folk air to the proceedings.

The straight D chord

The intro, verse, and interlude are all based around a straight D chord with a moving melody beneath it. The intro and interlude pattern includes some slightly tricky moves: while you hold and strum the D chord, use your pinky to hammer fret 4 on the G string. You'll need it again to hold fret 4 on the D string while letting the other strings ring — make sure it's out of the way. These first moves are omitted in the verse to make room for the vocal.

The bridge introduces a classic Beatles device: take the main chord and turn it minor, changing the mood to a darker tone, then back to major (bringing it back into the light) for the next verse.

The rest of the song is more of the same, a fun excursion into a world without chairs.

Patience *(page 154)*

A little patience, a lot of hair, and a cigarette dangling from your lips, and you'll be ready to play this song. (Just kidding; don't smoke — your hair might catch fire.) Guns N' Roses came along at the end of the glam-rock era, offering more of a gritty classic rock sound that helped win over listeners who appreciated their authenticity. "Patience," from the gigantic 1988 album *G N' R Lies*, shows their acoustic side, with guitarists Slash & Izzy Stradlin' doing the honors. Both rhythm and lead guitar are covered in a composite arrangement. I discuss the rhythm guitar first, then the optional lead.

It's "rock tuning" again! Refer to "About a Girl" for an explanation.

Rhythm guitar

Three basic sections (verse/chorus/outro) are varied throughout. The verse and chorus pattern establish themselves in the intro. The main strum pattern is a basic, "down, down–up, up–down–up," with ghost strums in between. The chorus pattern is played under the guitar solo. On the outro, a D chord morphs into a D/F♯ *inversion* — you're free to use your thumb to fret the low E string if you like (we won't tell anyone).

The lead guitar on this song contains a lot of *bends*, which don't always come easily on acoustic guitar. Don't chew up your fingers! Put extra light strings on your guitar if you want to tackle these parts.

Lead guitar

Lead guitar throughout this tune is played mostly in the G major *pentatonic scale* (a five-note major scale), with some *chromatic* and minor notes. This is acoustic guitar played like electric, with *bends*, *dyads*, and *vibrato* galore. The solo starts in what's known as a *blues box* between frets 8 and 12, then jumps down to another box at the bottom of the neck. Check the notation legend for lick decoding, and be patient with yourself!

Pink Houses *(page 165)*

Welcome to America's Heartland! John "the artist formerly known as Cougar" Mellencamp paints a vivid picture of small-town America in "Pink Houses," a Top 10 hit from the affirmative album *Uh-Huh* (1983). Guitarists Larry Crane and Mike Wanchic capture the musical spirit of Americana.

Another new tuning

Hold it! This tune is in open G tuning, an old blues tradition that was popularized in rock by Keith Richards of the Stones. Tune your low E string down to D, the A string down to G, and the high E string down to D. You're now ready to rock 'n' roll. Notice that some common chords have a different shape than usual in this tuning, but it allows you to play full barre chords with one finger!

The pickup

"Pink Houses" begins with a *pickup measure*, the first note coming in on the "and" of beat 4. If you play "correctly," you'll start with an upstroke, so the following notes and chords line up.

After that upstroke, slide up to fret 4, hit the open G, then strum "down, down–up–down–up, down, down–up, up–down (up)." (As always, take strum patterns as general guidelines.)

Verse strumming is straight ahead, until the F chord and a muted strum before the C *anticipates* the next beat. Notice that the first chorus has chords at the bottom of the neck, and the next chorus has full, one-finger barres — along with some nice *pull-offs*.

Now back up a bit, and notice the half-step *bend* just after coda 1. Bend it downward (toward the floor), but not too far — just enough so that it matches the pitch of the note one fret higher.

Signs *(page 173)*

Originally a hippie-hit in 1971 by Five Man Electrical Band, "Signs" was covered by the American rock band Tesla on their third album, the live *Five Man Acoustical Jam* (1990). Is the album name a coincidence? Nay. Guitarists Frank Hannon and Tommy Skeoch rock through this version with solid strumming and tasty licks.

There are three essential parts to learn (verse, chorus, and bridge), and within each there's a lot of chord movement. Give the chords a once-over, then jump in. The intro is a recurring hook, with an embellished D chord and a quick pair of passing chords leading to the verse.

The verse starts with *arpeggio* picking on a C chord with a descending bass note. The groovy fill just before the strumming is an outline of a D chord. Chords in the verse change a lot, but they are standard chords, played on the beat. The chorus is another story, with some chords coming in at upbeats with upstrokes (*anticipating* the beat ahead). On the second ending, notice the little off-beat thing that takes you into the bridge; this is a *chromatic* (one-note-at-a-time) riff, played in all upstrokes. Stop the strings between every pick to make it clean and tight.

Guitar solo

Got light strings? You need them for this solo, full of electric guitar-style *bends* on an "acoustical" instrument. It's played mostly in the D major *pentatonic scale* (a five-note scale in a major key), shifting between two "box" positions at frets 7 and 10. Within that there's *vibrato*, *slides*, *pull-offs*, and a classic bend trick: bend the B string at fret 10, hold that bend while you pick fret 10 on the next string, then pick the original bent string and release it back down. That's rock 'n' roll! As always, consult the guitar notation legend for technical explanations.

Space Oddity *(page 178)*

David Bowie captured the feeling of spaceflight (or perhaps a more psychological kind of trip) with this breakthrough hit, released in 1969 to coincide with the Apollo 11 moon landing, and appearing later on the album of the same title. The multi-talented singer/songwriter played acoustic guitar on the original.

Odyssey of chords

From the opening chord, you know this isn't your run-of-the-mill pop song. It's the shape of an E chord, played up a fret and letting all open strings ring out (flamenco-style!). Then notice the little *hammer-on* from inside the following E minor chord (pick the open string and "hammer" your finger on fret 2). The general strum pattern is: "down, up–down, down–up, up–down, up–down–up," but of course the strumming is a casual "feel thing."

The verse has its own chord oddities, including the C *inversion* (with a G on the bottom) and the D/F♯, to be played with your thumb wrapped around and fretting the low note. (Again, you're excused from the guitar teacher's advice, to keep the thumb behind the neck at all times.)

The bridge

Notice in the chorus how F turns to Fm, and back again — very classy. But wait, there's more! F turns to Fmaj7♯11 in the bridge, with open B and E strings in a variation of the intro. The bridge features some full barre chords higher up on the neck, moving back down to F.

The catchy interlude also starts with full barre chords. Hit the open E and mute between strums, by picking up the left hand (but not too far) and strumming across the "dead strings." Another fine chord appears later: D/E, best played with a barre on fret 2.

Another bit of muting happens under the line, "circuit's dead, there's *something wrong.*" The pinky reaches over to fret 3 on the E string, and it should naturally touch the A string just enough to keep it silent. From here on, you're on your own, just like Major Tom "floating round [his] tin can."

Tangled Up in Blue *(page 186)*

Folk legend Bob Dylan, after his post-folkie phase, always came back to the acoustic guitar. "Tangled Up in Blue," a popular song from the 1975 *Blood on the Tracks* album, tells a love story in a shifting timeline over a recurring three-part musical structure — Dylan's poetic take on the concepts behind the cubist art movement. Without getting into deep analysis of its lyrics, you can have fun playing this infectious tune.

Supportive strumming

Strumming is casual throughout. Generally, play the bottom one or two notes of each chord, then strum the rest of the chord for a couple beats. The intro establishes the feel in fast sixteenth-note strums of A to Asus4, which is simply an A chord with the top note moved up a fret. That note gets pulled off sometimes when returning to the A.

The verse straightens out the strum pattern. Just lift your fingers off the A and strum open strings for the G. At one point the strumming goes to an "oom-pah" pattern, all downstrokes, under the line "I was standin' . . . " There the chords start moving more, but they're all in pretty standard barre and open positions.

Short measure

There's a measure of 2/4 at the line "tangled up in blue." The short measure is just the transcriber's way of counting a section that's naturally shorter to accommodate the lyrics.

The same sections keep repeating in slight variation while the story continues. Let this song be an exercise in letting go of strict structure, while still playing tastefully to support the song.

Tears in Heaven *(page 193)*

Eric Clapton's song to his deceased son Conor, "Tears in Heaven," was first heard on the soundtrack to the 1991 movie *Rush*. It's also featured on the Grammy award–winning *Unplugged* album. Clapton takes a detour from his usual blues-based picking in favor of a sensitive finger-style approach.

The pickup

The song has three basic sections — verse, chorus, and bridge — with an intro/interlude that acts like a turnaround between them. The intro begins with a partial *pickup measure*, starting on an *upbeat*. Count "one-and, two-and, three-and, four-*and*" — the lick that starts the tune comes in on the last "and," while your tapping foot is *up* in the air.

Pick with your thumb and the next three fingers. The verse chords are not barres, but classical-style positions with bass notes played by the thumb. Review them first, then throw in the frills, like the quick *hammer-on/pull-off* lick that happens over the A chord (hold the chord with one finger and just tap fret 3 with another). Notice how the F#m chord *anticipates* the next measure.

Finger tips

To play the sliding fill after "Would you know my name," start with your ring finger barring both strings. Slide up to fret 7, then play the next pair of notes with your index finger. Play the next lick however you choose, as long as you end up with middle and ring fingers on the frets — then you're in position to play the following D/F# chord.

The chorus has partial barre chords, played in consistent arpeggios. The first ending has a fun fill, played by holding down an A chord with the index finger and slapping other fingers down on the frets shown.

Two guitars in one

The guitar solo is a *composite* part (two guitars arranged for one). Let the A string ring out while you play the upper notes, then jump down again for chords, and quickly jump back up for the *dyads* (two-note chords) that follow. Carry on with more of the same.

Thick As a Brick *(page 200)*

Jethro Tull (a band, not a person) is one of the giants of British progressive rock that thrived in the 1970s and still makes music today. Tull's unique sound mixes classical, rock, and blues influences with more than a little English/Celtic folk. From the 1972 "concept" album of the same name, "Thick As a Brick" features the acoustic strumming of singer/songwriter/flautist Ian Anderson and Martin Barre's electric soloing.

Capo III

"Capo III" is not the name of a medieval Pope. See "Free Fallin'" for the lowdown, then put your capo on fret 3.

The *6/8 time signature* has a kind of natural *shuffle feel*. There are six beats to every measure, and an eighth note gets one beat. As in "Norwegian Wood," it lends a kind of Celtic folk air to the proceedings.

Figure out the intro and verse chord positions first so you'll know which fingers to use where. The first measure introduces some fast *arpeggio* picking, best done with a repeated "down–down–up." This is followed by some G chord strums. (Notice the addition of a *hammer-on* to this riff later in the verse.) Measure 3 is the same as measure 1, moved up in position. The first part gets repeated between strums of the verse pattern, which is best played "down, down–up–down–up."

The chorus is strummed, but don't miss the moving notes within the D and A chords. (Fret the A with three fingers to accommodate this.) The bridge continues with strumming and a nice added flourish of hammer-ons when the vocals break. The outro is basically the same as the picked and strummed intro, but moved up to fret 5.

Extra credit

Now, try playing this song while standing on one foot in the style of Mr. Anderson! (Just kidding.)

3 AM (page 208)

Matchbox 20 (also known as the lowercase matchbox twenty) is the modern American pop band whose melody-driven songs have taken the airwaves by storm. They released their first album, *yourself or someone like you*, in 1996, spawning many hits including the upbeat "3 AM." It features the synchronized strumming of Kyle Cook (lead guitar) and Adam Gaynor (rhythm).

"Capo I" sounds like the name of another alternative pop band, but (so far) it's not. Refer to "Free Fallin'" to find out what it really is, then clamp it on fret 1.

Hammer time

The intro establishes the strumming pattern. Start strumming "down, up–down–up–down." Right after you hit the Cadd9 chord, *hammer-on* the second fret with your first finger. On the straight strumming part, let your hand bounce in sixteenth notes.

The verse is full of more hammer-ons that logically follow the chord positions. The D–C move repeats, then it's into the chorus, a festival of *triads* (three-note chords). Pick up your fretting fingers and mute the strings wherever there's a rest. Notice that Em nicely substitutes for G on the last time through the pattern.

Harmonic alert!

The interlude has the same moves as the intro, and the following verse has a new twist: *harmonics* over the line "she thinks happiness . . . " With one finger, barely touch the strings at fret 7 (actually fret 8 in non-capo reality) while picking. Then comes a *crescendo*, as shown by the two bisecting lines under the staff; gradually play louder and louder to build up to the final chorus.

Time in a Bottle (page 217)

Jim Croce, one of the giants of the singer/songwriter movement of the '70s, left us all too soon with a legacy of ballads and down-home pop songs. A #1 hit from the 1972 album *You Don't Mess Around With Jim*, "Time in a Bottle" demonstrates Croce's skills as a composer, poet, and a refined acoustic fingerpicker.

3/4 time

This is the same feel used in "Annie's Song" in which there are three beats per measure and a quarter note gets one beat. It's great for serenading your loved one from beneath a balcony.

Finger food

This song is fingerpicked classical-style, with the thumb, index, and middle fingers playing *arpeggios* (our favorite word) in a fanlike motion, one finger per string. Get familiar with the chord positions, and notice that the low notes start descending under a static chord (Dm). Just hold the chord on top with your first three fingers, and stretch your pinky over to hit fret 4, then 3. The chord starts changing after that to allow other fingers to cover the bass. All your fingers get involved on the two-note chords that follow. Generally think "one finger per fret," but use whatever digits get the job done. (Extra Tip: a one-finger barre at the end of the intro makes it easier to play the grace notes.)

The verse is an expansion of the intro pattern, and the bridge is a clever change to D major. This time, you'll need to barre four strings with one finger when you hit the Bm7.

Finally, the very cool outro has *harmonics* played over a dissonant chord. (Harmonics are discussed in "Angie," and in the guitar notation legend.) Keep the chord ringing as much as possible while you "chime" on the D and G strings at fret 7.

To Be With You *(page 221)*

"Pop" goes the shredder! Mr. Big was an American pop/rock band made up of some of the most heroic technical virtuosos of the 1980s *shred-rock* scene. Their 1992 acoustic hit, "To Be With You," shows them moderating their blazing chops in favor of catchy melodies and lyrical pop songwriting. The song was a #1 hit from their 1991 album, *Lean Into It.* Guitarist Paul Gilbert strums and picks with a tasteful melodic flair.

The verse

Gilbert jumps right into the verse with a full C♯m7 barre chord, alternating with folky chords in a straight-ahead strum pattern, roughly: "down, (down,) down, down–up." As always, try to feel it rather than play exactly as shown.

In the chorus, a bass note follows vocals while the first chord is held out. Strum the E chord, and while holding, reach up with your middle finger to hit fret 2, then your pinky for fret 4. Carry on.

The solo

The optional solo happens over the chorus pattern. Should you choose to play it, put your pick between your teeth or wherever you can find it again. You can choose which fingers to use, as long as you pluck hard. Playing *double stops* that follow the melody, add *slides* and *hammer-ons* where shown. Where you see *vibrato* on a double stop, wiggle the strings *upward*, so you don't pull the high E string off the neck. The solo ends with *harmonics* on fret 12 (they were introduced in "Angie"); let them ring out while you play the following slide, country-style. Tasty!

On the final chorus, notice the mark of a true rock ballad: the *key change*. In this case, it makes things easier to play, so just follow the chords. The song returns to the original key and slows down (*ritards*) in the outro.

Wanted Dead or Alive *(page 227)*

Ah, twelve-string guitars. They're best played by cowboys whilst riding on steel horses with six-strings on their backs. Bon Jovi was one of few bands to emerge from the arena rock/"hair band" scene of the '80s to become an enduring force in pop music — with help from a good barber and great songs like this one. "Wanted Dead or Alive" was the third single from their 1986 smash album, *Slippery When Wet.* It features the jangly twelve-string and bluesy lead playing of guitarist Richie Sambora.

The twelve-string

A twelve-string guitar is pretty much the same as a six-string, but with *double courses* — two strings where there's usually one — some of which are tuned in octaves, some in unison. That's why it sounds so full and jingly, but it's no crime to play this part with just six wires.

"Wanted" starts with some moving *dyads* (two-note chords) over a D string *drone* — a static note played under a moving melody. Technical info aside, you're just moving a couple of chord shapes across the fretboard to outline a D minor scale, and letting the open D string ring out under the moving chords. (Skip the B string.) Then comes a bluesy lick with a quarter-step *bend*; just pull the string *downward* (toward the earth) slightly after you pick it (this recurs throughout the song).

The progression

The verse gets extra jangly with chord strums and fills. Learn the chords first, then try throwing in the extra notes. The progression is a rock standard, moving between a D and two variations of a G chord shape (Cadd9 and G) — until the end of the pattern, where there's a quick move from a G chord to a full F barre. There's no way to do this without rearranging all of your fingers, so bite the proverbial bullet and work on playing it smoothly. Likewise for the chorus, learn to strum all chords before you throw in the decorations.

When the Children Cry (page 234)

The 1980s rock school of hairspray and spandex produced more than its share of noteworthy music from top-class guitarists, including Vito Bratta of White Lion. Bratta was best known for melodic and humanly impossible guitar solos, but he shows his fingerstyle acoustic chops on this heartfelt anti-war anthem from WL's 1987 album *Pride*.

Fingerpickin' good

The classical-style intro includes a melody playing over static open strings. There's no way around using your fingers on this one; the thumb plucks all bass notes, and any combination of fingers can play the chords and melody. When you get into the chord changes, find the chord positions first — notice that the Bm is a full barre chord, and the rest involve open strings — then work out the picking patterns. The little flourish of notes just before the verse is a hint of what's to come: grace notes and decorations galore. After the quick *hammer-on* and *pull-off* over the D chord, what he's doing is sliding up to different positions of the chord and ending with plucked *harmonics* (see "Angie" for an intro to harmonics).

Pace yourself!

In the verse, wherever you see a slurred triplet ⌐³⌐ , start out just playing the first note of the group of three. Do this until you know the basic picking pattern, then try adding the decorations. Same deal with the pre-chorus and chorus, equally frilly in their own right; leave out the grace notes until you're confident with the chords and fingerpicking.

While your friend with the whammy bar–equipped, Strat-style guitar plays the solo, you can continue with the verse pattern. The rest of the song consists of variations on the same pre-chorus and chorus parts, ending with the same flourish and harmonics that closed out the intro.

You've Got a Friend (page 242)

How better to wrap up this collection than with a friendly song from the understated giant of mellow guitar, James Taylor? Written by fellow singer/songwriter Carole King, "You've Got a Friend" was the first single from JT's 1971 album *Mud Slide Slim and the Blue Horizon*.

Return of the capo

Where did you put your capo? Find it now, and refer to the song "Landslide" if you need a quick primer on capo notation. Here it's clamped on fret 2, so what the tab calls "3" is actually fret 5, and so on.

With that in mind, start with your hand pretty much in a G chord position — third finger on the low E string, pinky on the high E. Fingerpick the notes and let the strings ring out through the chord changes. It's mostly a series of *arpeggios* (chords played one note at a time) mixed with plucked chords and fills. For picking, you're best off using the thumb for all bass notes, and the next three fingers for all the "upper" notes. Most of the chords are at the bottom of the neck, except for the occasional barre chord two frets up from the capo. If the picking doesn't feel natural, the best advice is always to learn the chords first — maybe just strumming them through the song — then work out the picking when you have the changes down.

A touch of blues

It's more of the same until the middle of the chorus: Every time you see the lyric, "all you've got to do is call," that's your cue to break into a blues fill! It's played in the minor *pentatonic* (five-note) *scale*, and you can pick it with any combination of fingers — thumb and forefinger work well for some, but it's up to you.

You'll notice that the part has more and more notes as the song goes on, but the chord shapes stay the same, and most fills happen "inside" the chords. Take your time learning it, and you'll get the hang of throwing in those tasty little ornaments that are the James Taylor trademark.

About a Girl

Words and Music by Kurt Cobain

Tune down 1/2 step:
(low to high) Eb-Ab-Db-Gb-Bb-Eb

Intro
Moderately ♩ = 122

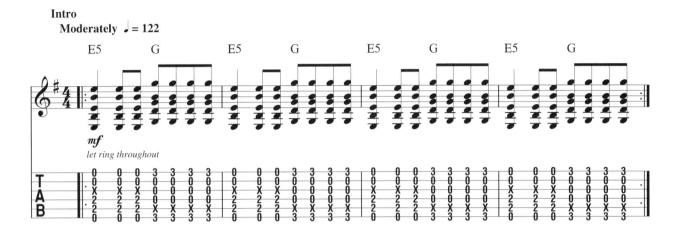

mf
let ring throughout

Verse

1., 3. I   need an   eas - y   friend, _   I   do,   with an
2. *See additional lyrics*

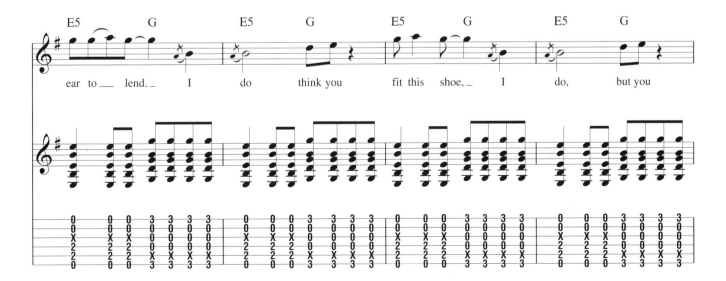

ear to _ lend. _   I   do   think you   fit this   shoe, _   I   do,   but you

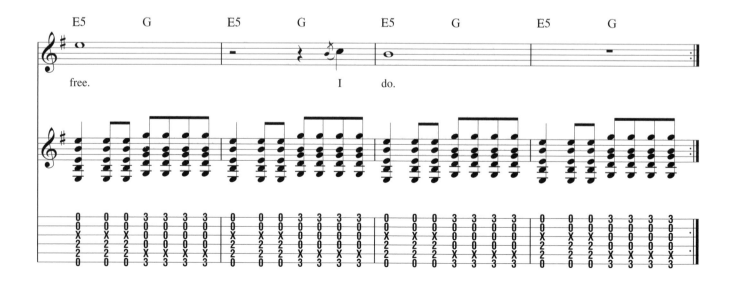

Guitar Solo

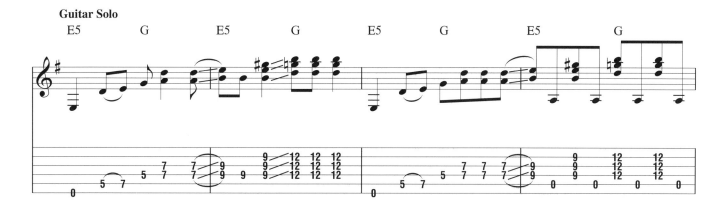

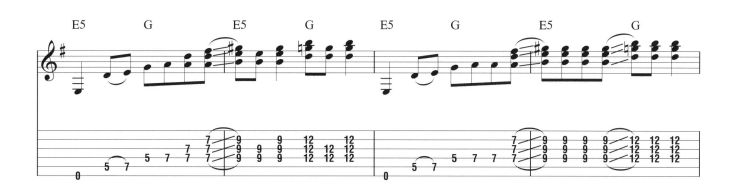

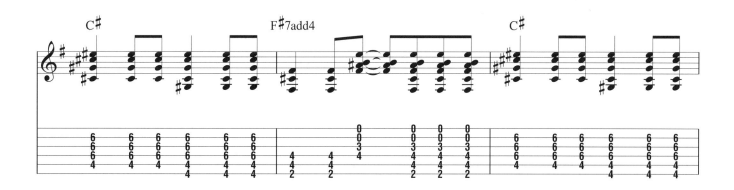

D.C. al Coda
(no repeats)

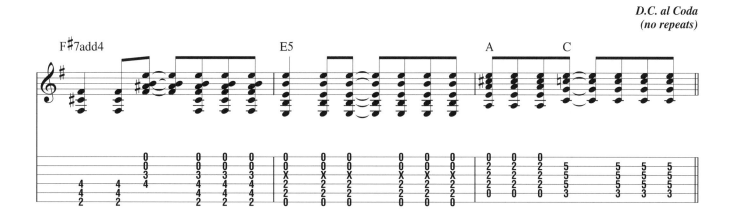

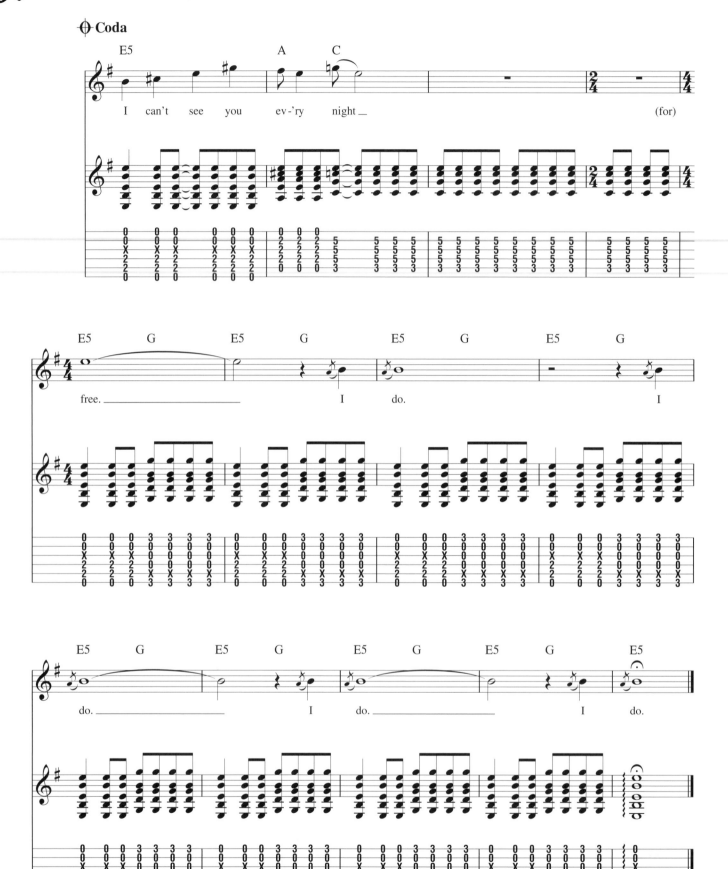

Additional Lyrics

2. I'm standing in your line,
   I do, hope you have the time.
   I do, pick a number to,
   I do, keep a date with you.

Across the Universe

Words and Music by John Lennon and Paul McCartney

Tune down 1/2 step:
(low to high) Eb-Ab-Db-Gb-Bb-Eb

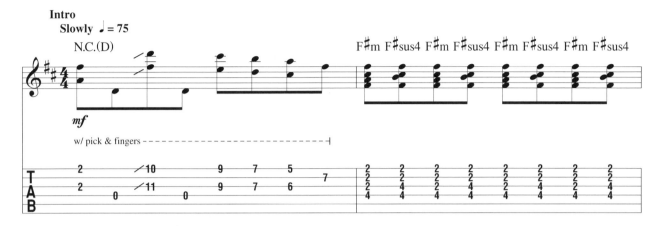

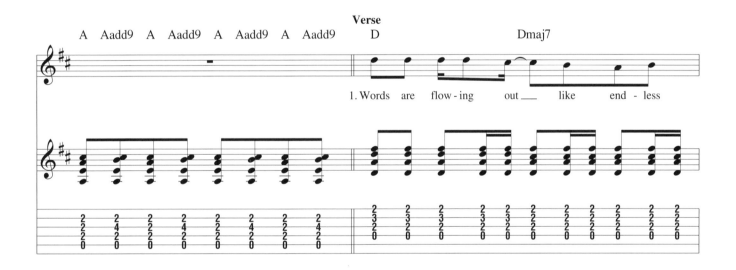

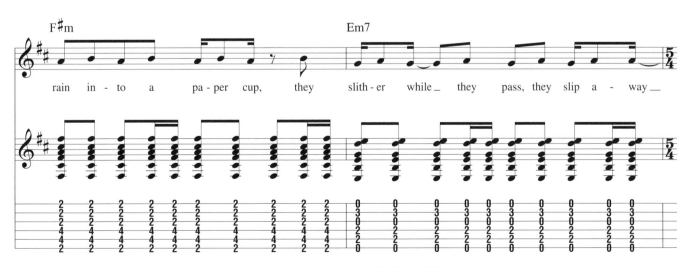

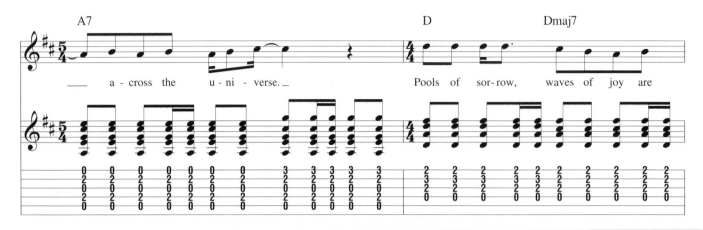

a - cross the   u - ni - verse. ___   Pools of   sor-row,   waves of   joy are

drift-ing through my   o-pened mind, __   pos - sess-ing   and ca - ress-ing   me. __

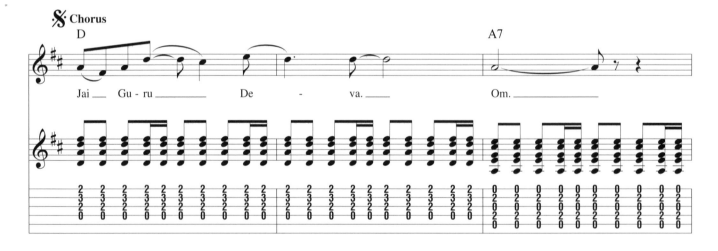

Jai __ Gu - ru _____   De - va. _____   Om. _____

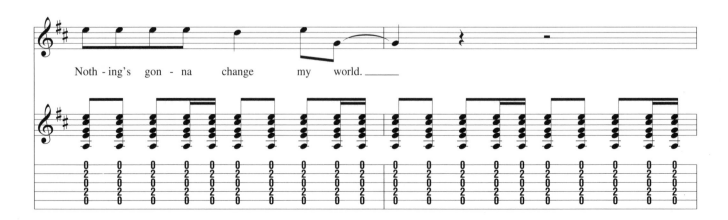

Noth - ing's gon - na   change   my   world. _____

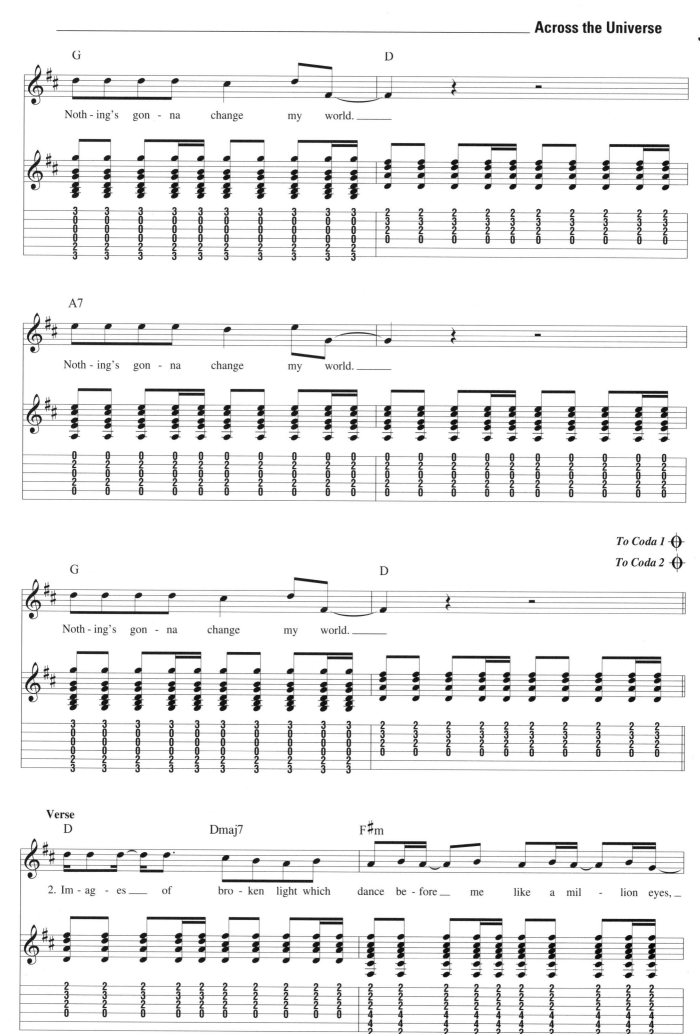

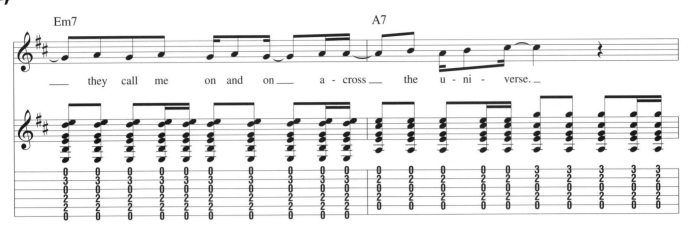

they call me on and on___ a - cross ___ the u - ni - verse.___

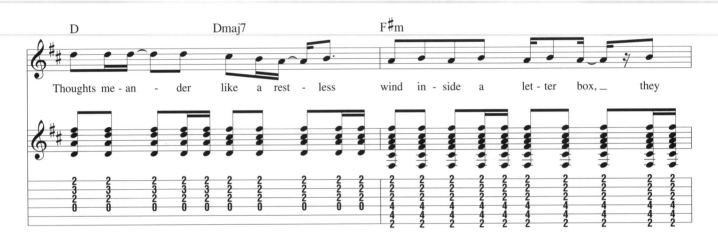

Thoughts me - an - der like a rest - less wind in - side a let - ter box, ___ they

D.S. al Coda 1

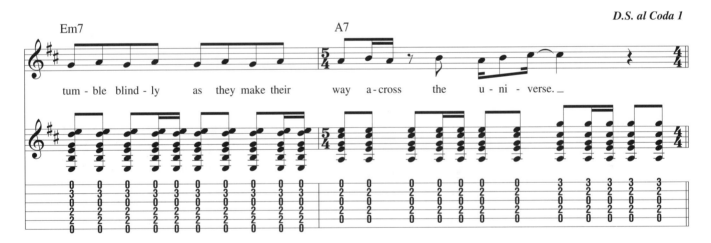

tum - ble blind - ly as they make their way a - cross the u - ni - verse. ___

Coda 1

Verse

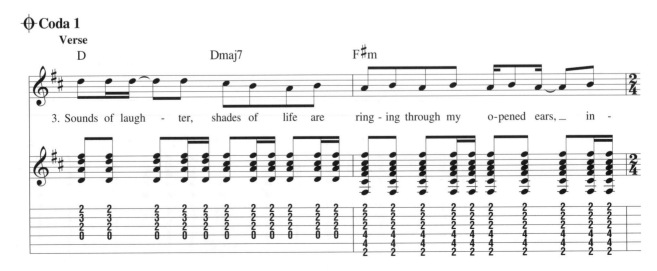

3. Sounds of laugh - ter, shades of life are ring - ing through my o - pened ears, ___ in -

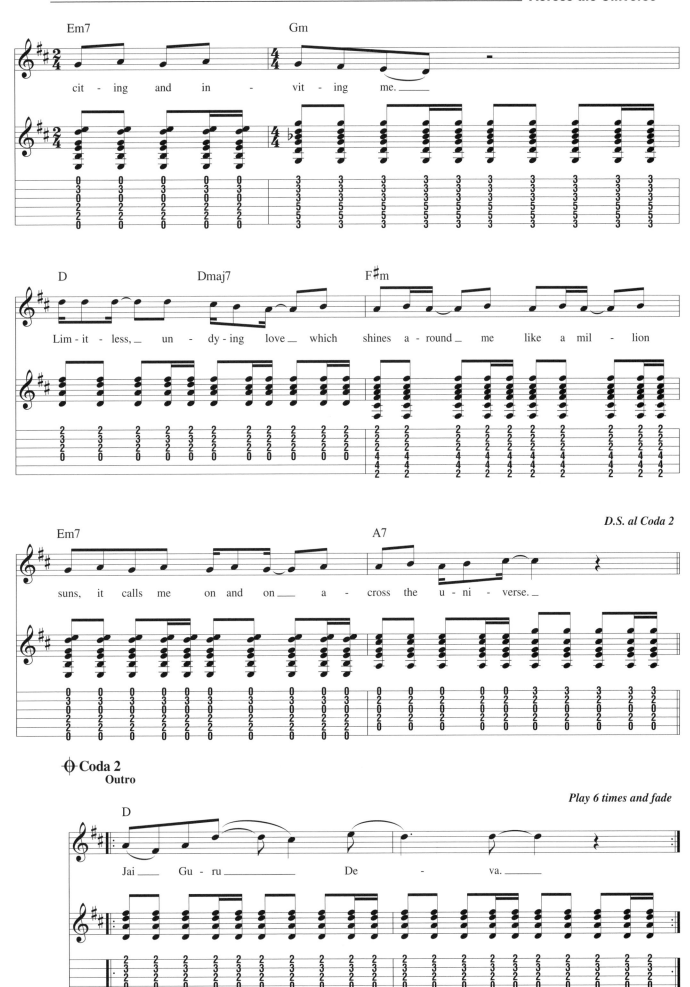

Angie

Words and Music by Mick Jagger and Keith Richards

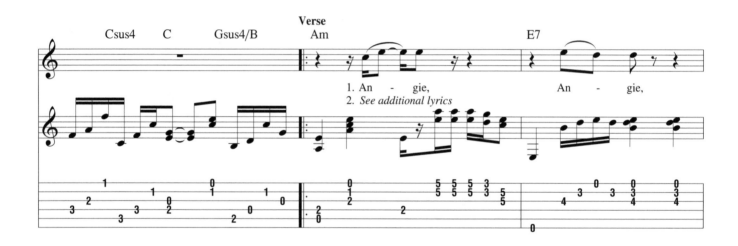

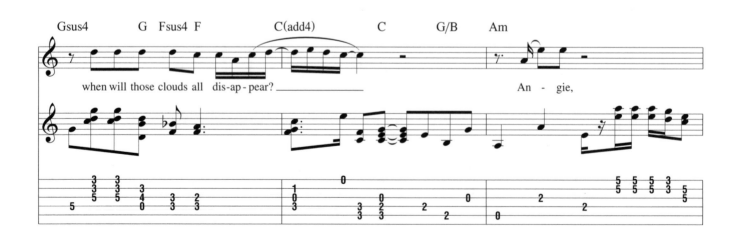

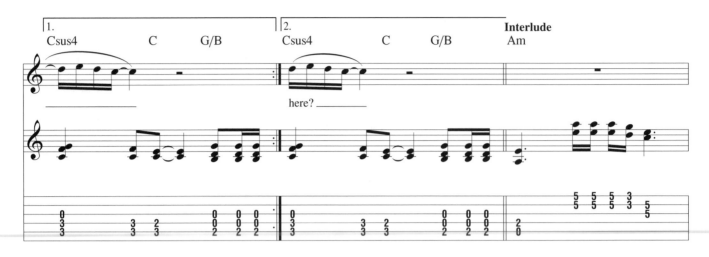

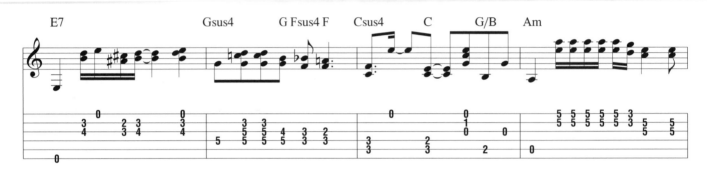

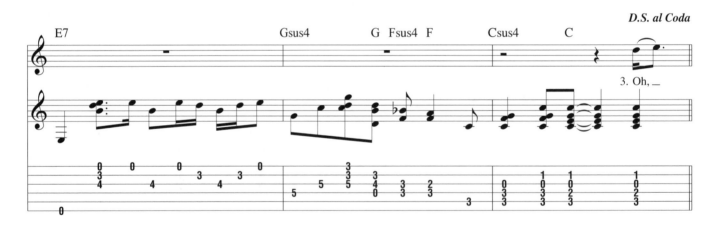

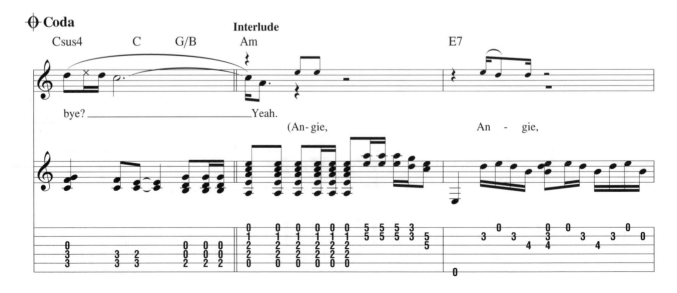

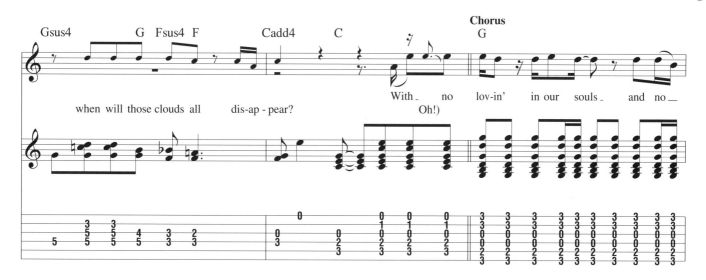

when will those clouds all dis-ap - pear?

Chorus

Oh!) With no lov-in' in our souls and no

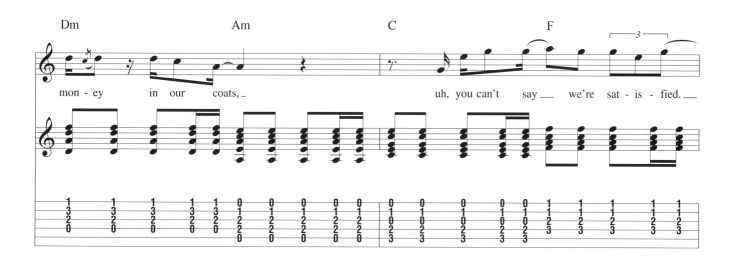

mon - ey in our coats, uh, you can't say we're sat - is - fied.

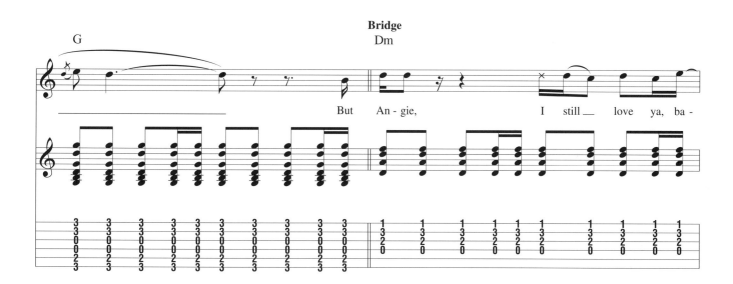

Bridge

But An - gie, I still love ya, ba -

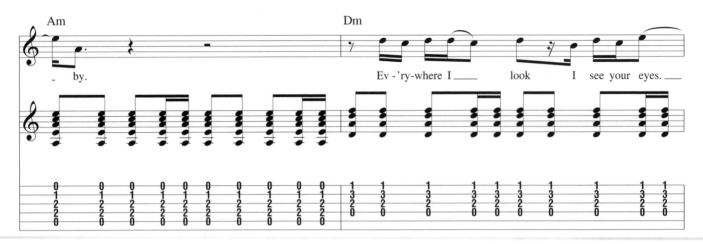

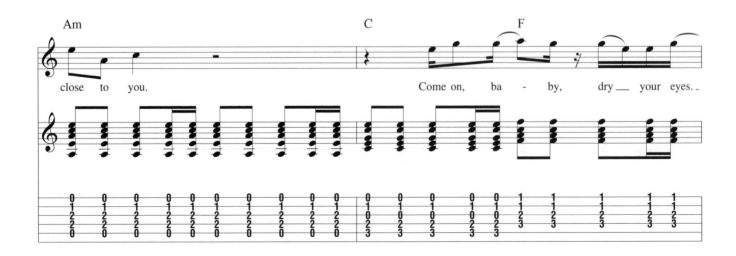

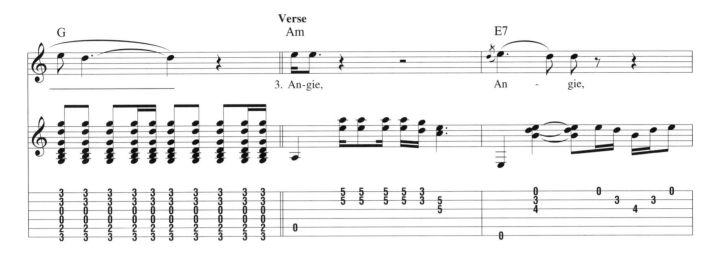

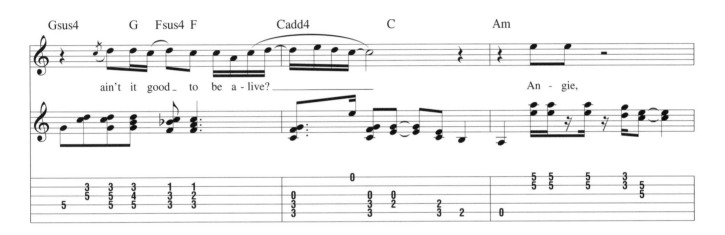

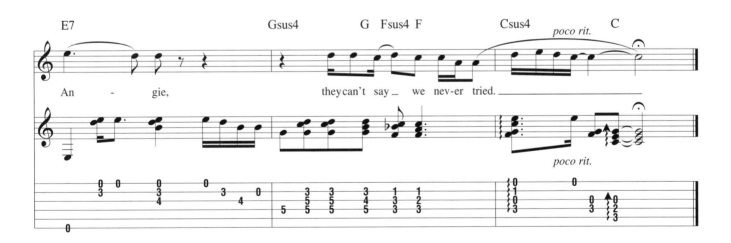

Additional Lyrics

2. A-Angie, you're beautiful, yes,
   But ain't it time we said goodbye?
   A-Angie, I still love ya.
   Remember all those nights we cried?

Chorus 2. All the dreams we held so close
   Seemed to all go up in smoke.
   Uh, let me whisper in your ear.
   Whispered: Angie, Angie,
   Where will it lead us from here?

Chorus 3. Oh, Angie, don't you weep,
   All your kisses still taste sweet.
   I hate that sadness in your eyes.
   But Angie, Angie,
   A-ain't it time we said goodbye?

Annie's Song

Words and Music by John Denver

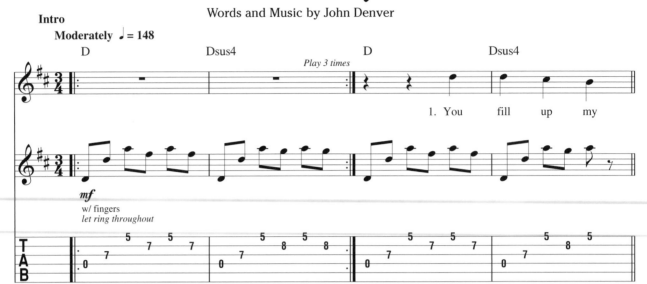

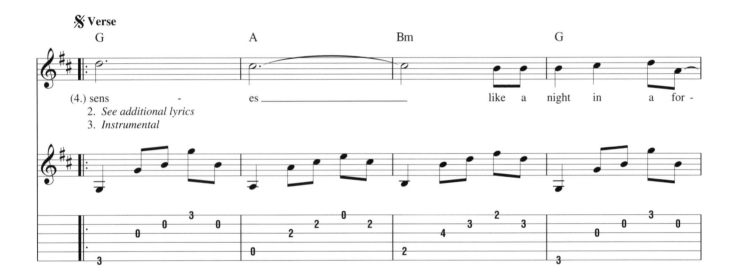

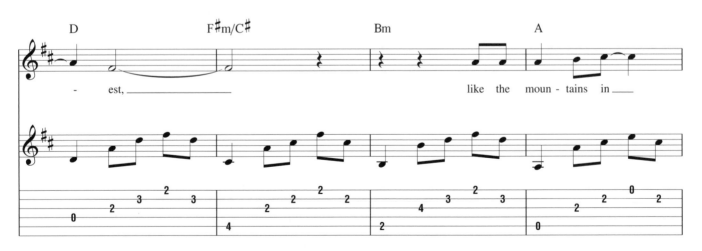

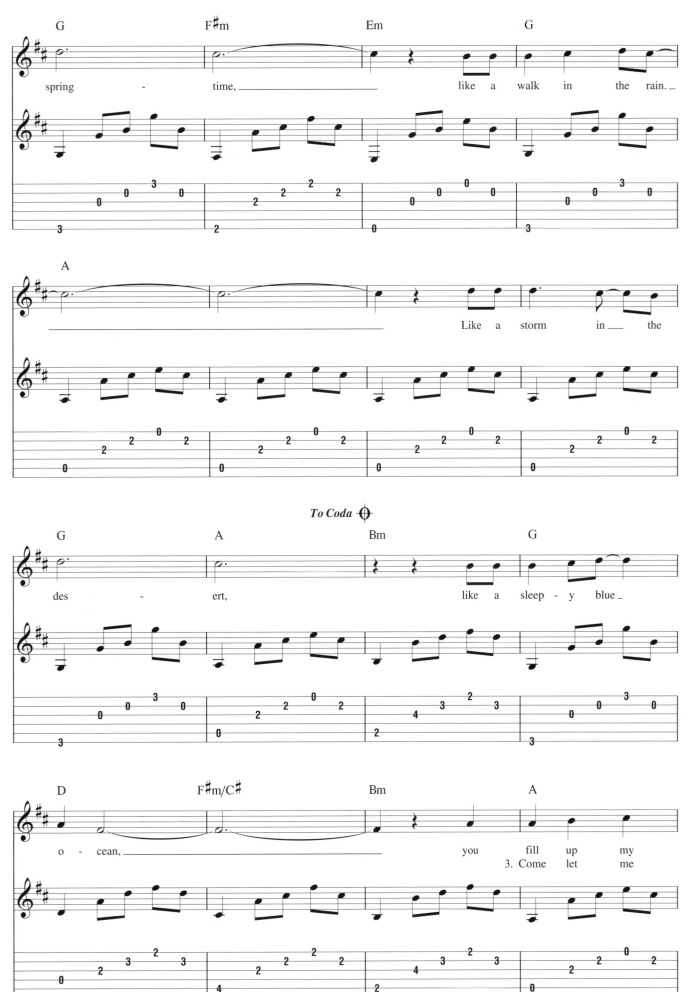

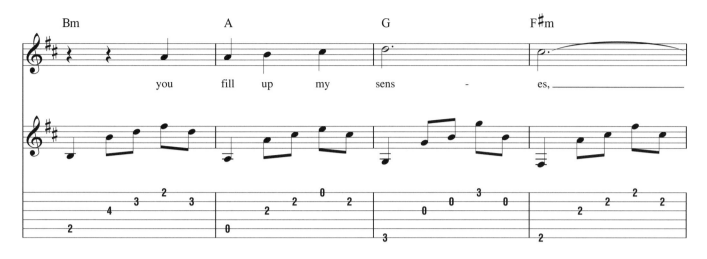

you fill up my sens - es, _____

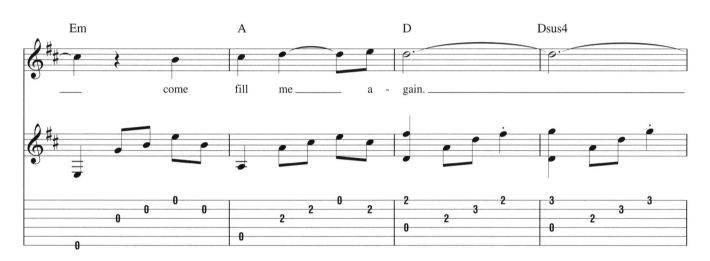

_____ come fill me _____ a - gain. _____

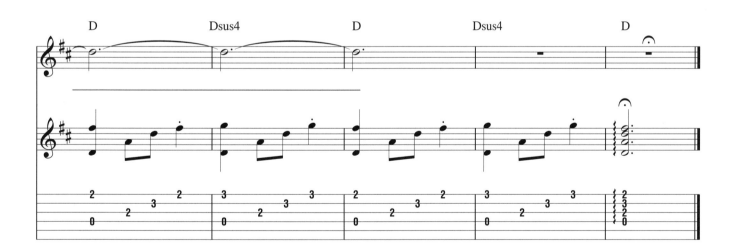

Additional Lyrics

2. Come let me love you,
   Let me give my life to you,
   Let me drown in your laughter,
   Let me die in your arms,
   Let me lay down beside you,
   Let me always be with you.
   Come let me love you,
   Come love me again.

Behind Blue Eyes

Words and Music by Pete Townshend

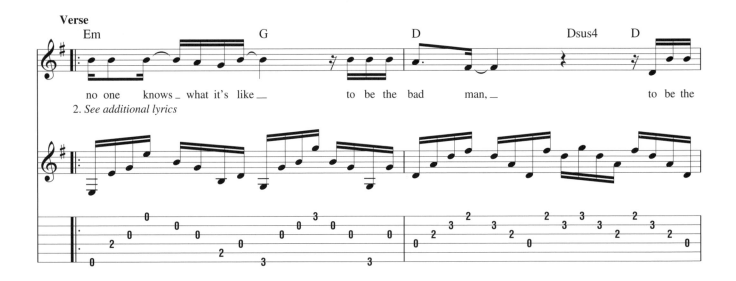

no one   knows _ what it's like _   to be the bad   man, _   to be the

2. *See additional lyrics*

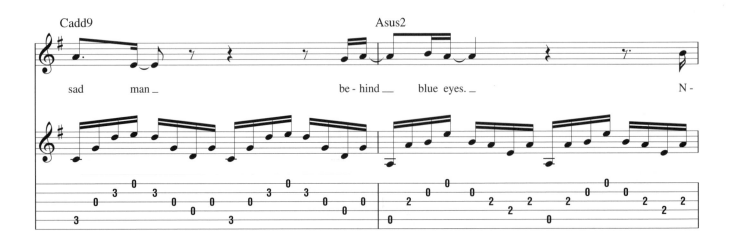

sad   man _   be - hind _ blue eyes. _   N-

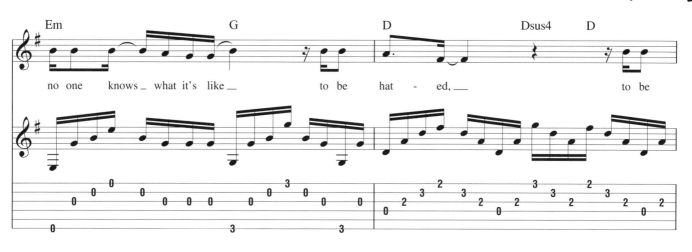

no one   knows _ what it's like _   to be   hat - ed, ___   to be

fat - ed ___   to tell - ing on - ly lies.   But   my

Chorus

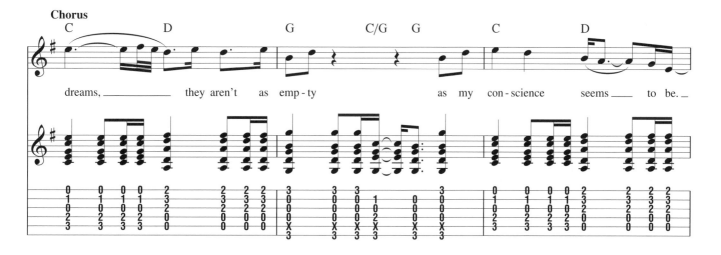

dreams, _____ they aren't   as   emp - ty   as   my   con - science   seems ___ to be. _

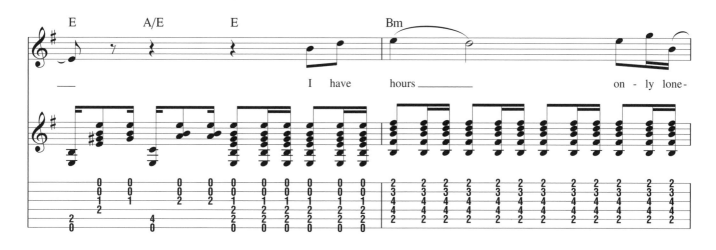

___   I   have   hours _____   on - ly lone-

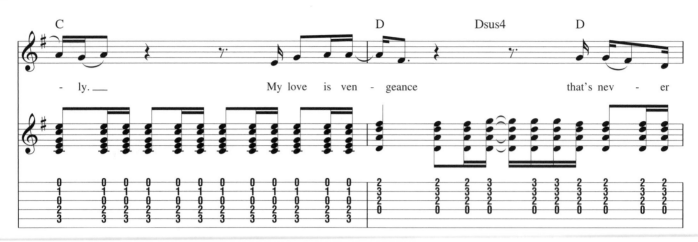

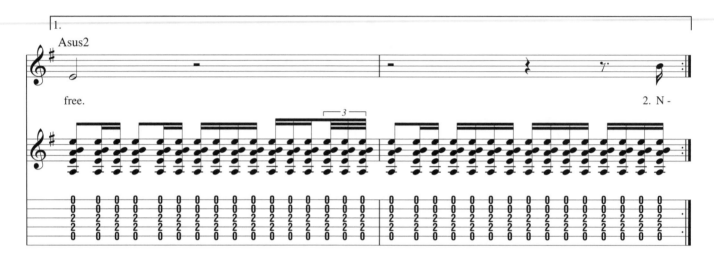

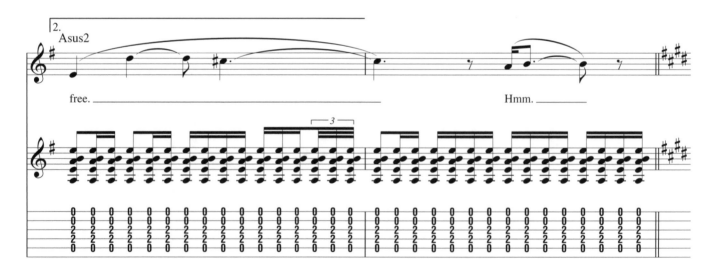

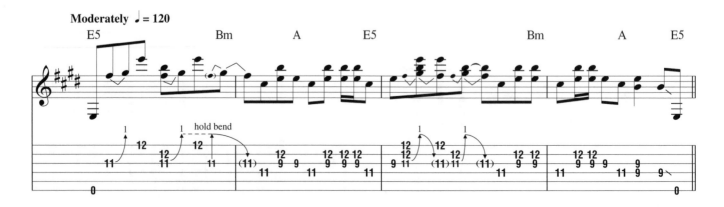

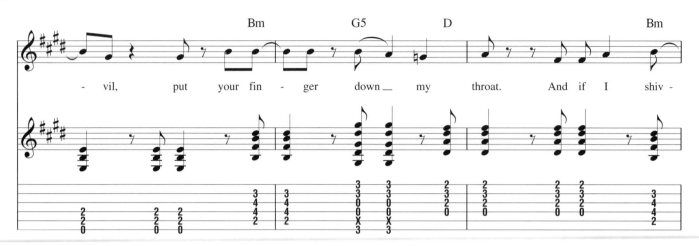

- vil,   put   your fin - ger   down __ my   throat.   And if I   shiv -

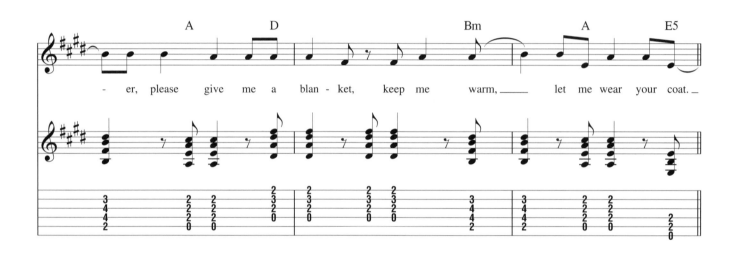

- er,   please   give   me a   blan - ket,   keep   me   warm, ___   let   me wear   your   coat. __

Interlude

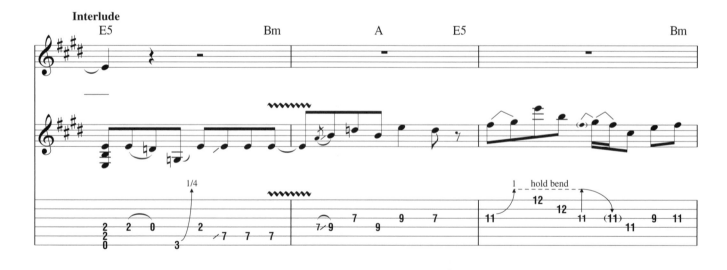

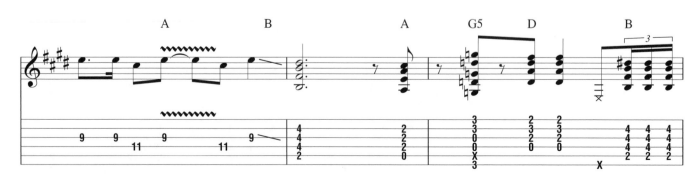

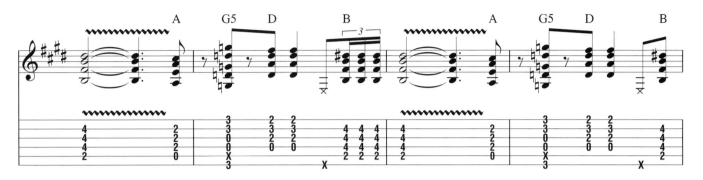

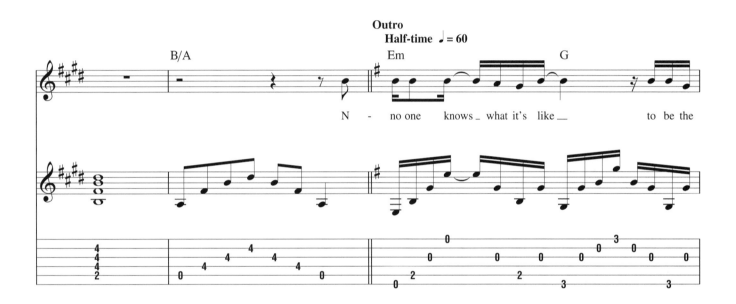

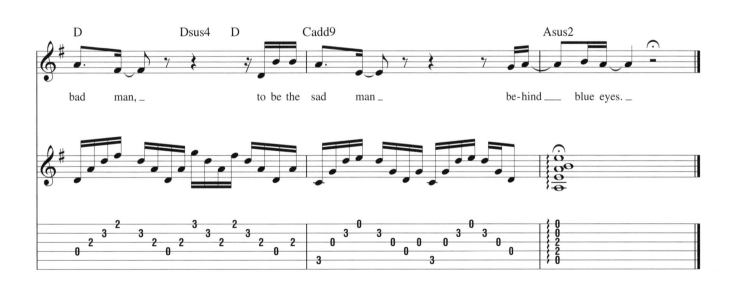

Additional Lyrics

2. N-no one knows what it's like to feel these feelings
Like I do, and I blame you.
N-no one bites back as hard on their anger,
None of my pain and woe can show through.

Best of My Love

Words and Music by John David Souther, Don Henley and Glenn Frey

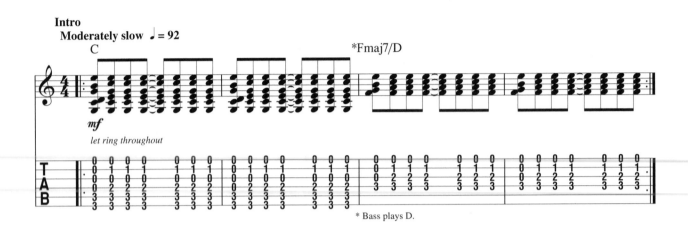

* Bass plays D.

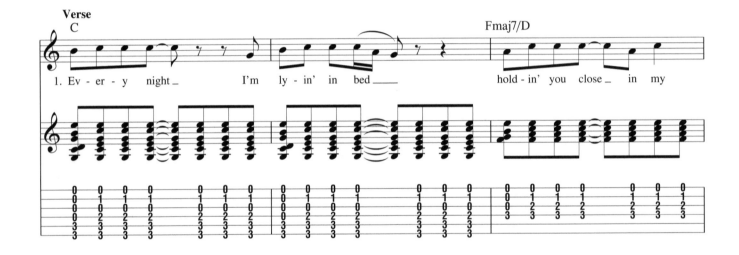

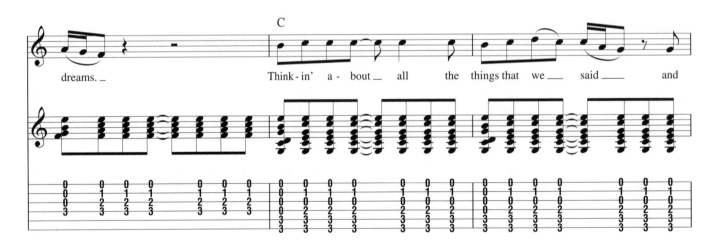

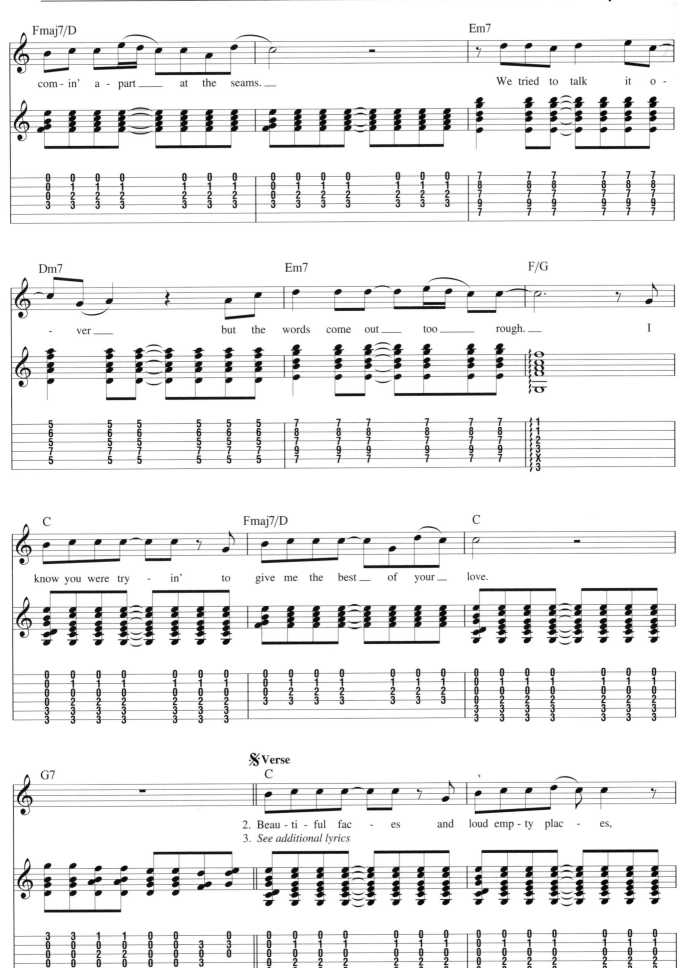

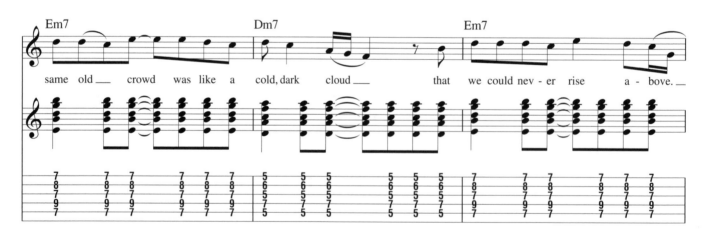

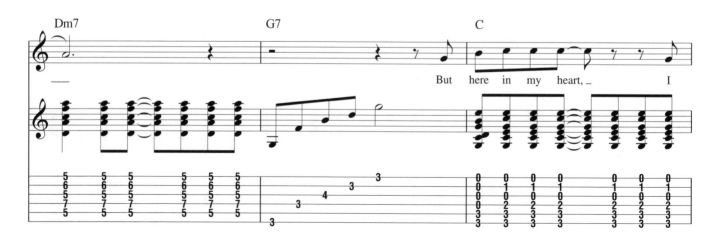

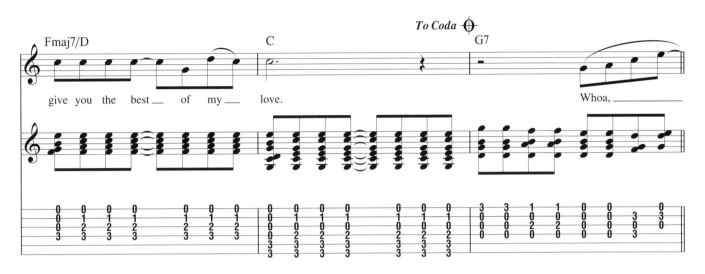

give you the best __ of my __ love.   Whoa, _____

Chorus

sweet dar - lin',   you get the best of my
(You get the best of my __ love.)

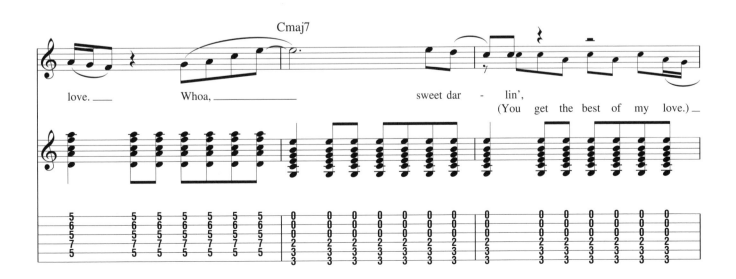

love. __   Whoa, _____   sweet dar - lin',
(You get the best of my love.) __

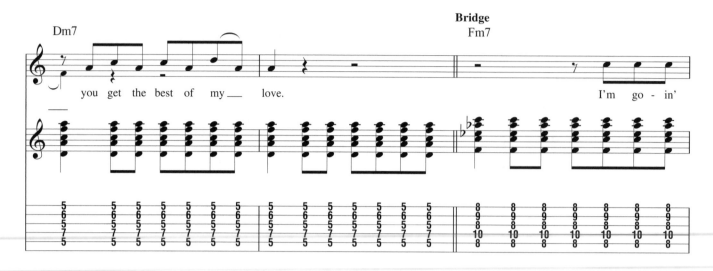

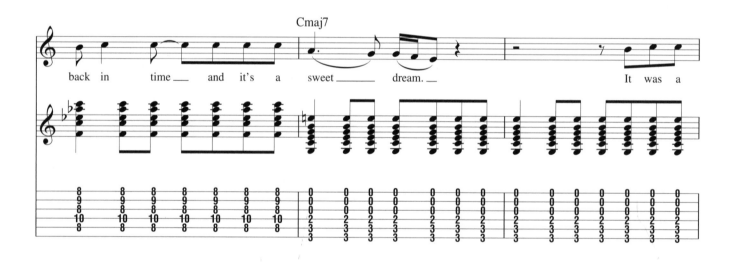

⊕ **Coda**

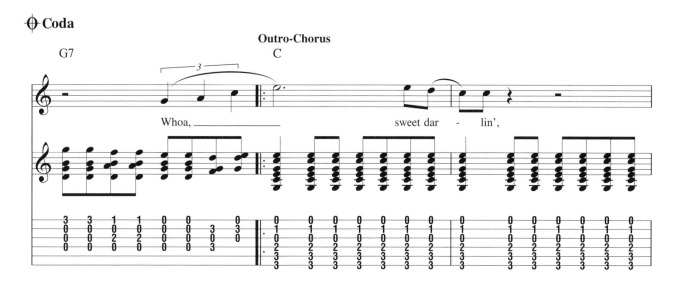

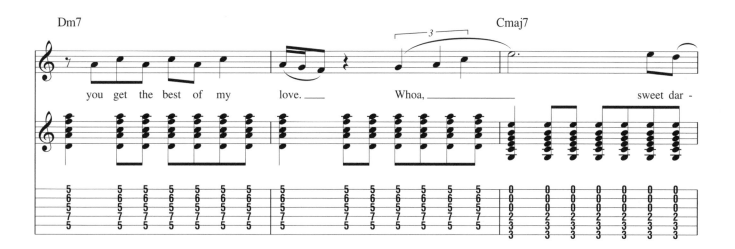

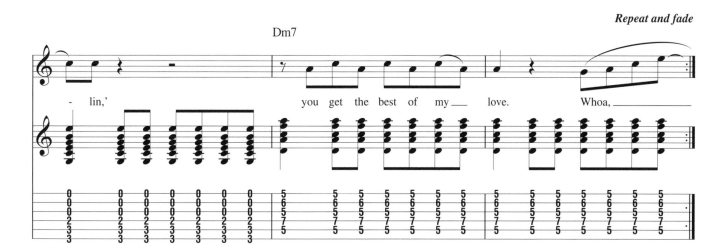

Additional Lyrics

3. But ev'ry morning I wake up and worry
What's gonna happen today.
You see it your way and I'll see it mine,
But we both see it slippin' away.
You know we always had each other, baby.
I guess that wasn't enough.
Oh, oh, but here in my heart,
I give you the best of my love.

Blackbird

Words and Music by John Lennon and Paul McCartney

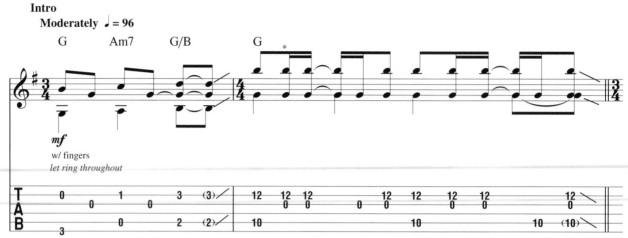

*Strum upstemmed notes w/ index finger of pick hand
whenever more than one upstemmed note appears.

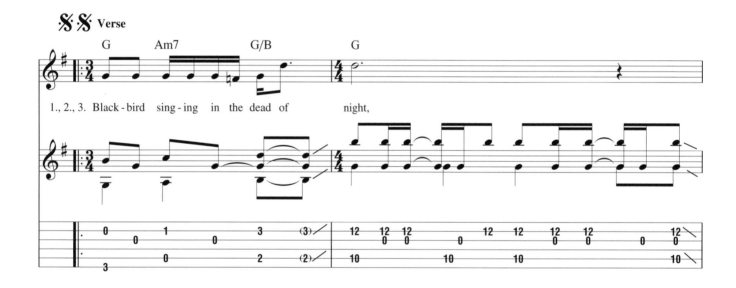

1., 2., 3. Black-bird sing-ing in the dead of night,

1., 3. take _ these bro-ken wings _ and learn _ to fly. _
2. take _ these sunk-en eyes _ and learn _ to see. _

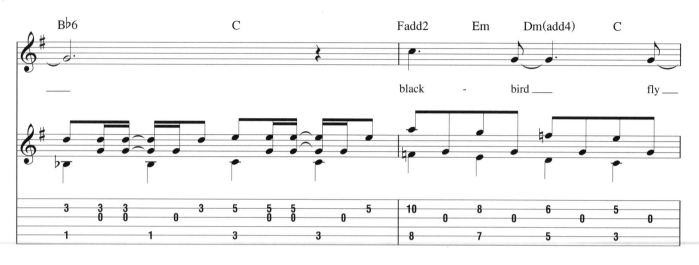

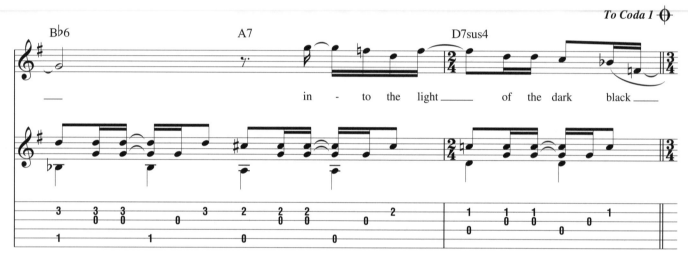

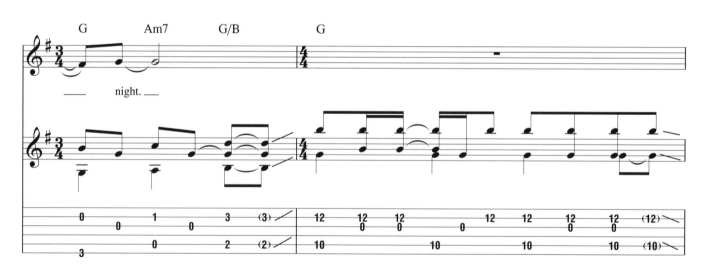

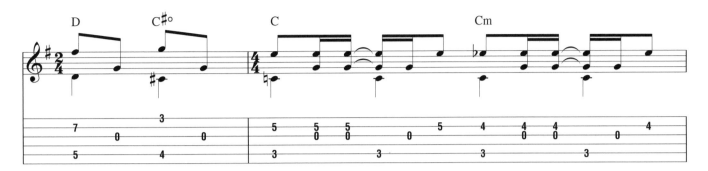

D.S. al Coda 1

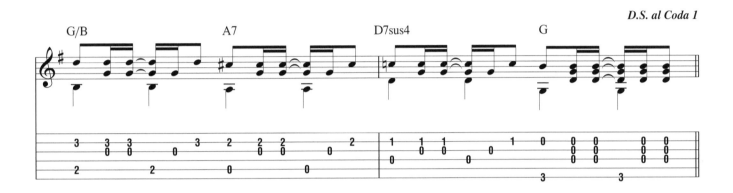

Coda 1

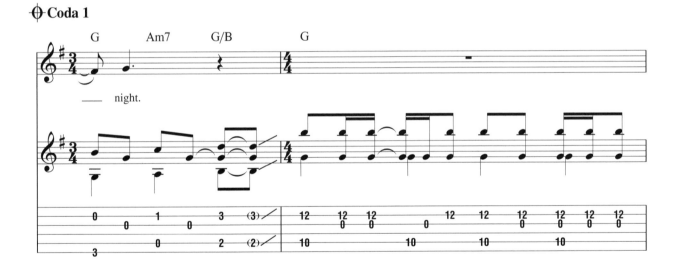

D.S.S. al Coda 2

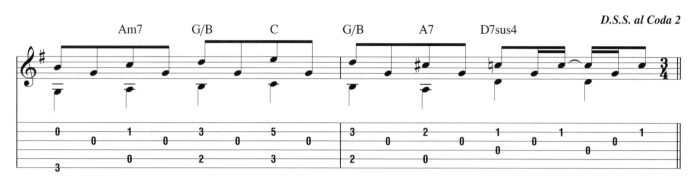

⊕ Coda 2

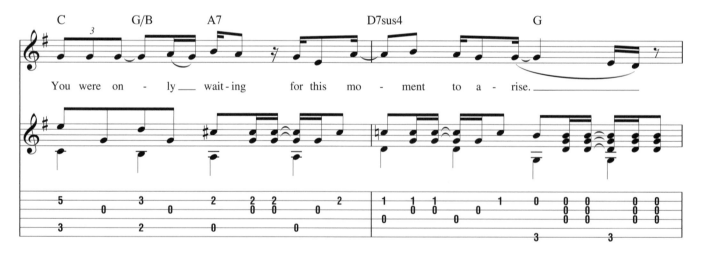

you were on - ly wait - ing   for this mo - ment   to a - rise. __

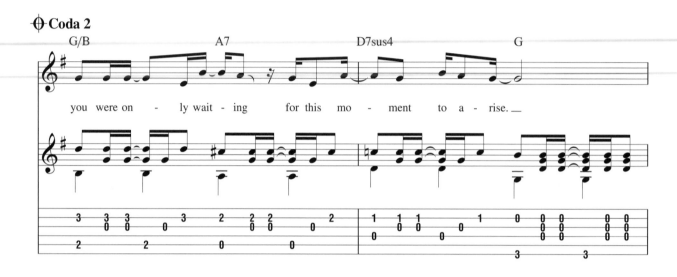

You were on - ly __ wait - ing   for this mo - ment   to a - rise. _____

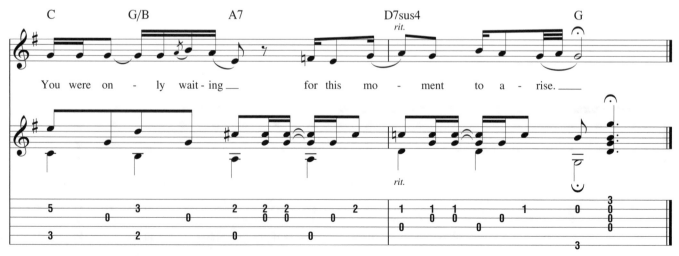

You were on - ly wait - ing __   for this mo - ment   to a - rise. __

Crazy Little Thing Called Love

Words and Music by Freddie Mercury

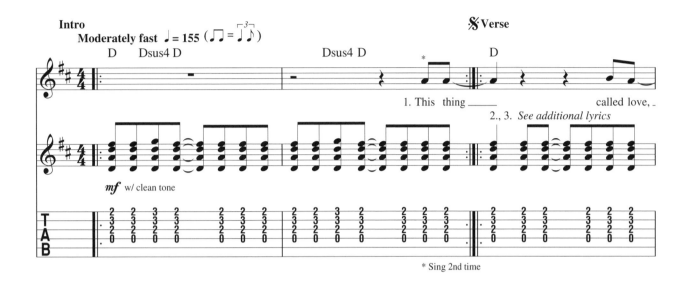

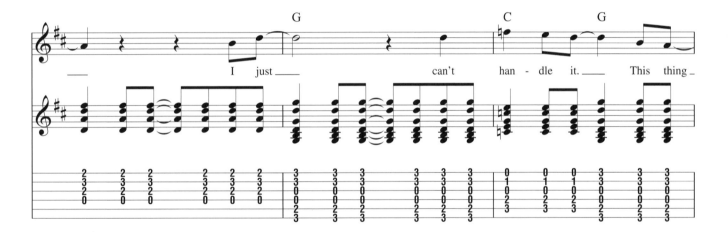

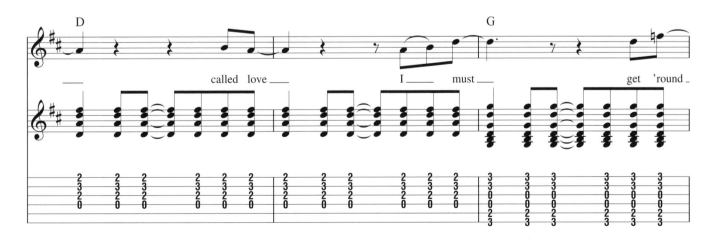

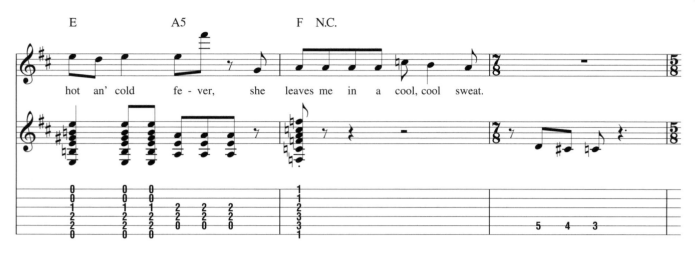

D.S. al Coda 1

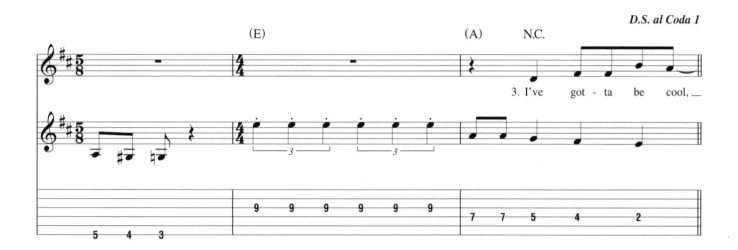

Coda 1

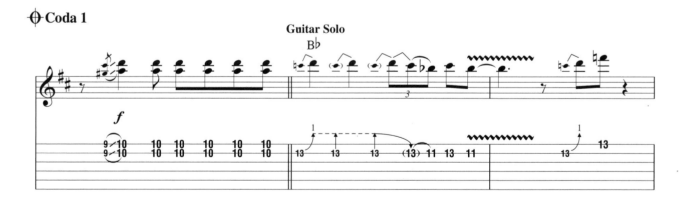

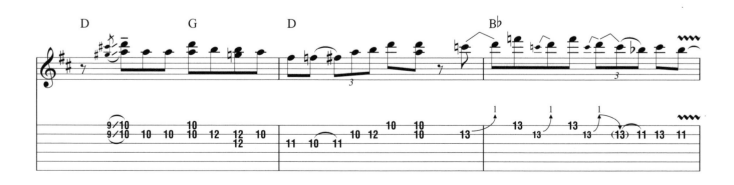

Additional Lyrics

2. A this thing called love
   It cries in a cradle all night.
   It swings, it jives,
   Shakes all over like a jellyfish.
   I kinda like it.
   Crazy little thing called love.

3. I've gotta be cool, relax,
   Get hip, get on my tracks.
   Take a back seat, hitchhike,
   Take a long ride on my motorbike
   Until I'm ready.
   Crazy little thing called love.

Drive

Words and Music by Brandon Boyd, Michael Einziger, Alex Katunich, Jose Pasillas II and Chris Kilmore

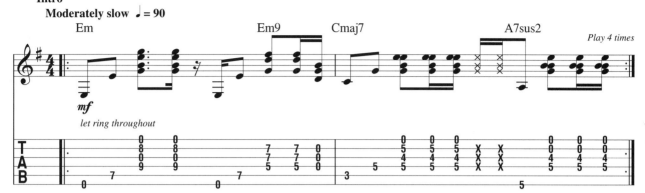

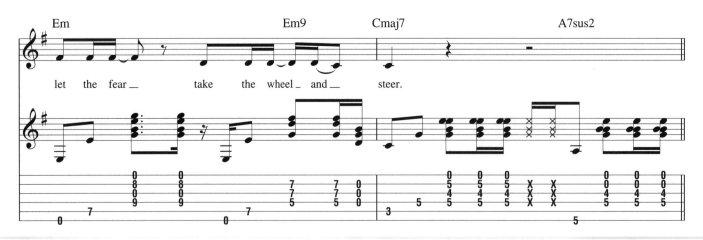

let the fear ___ take the wheel ___ and ___ steer.

Pre-Chorus

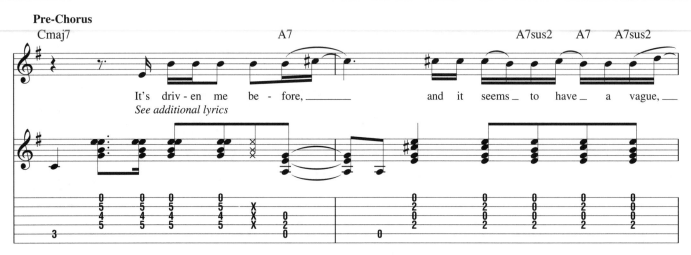

It's driv-en me be-fore, _____ and it seems ___ to have ___ a vague, ___
See additional lyrics

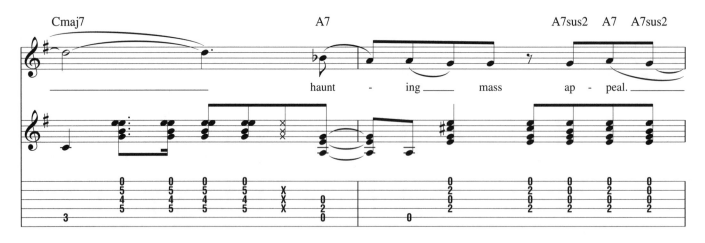

_____ haunt - ing ___ mass ap - peal. ___

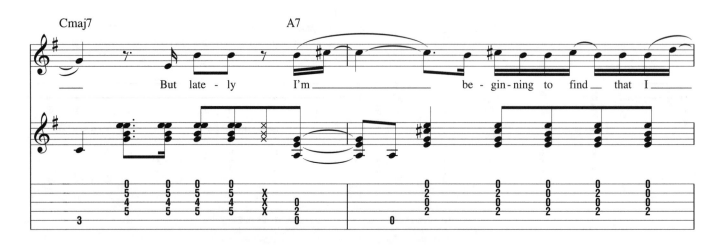

___ But late - ly I'm _____ be - gin-ning to find ___ that I ___

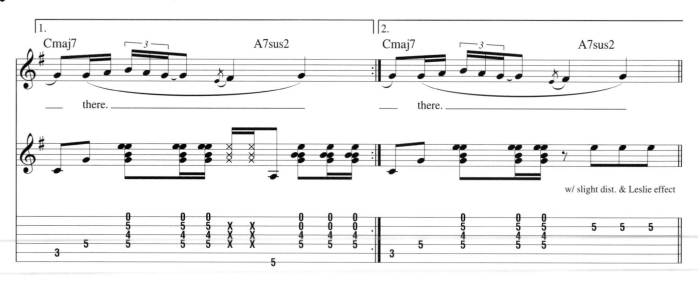

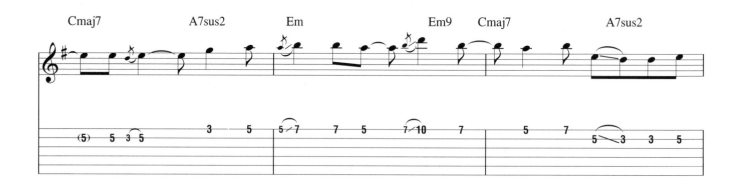

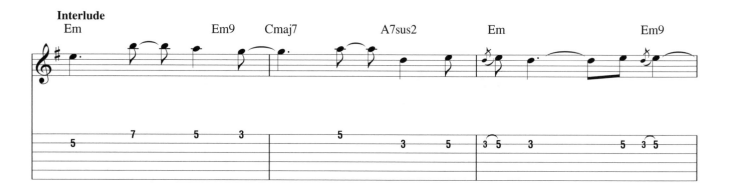

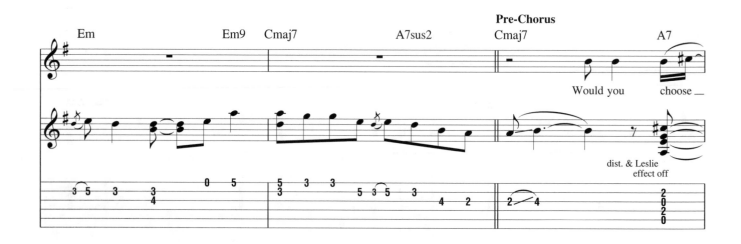

*Rub edge of pick down the strings,
producing a scratchy sound.

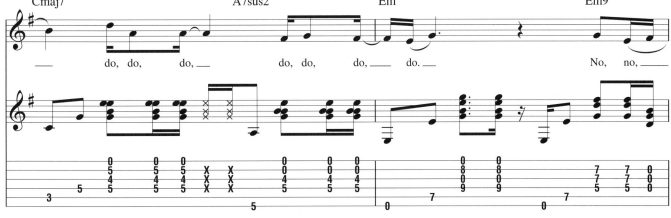

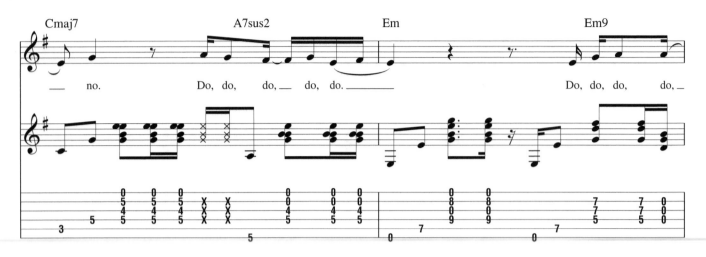

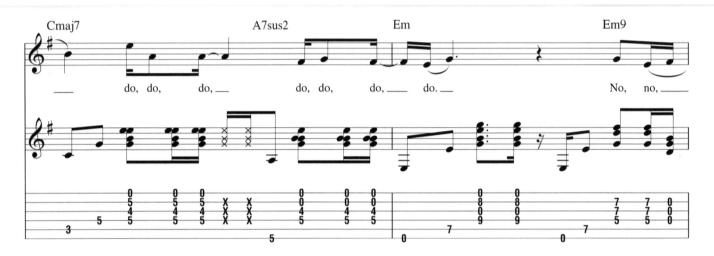

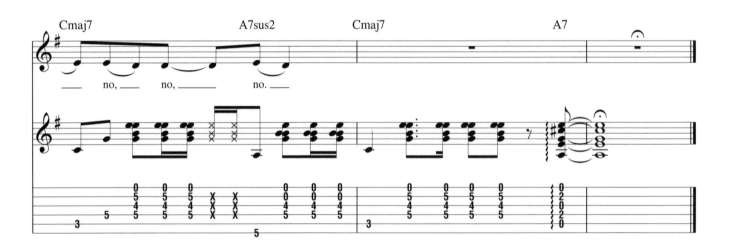

Additional Lyrics

2. So if I decide to waiver the
Chance to be one of the hive,
Will I choose water over wine
And hold my own and drive?
Oh, oh, oh.

Pre-Chorus It's driven me before,
And it seems to have a vague,
Haunting mass appeal.
But lately I'm beginning to find
That when I drive myself my light is found.

Dust in the Wind

Words and Music by Kerry Livgren

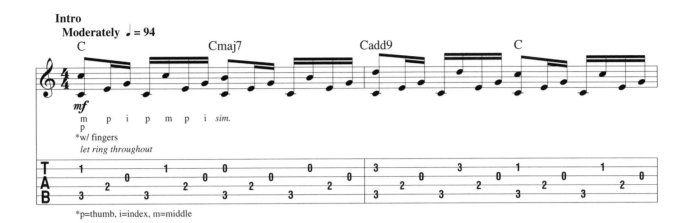

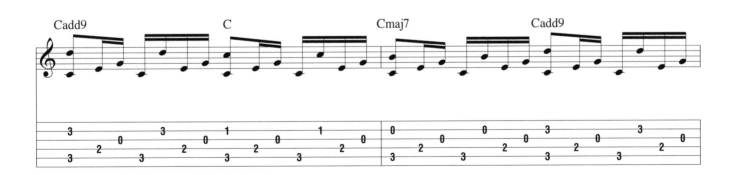

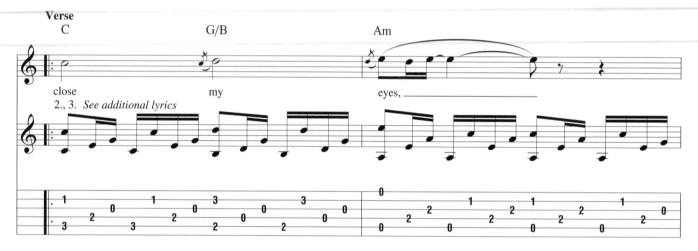

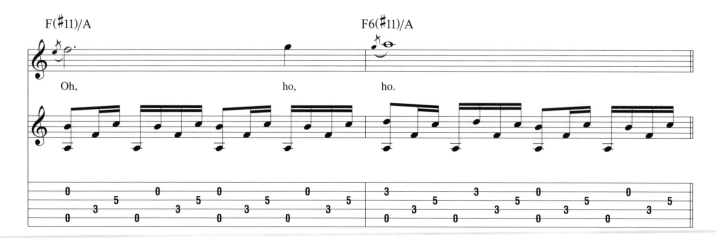

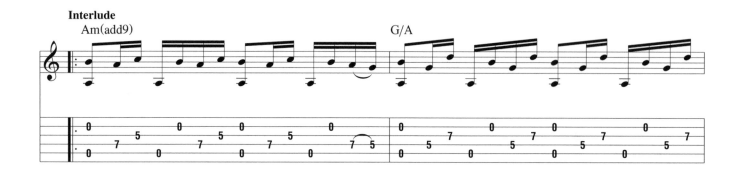

2nd time, D.C. al Coda

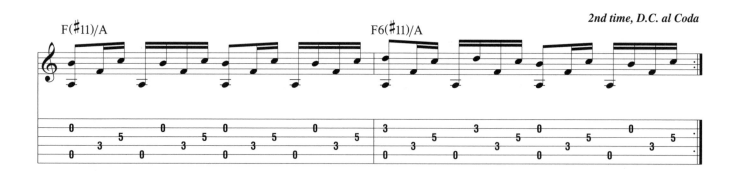

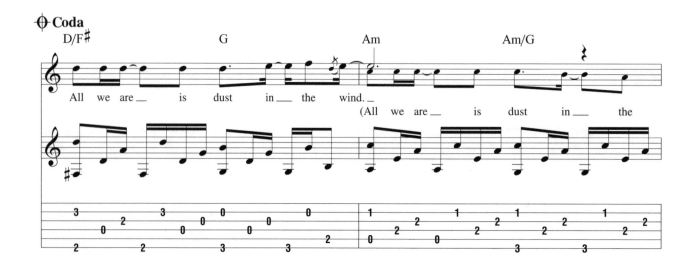

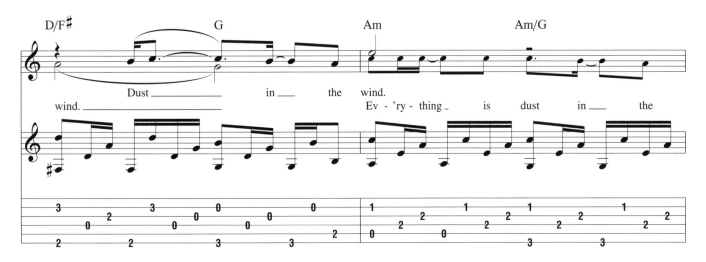

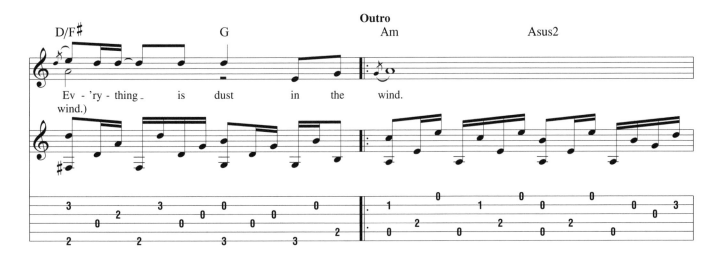

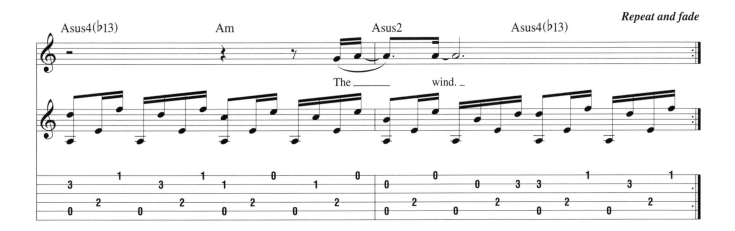

Additional Lyrics

2. Same old song.
    Just a drop of water in an endless sea.
    All we do
    Crumbles to the ground though we refuse to see.

3. Now don't hang on,
    Nothing lasts forever but the earth and sky.
    It slips away
    And all your money won't another minute buy.

Fly to the Angels

Words and Music by Mark Slaughter and Dana Strum

Tune down 1 step:
(low to high) D-G-C-F-A-D

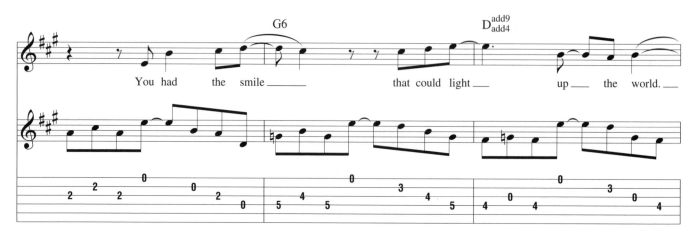

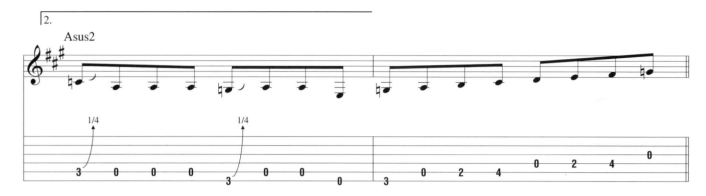

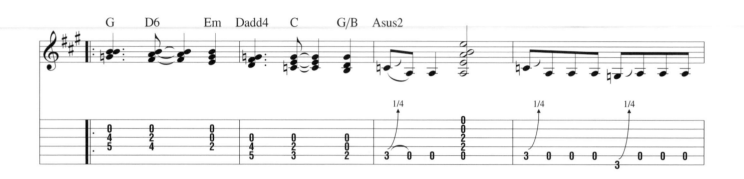

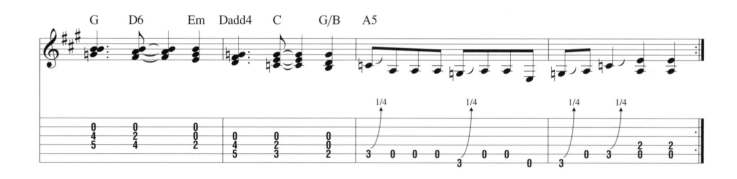

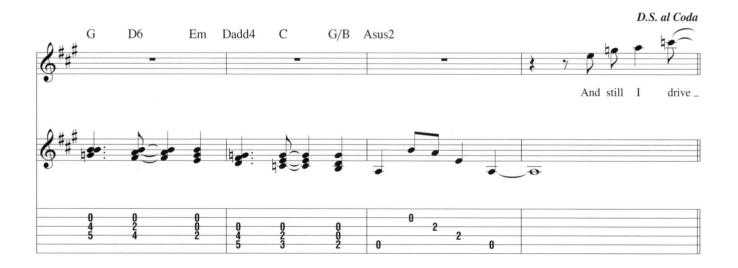

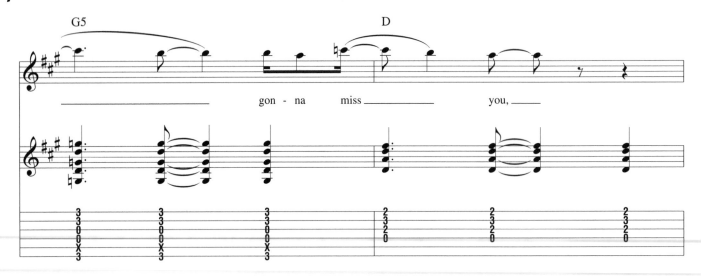

Asus2
let ___ you ___ go, ___ 'cause now you've got to
w/ dist.
Chorus
G5
D5
fly, ___ fly to the an -
Asus2
G5
- gels. ___ Heav - en a - waits ___ your heart ___ and
1/4
D5
Asus2
flow - ers bloom ___ in your name. ___ Whoa, ___ you've got to fly, ___
1/4

gon - na   miss _____   you, _____

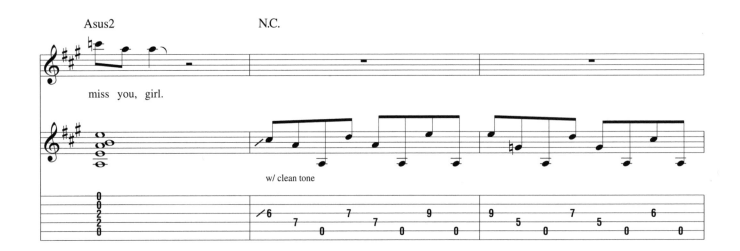

miss   you,   girl.

w/ clean tone

Additional Lyrics

2. You know it hurts me way deep inside
   When I turn and look and find that you're not there.
   I try to convince myself that the pain,
   The pain, it's still not gone.

Free Fallin'

Words and Music by Tom Petty and Jeff Lynne

Capo I

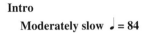

Intro

Moderately slow ♩ = 84

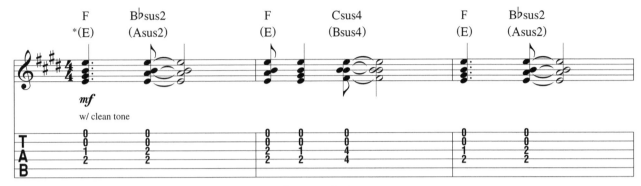

*Symbols in parentheses represent chord names respective to capoed guitar.
Symbols above reflect actual sounding chords. Capoed fret is "0" in tab.

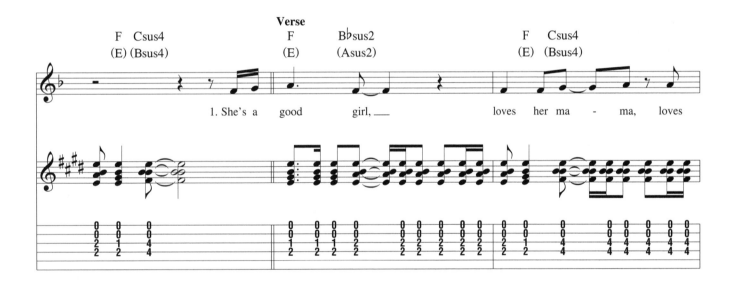

1. She's a good girl, ___ loves her ma - ma, loves

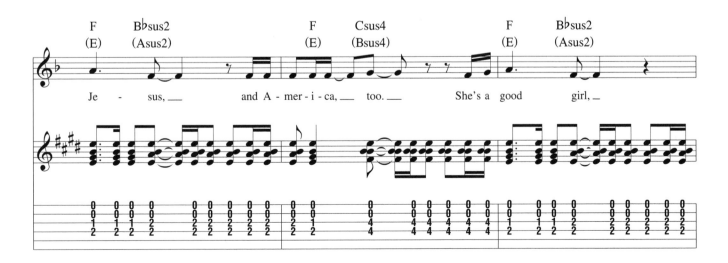

Je - sus, ___ and A - mer - i - ca, ___ too. ___ She's a good girl, ___

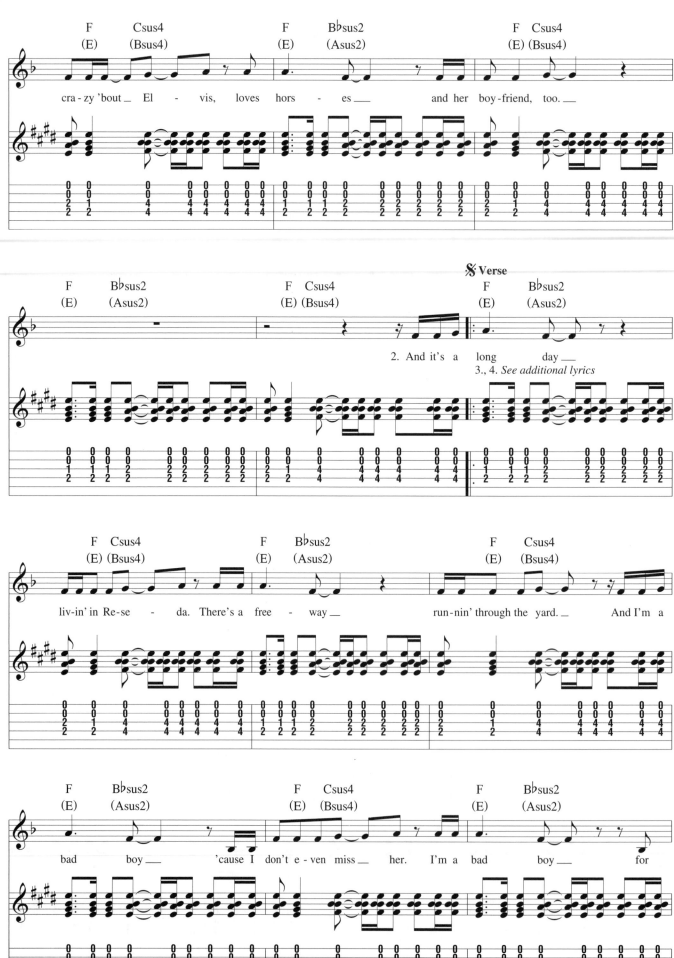

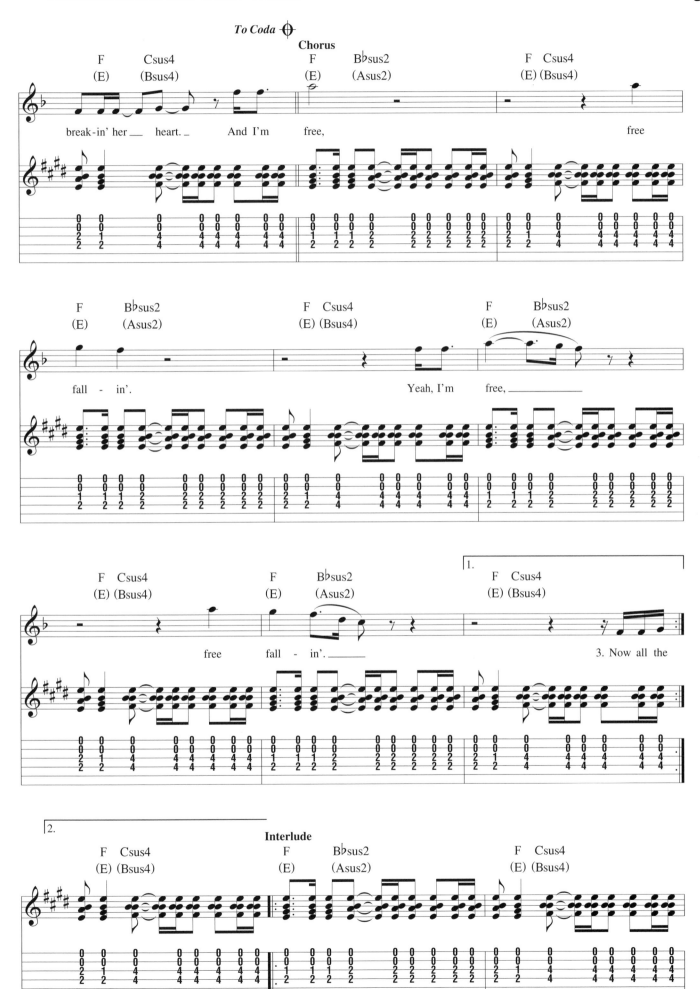

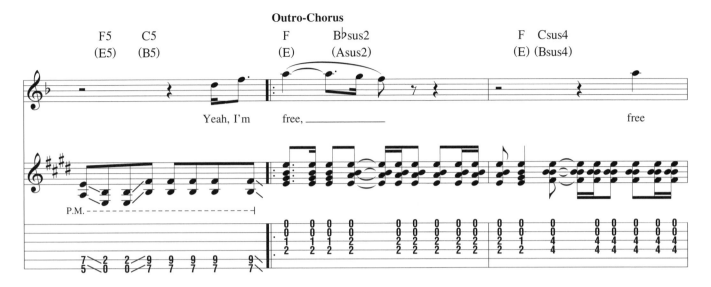

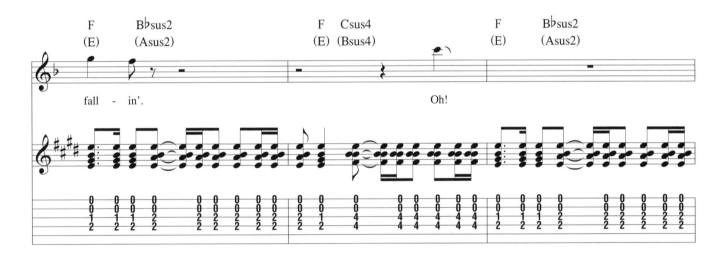

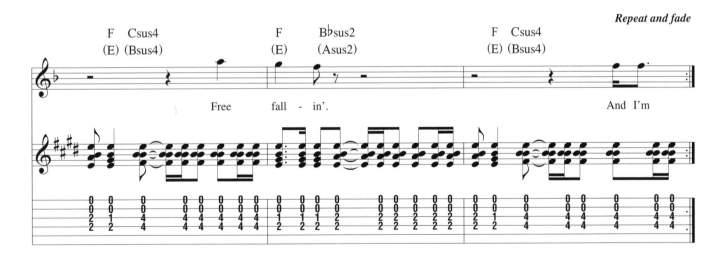

Additional Lyrics

3. Now all the vampires walkin' through the valley
Move west down Ventura Boulevard.
And all the bad boys are standin' in the shadows,
And the good girls are home with broken hearts.

4. I wanna glide down over Mulholland,
I wanna write her name in the sky.
I'm gonna free fall out into nothin',
Gonna leave this world for a while.

I'd Love to Change the World

Words and Music by Alvin Lee

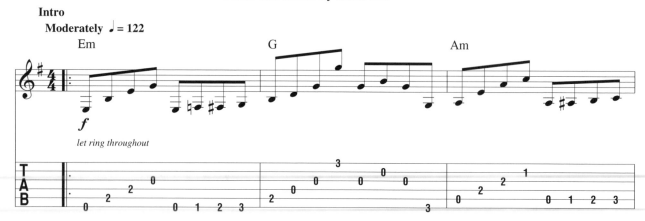

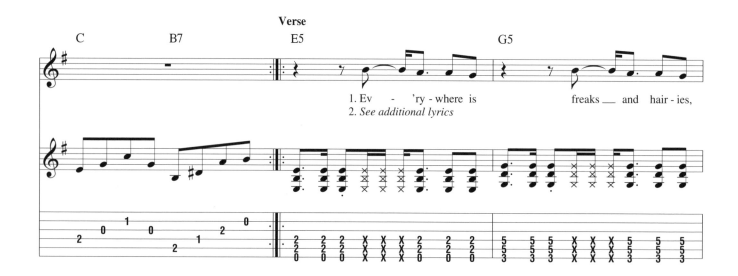

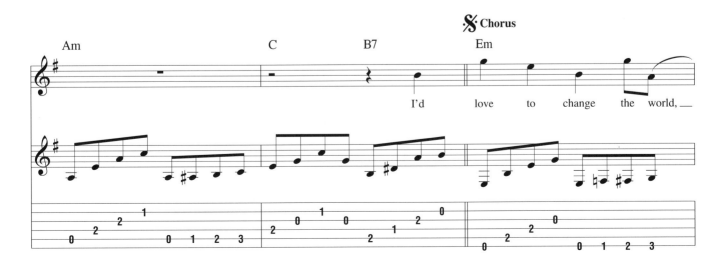

Guitar Solo

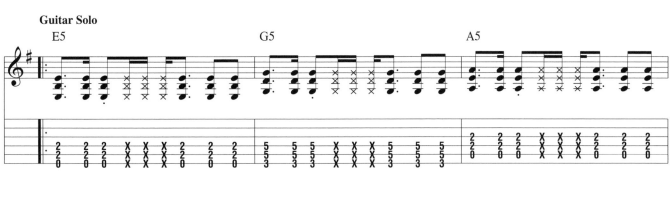

Bridge

World _ pol - lu - tion

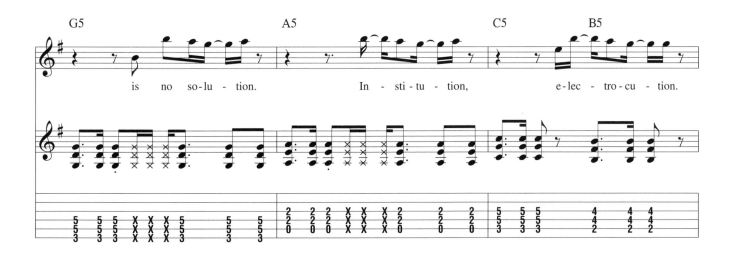

is   no   so-lu - tion.   In - sti-tu - tion,   e-lec - tro-cu - tion.

There's black or white, _   rich or   poor. __   Gov-er - nors, _

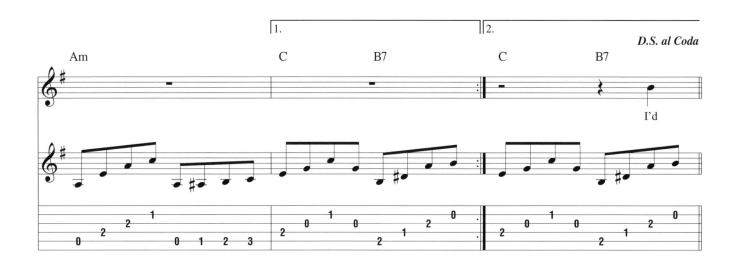

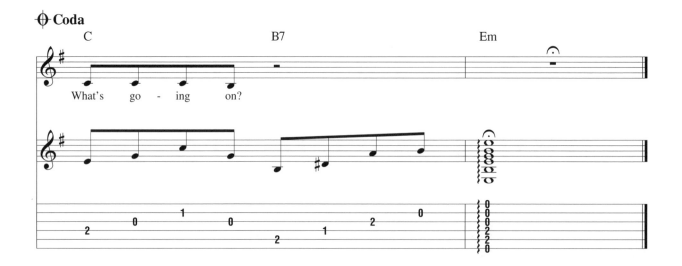

Additional Lyrics

2. Population keeps on breeding.
   Nation bleeding, still more feeding economy.
   Life is funny; skies are sunny.
   Bees make honey; who needs money?
   Monopoly.
   No, not for me.

Iris

from the Motion Picture CITY OF ANGELS
Words and Music by John Rzeznik

Tuning:
(low to high) B♭-D♭-D-D♭-D♯-D

Intro
Moderately slow ♩ = 51

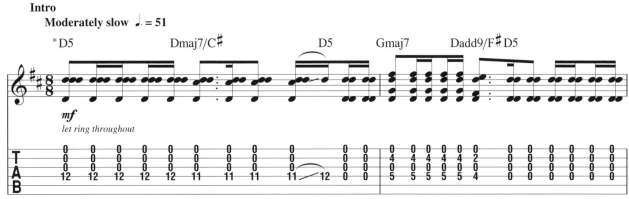

*Chord symbols reflect implied harmony.

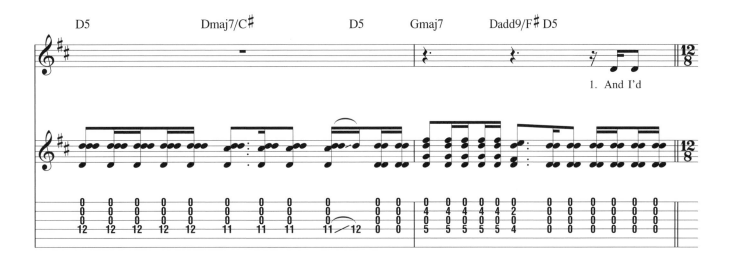

1. And I'd

Verse

give up for-ev - er to touch _ you   'cause I   know _ that you feel _ me some - how.   You're the clos-

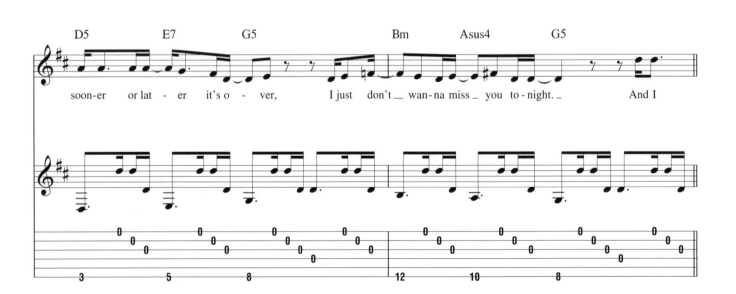

§ **Chorus**

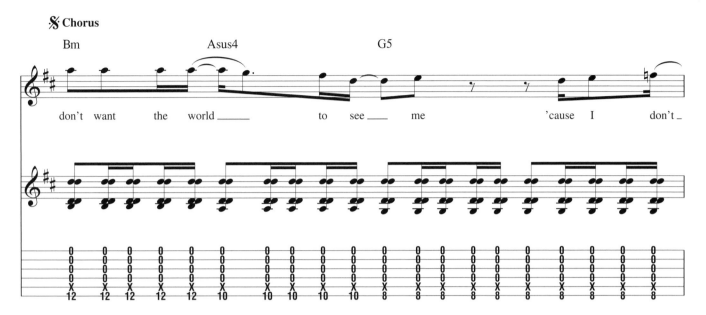

don't want the world _____ to see ___ me 'cause I don't _

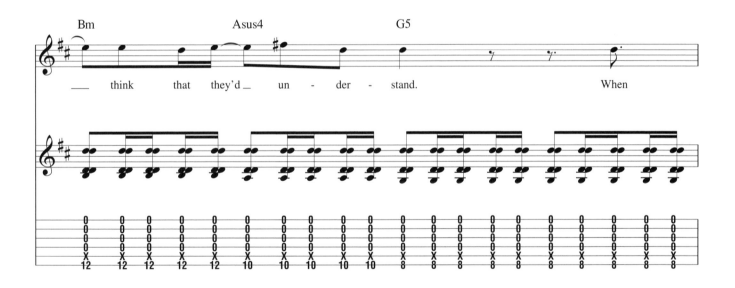

___ think that they'd _ un - der - stand. When

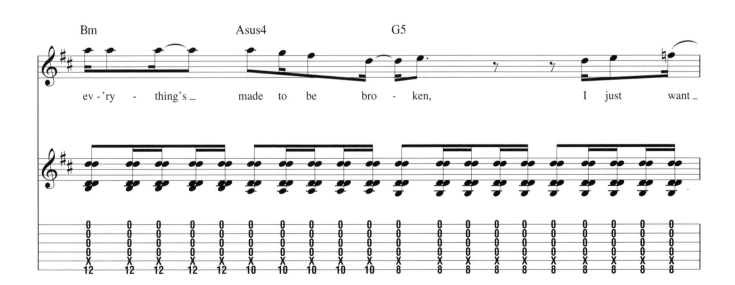

ev -'ry - thing's _ made to be bro - ken, I just want _

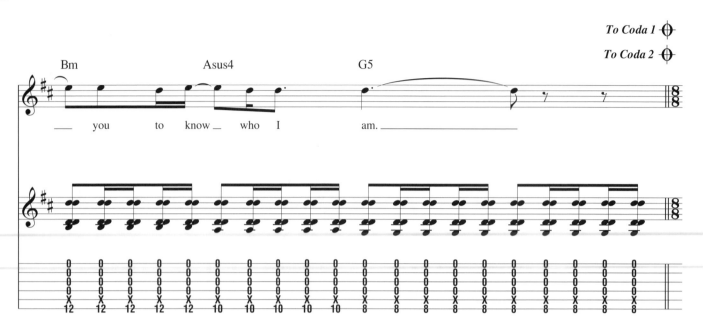

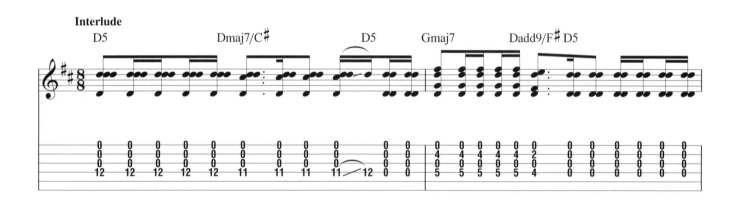

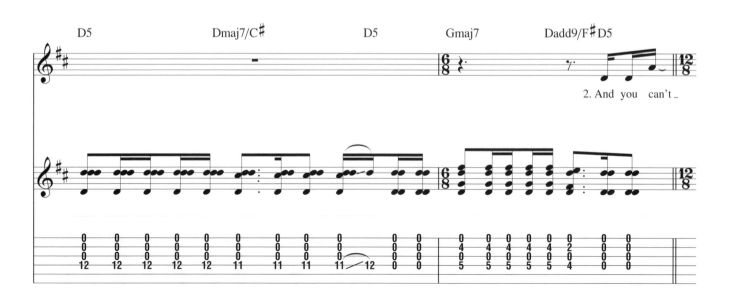

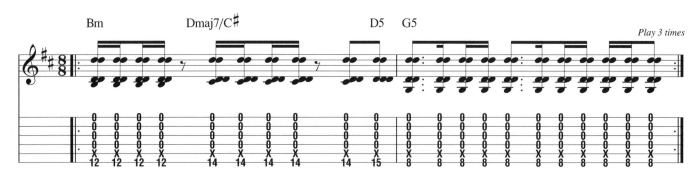

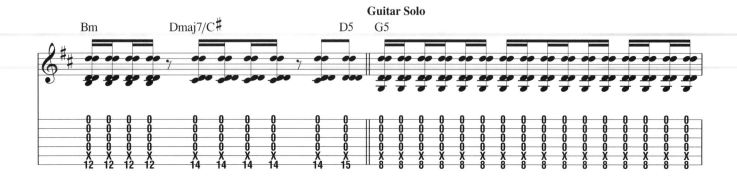

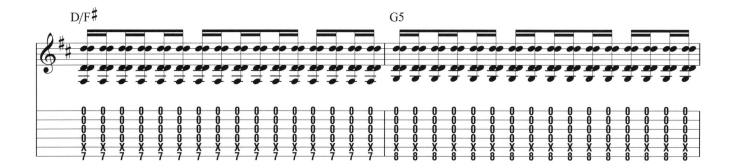

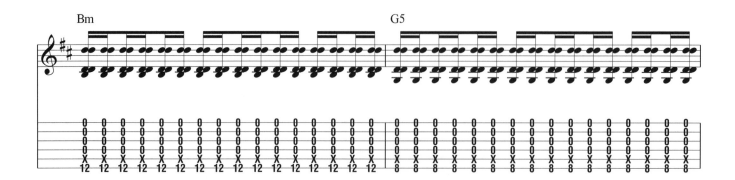

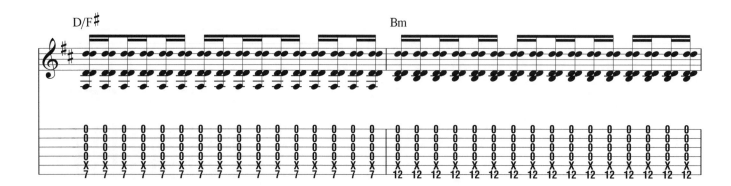

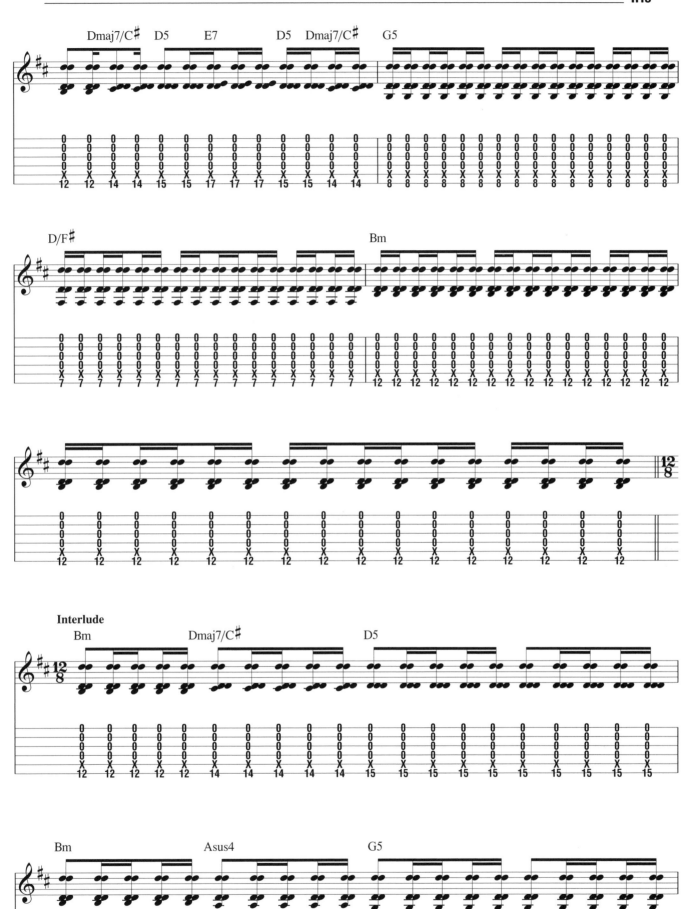

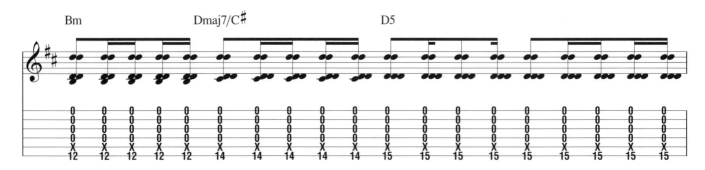

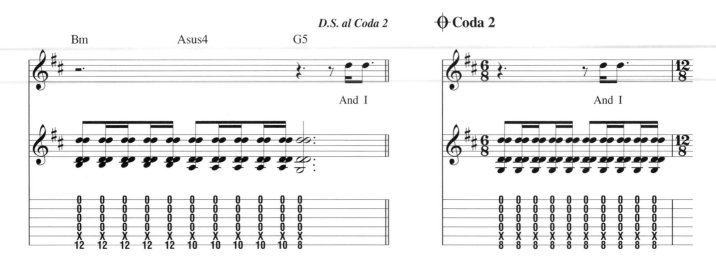

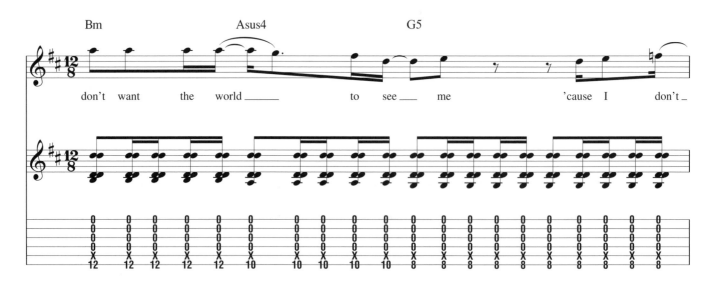

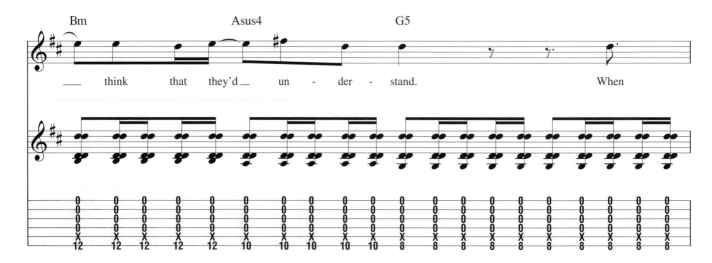

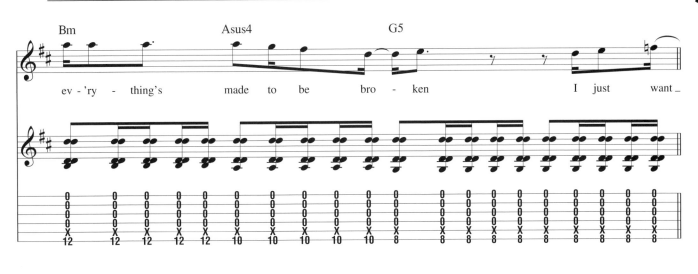

ev-'ry - thing's made to be bro - ken I just want

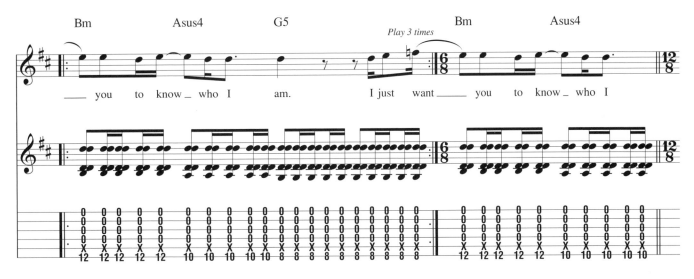

_____ you to know _ who I am. I just want _____ you to know _ who I

Outro

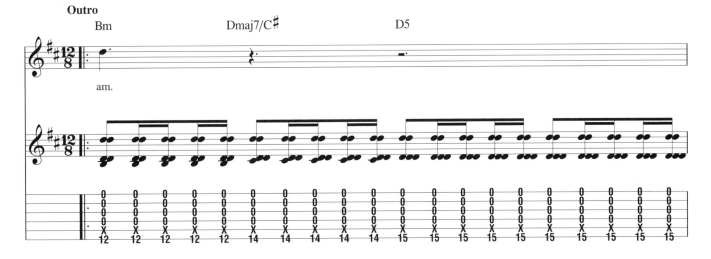

am.

Repeat and fade

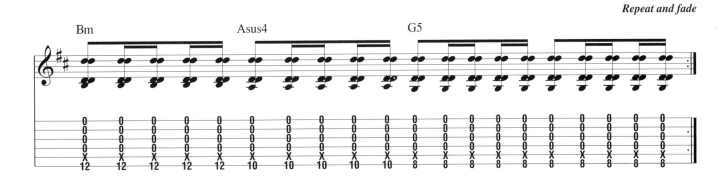

Landslide

Words and Music by Stevie Nicks

Capo III

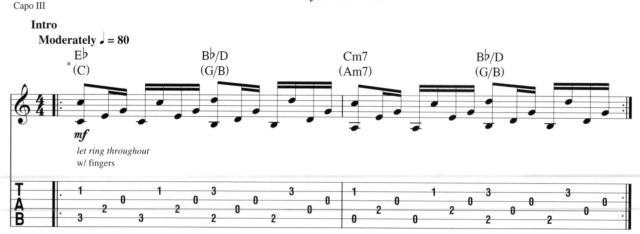

*Symbols in parentheses represent chord names respective to capoed guitar.
Symbols above reflect actual sounding chords. Capoed fret is "0" in tab.

Verse

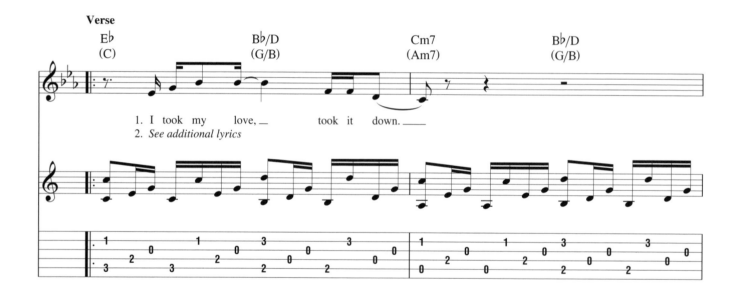

1. I took my love, __ took it down. __
2. *See additional lyrics*

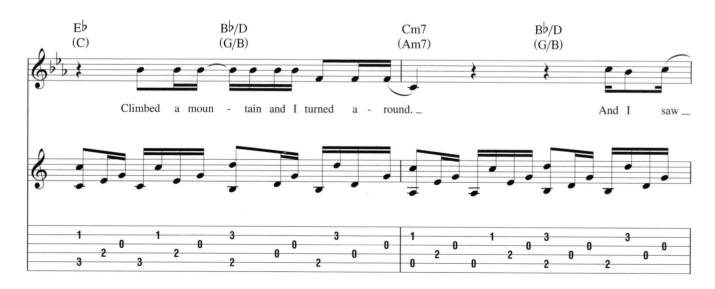

Climbed a moun - tain and I turned a - round. __ And I saw __

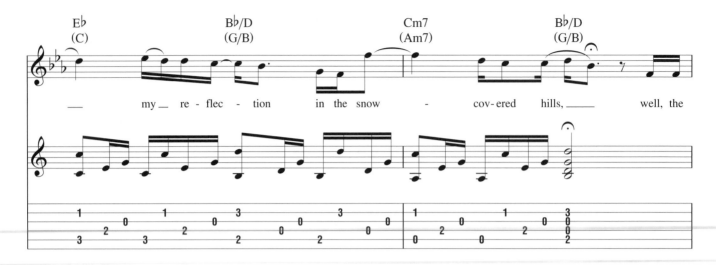

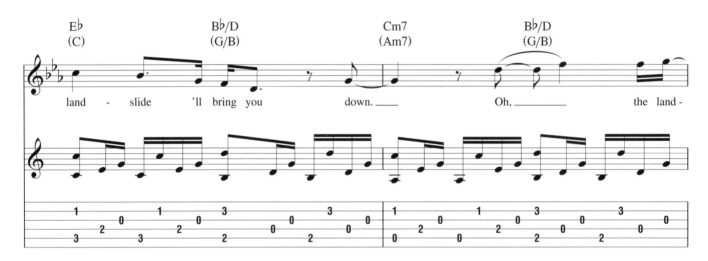

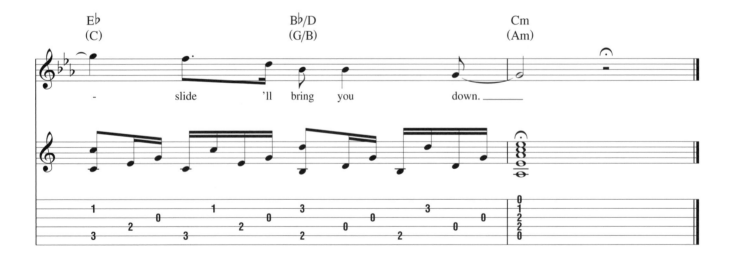

Additional Lyrics

2. Oh, mirror in the sky, what is love?
   Can the child within my heart rise above?
   Can I sail through the changing ocean tides?
   Can I handle the seasons of my life? Mm.

Layla

Words and Music by Eric Clapton and Jim Gordon

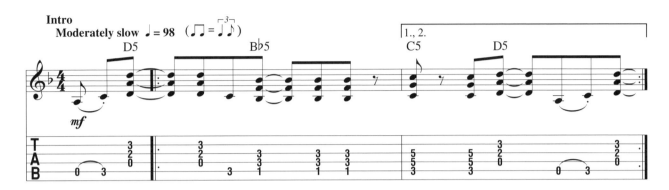

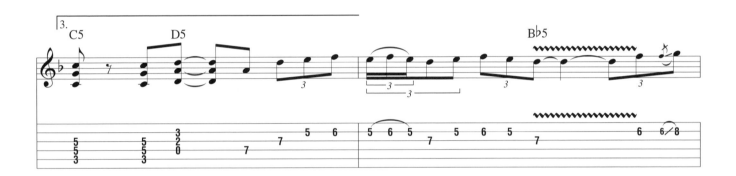

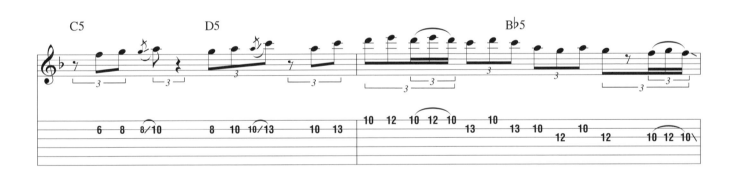

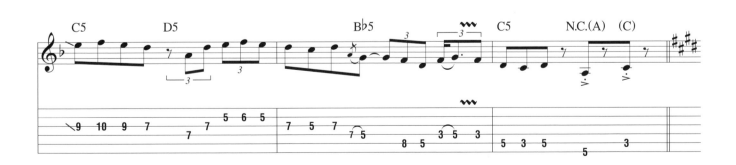

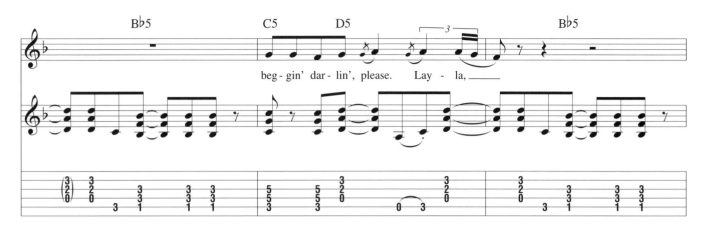

beg - gin' dar - lin', please.   Lay - la, _____

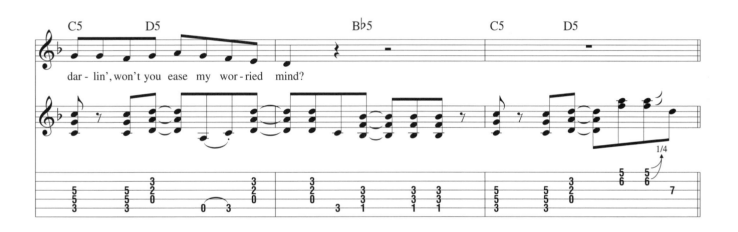

dar - lin', won't you ease my wor-ried mind?

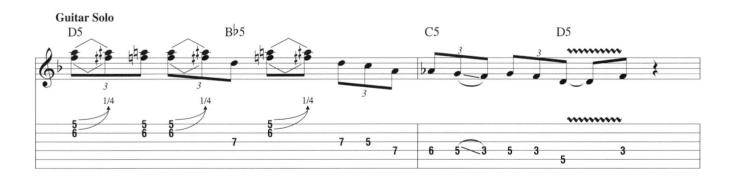

Guitar Solo

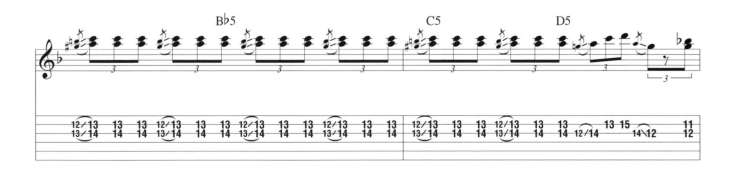

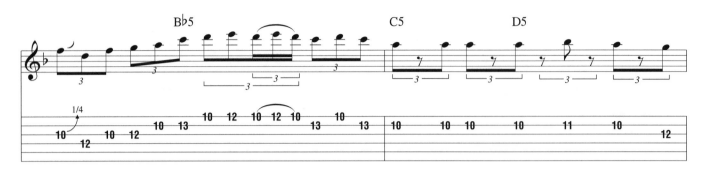

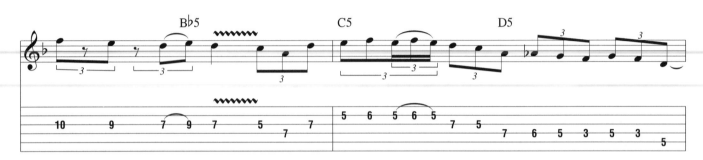

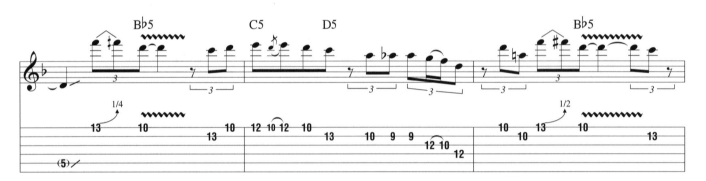

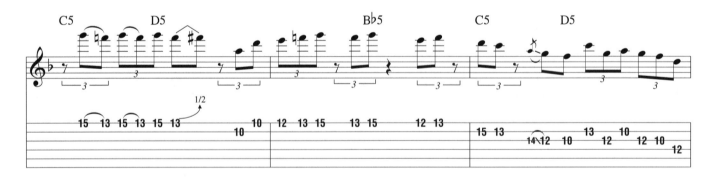

D.S. al Coda

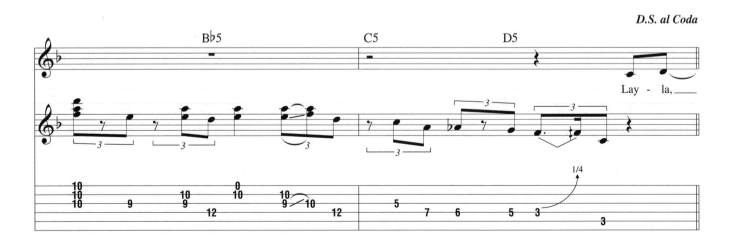

Lay - la, ___

Additional Lyrics

2. Make the best of the situation,
   Before I fin'ly go insane.
   Please don't say we'll never find a way.
   Tell me all my love's in vain.

Leaving on a Jet Plane

Words and Music by John Denver

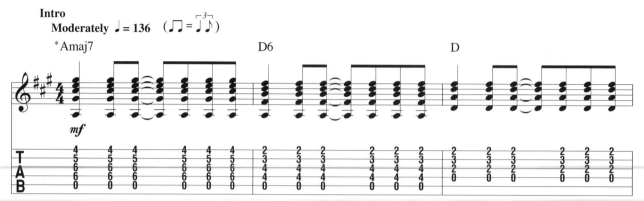

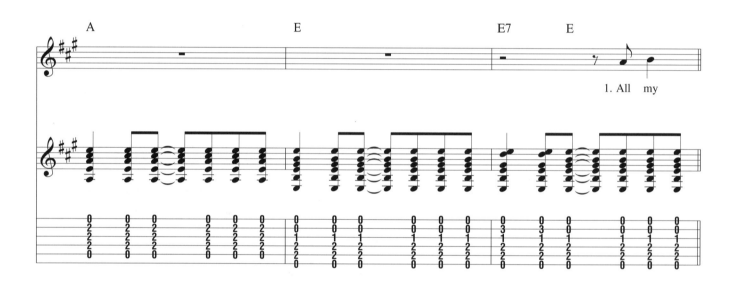

*Bass plays E, next 2 meas.

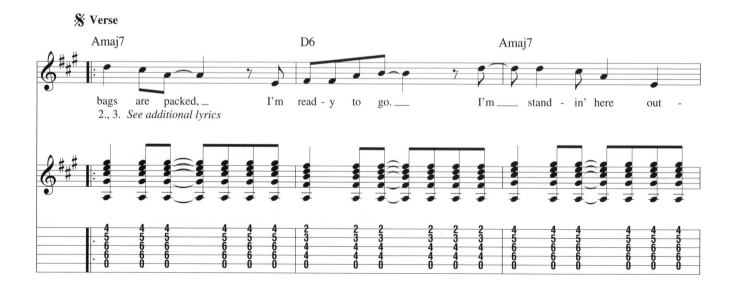

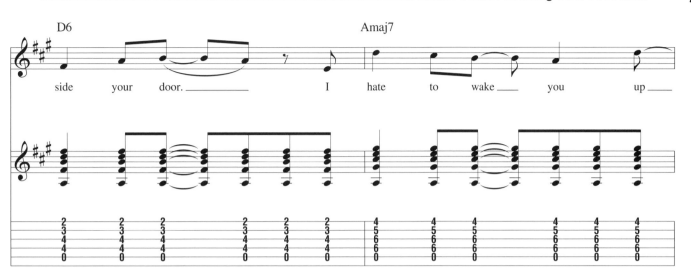

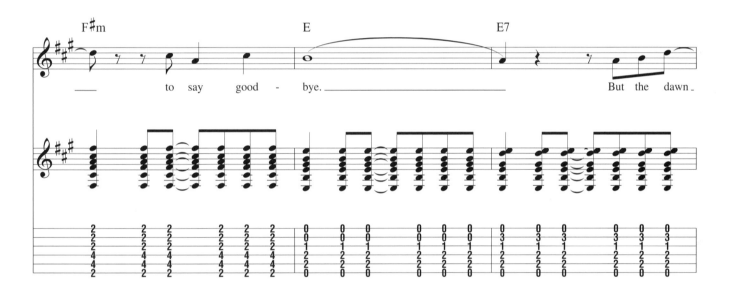

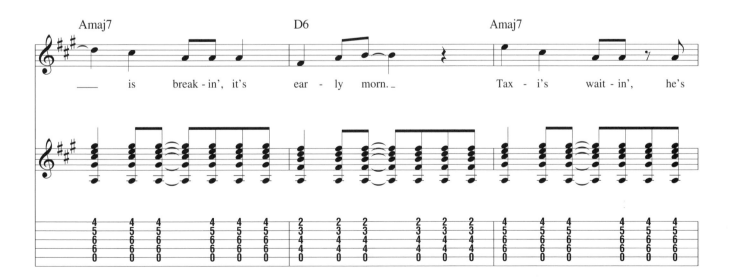

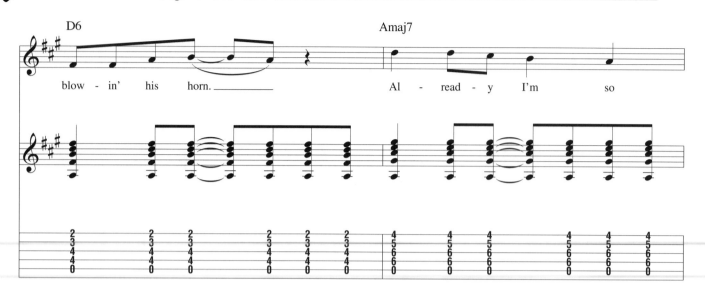

blow - in' his horn. _____ Al - read - y I'm so

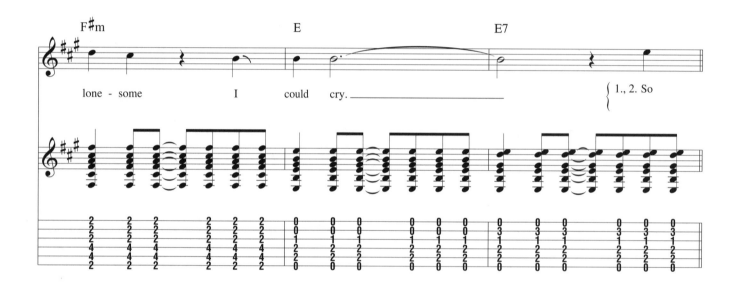

lone - some I could cry. _____ { 1., 2. So

Pre-Chorus

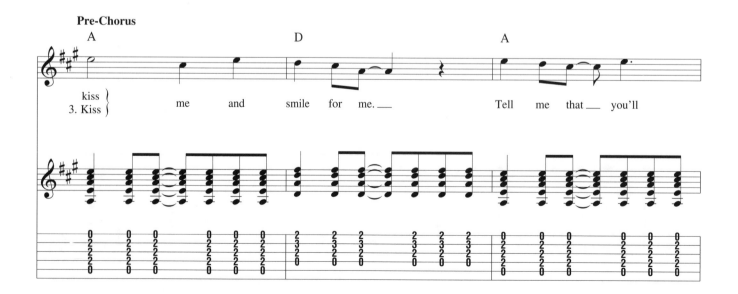

kiss } me and smile for me. __ Tell me that __ you'll
3. Kiss }

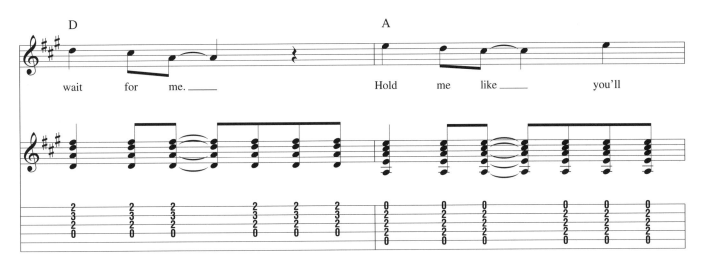

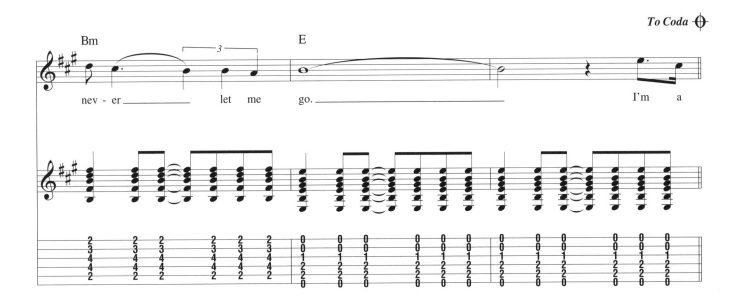

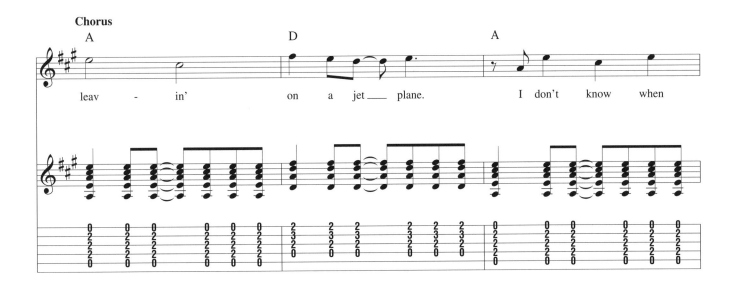

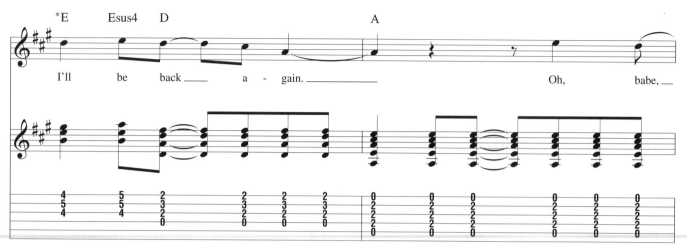

I'll   be   back ____ a - gain. _____   Oh,   babe, __

*Bass plays A this meas.

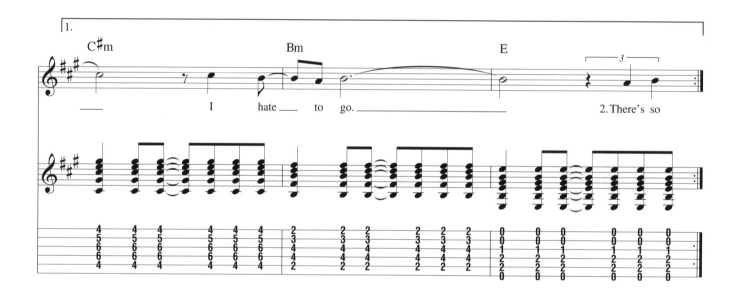

____   I   hate ___ to   go. _____   2. There's so

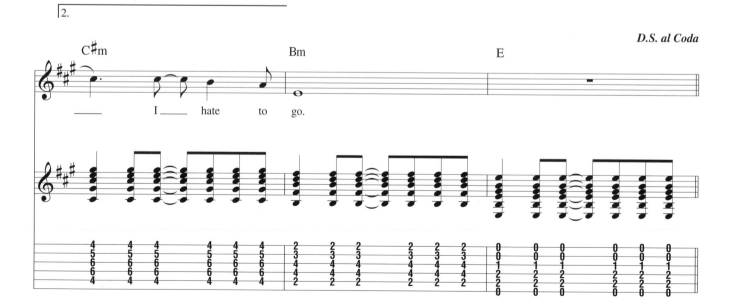

D.S. al Coda

____   I ___ hate   to   go.

Coda

Outro-Chorus

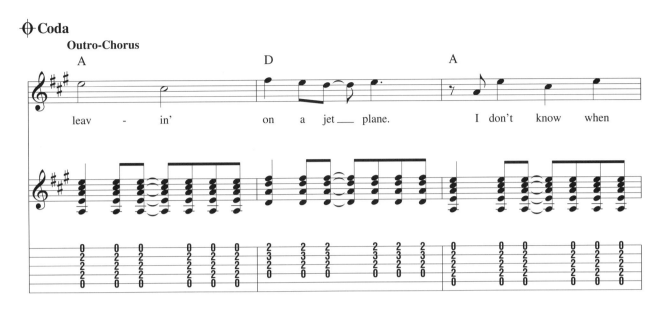

leav - in' on a jet ___ plane. I don't know when

*Bass plays A this meas.

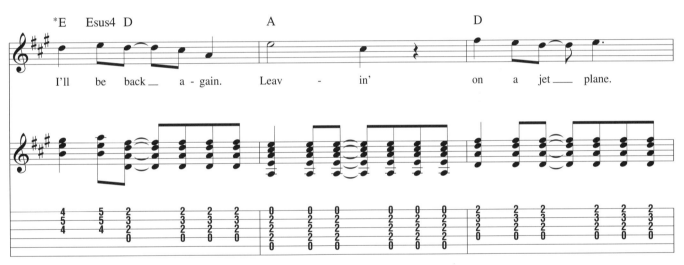

I'll be back ___ a - gain. Leav - in' on a jet ___ plane.

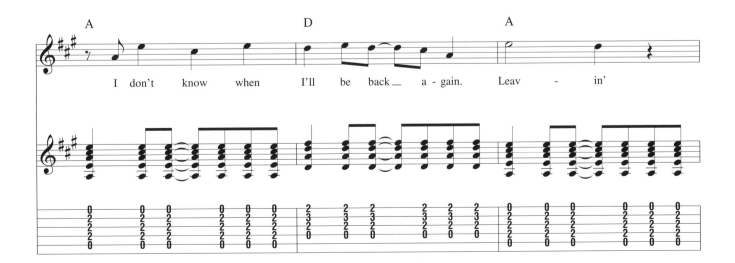

I don't know when I'll be back ___ a - gain. Leav - in'

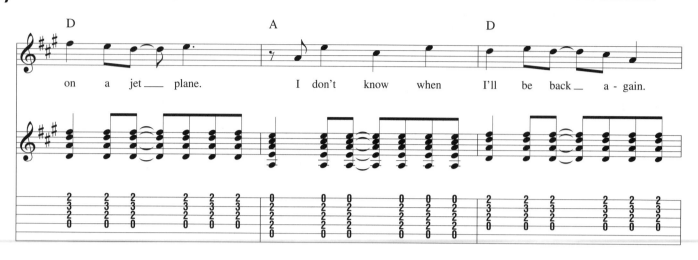

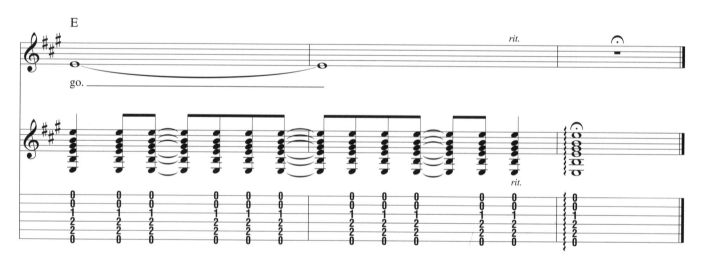

Additional Lyrics

2. There's so many times I've let you down,
   So many times I've played around.
   I tell you now, they don't mean a thing.
   Ev'ry place I go I think of you,
   Ev'ry song I sing I sing for you.
   When I come back I'll wear your wedding ring.

3. Now the time has come to leave you.
   One more time, let me kiss you.
   Then close your eyes, I'll be on my way.
   Dream about the days to come
   When I won't have to leave alone,
   About the time I won't have to say:

Love of a Lifetime

Words and Music by Bill Leverty and Carl Snare

Tune down 1/2 step:
(low to high) E♭-A♭-D♭-G♭-B♭-E♭

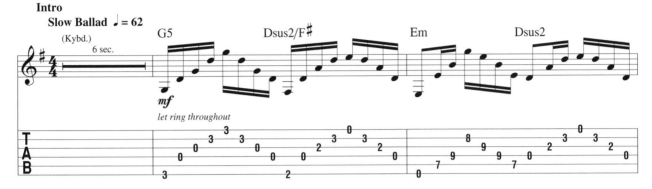

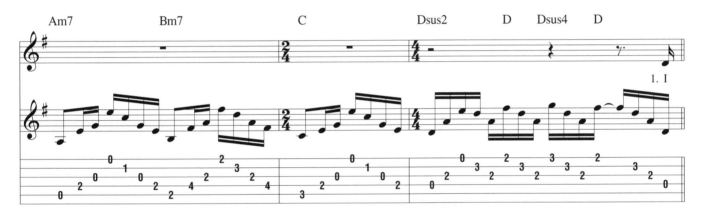

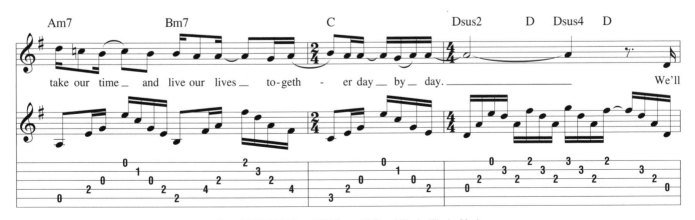

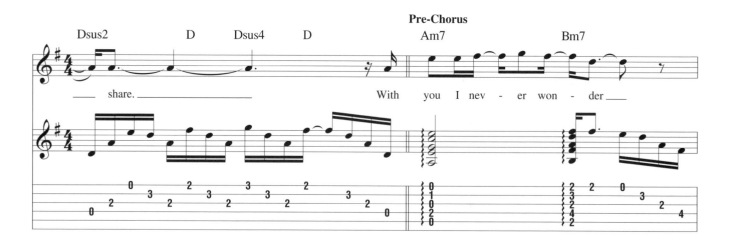

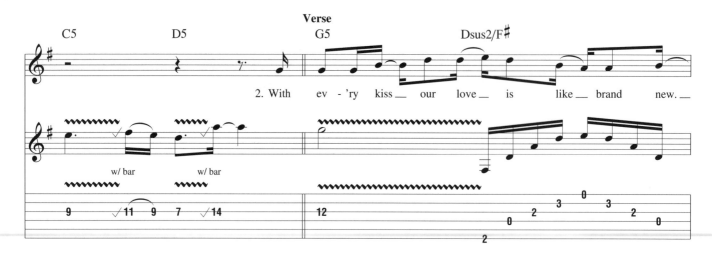

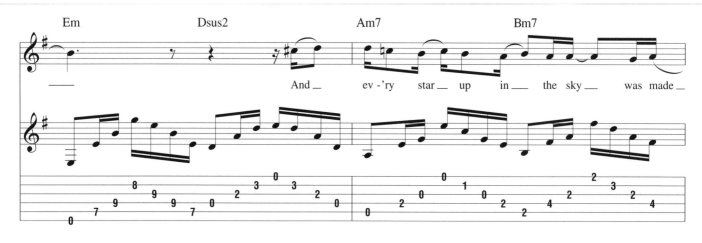

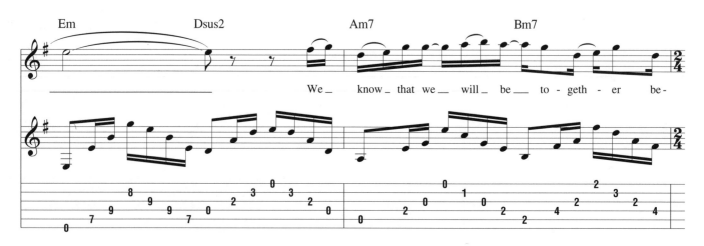

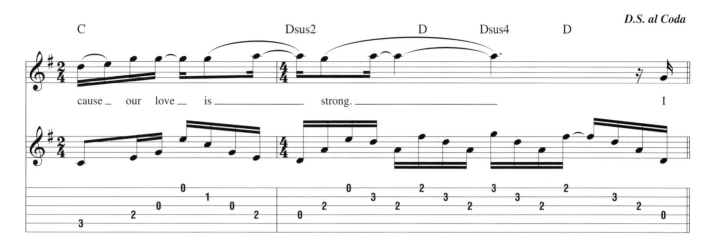

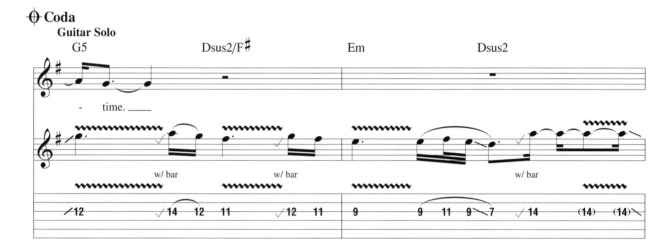

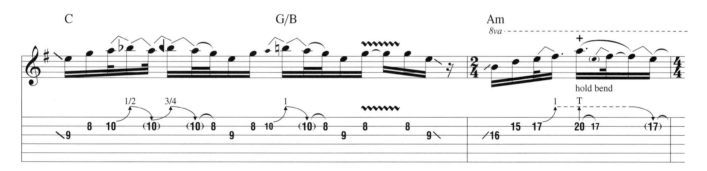

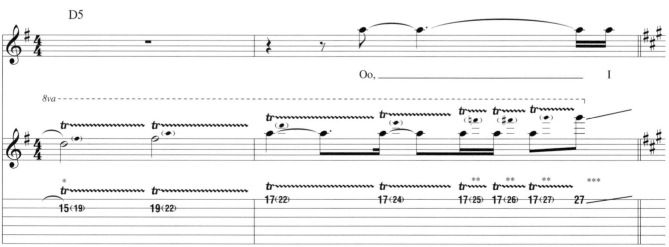

*Tap higher note w/ edge of pick.

**Hypothetical fret location. ***Slide w/
edge of pick.

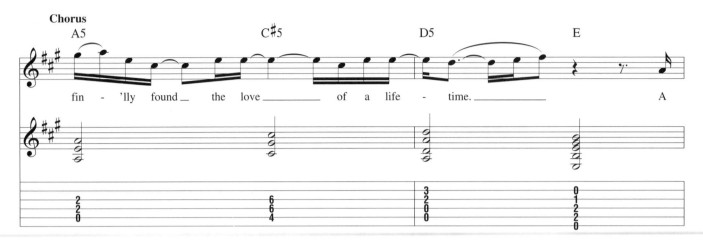

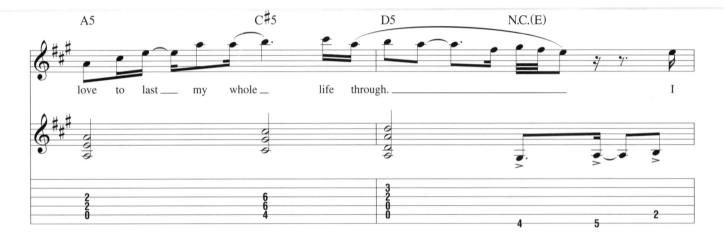

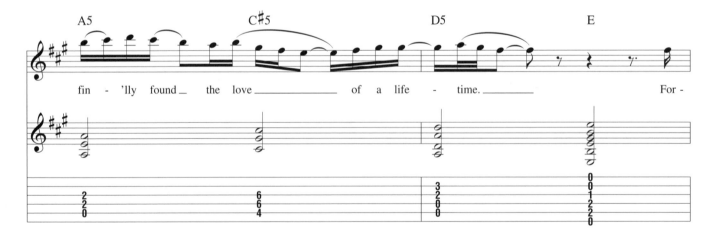

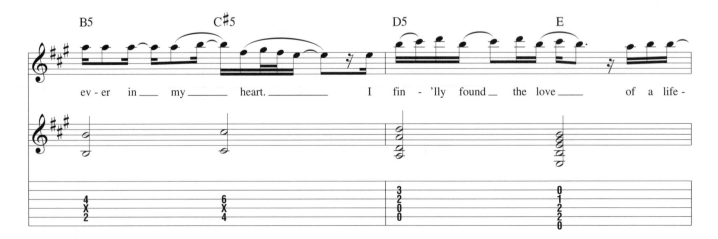

Maggie May

Words and Music by Rod Stewart and Martin Quittenton

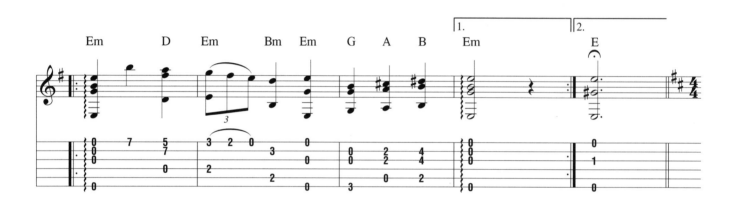

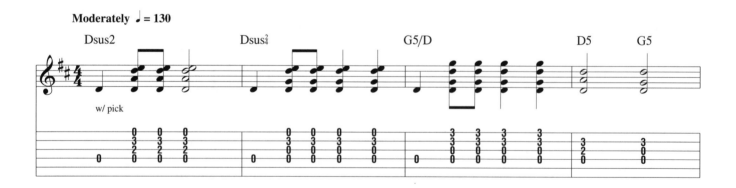

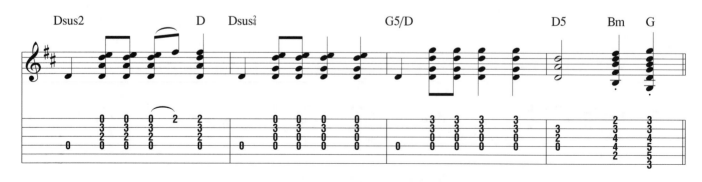

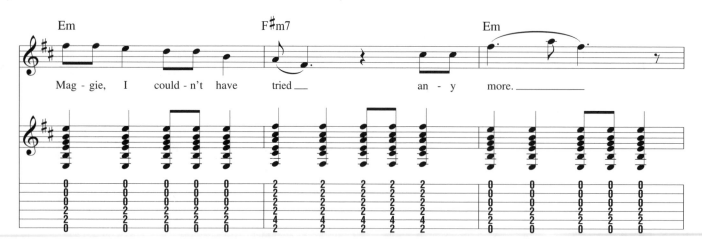

Mag - gie, I could - n't have tried ___ an - y more. ___

2nd & 3rd times, substitute Fill 1
4th time, substitute Fill 3

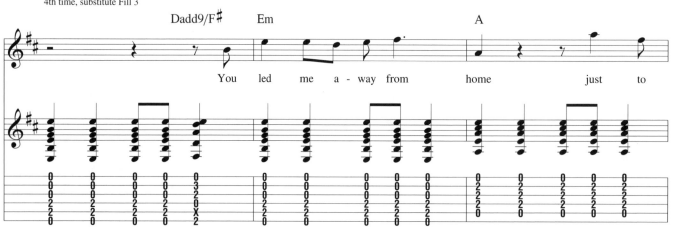

You led me a - way from home just to

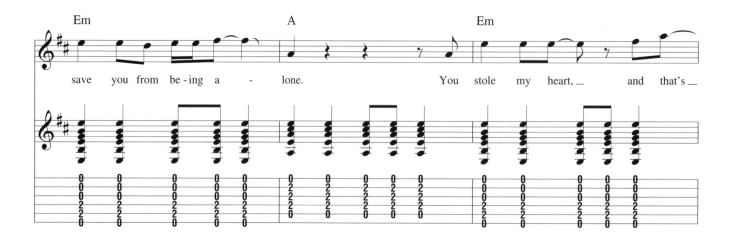

save you from be - ing a - lone. You stole my heart, ___ and that's ___

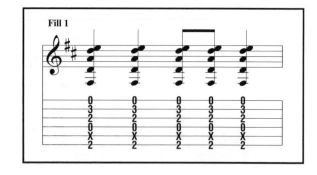

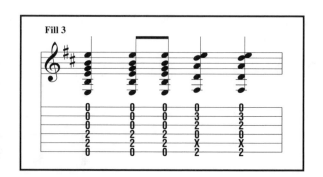

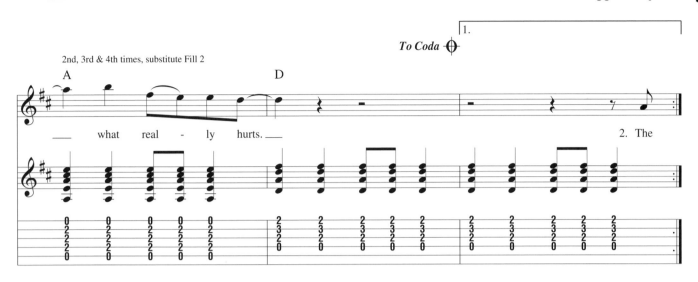

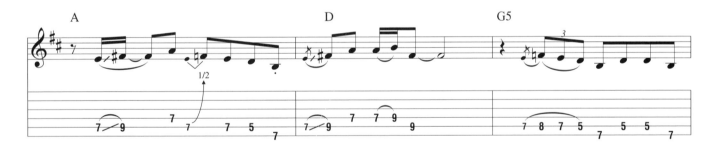

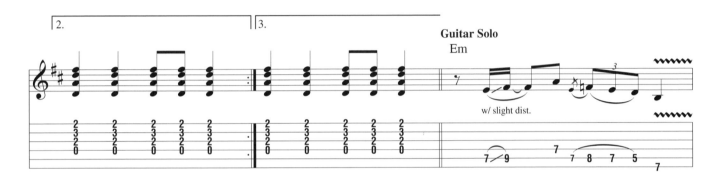

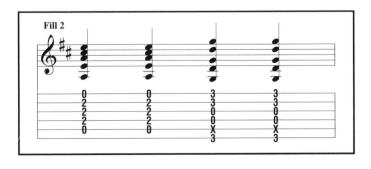

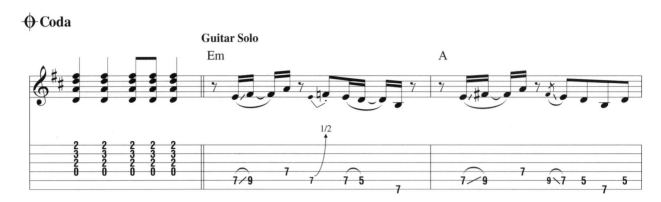

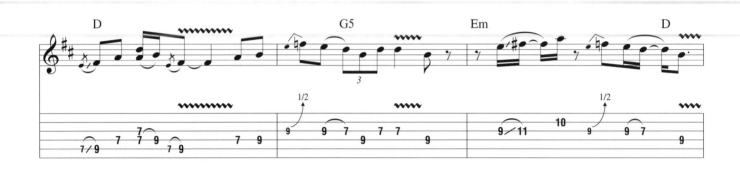

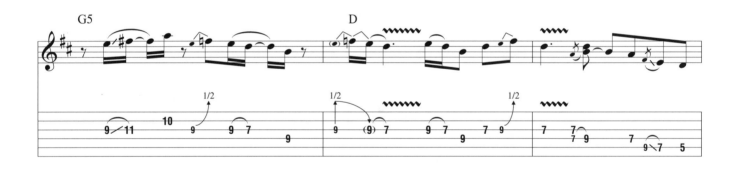

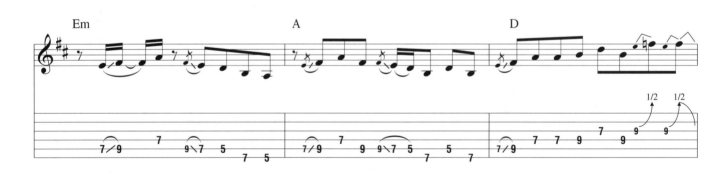

Mandolin Solo

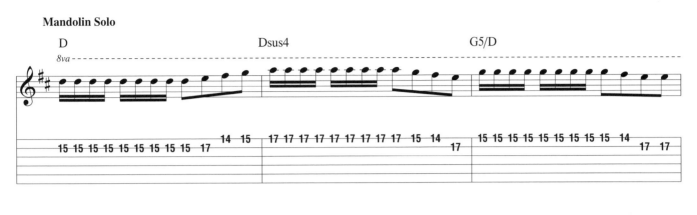

*Bass plays E.

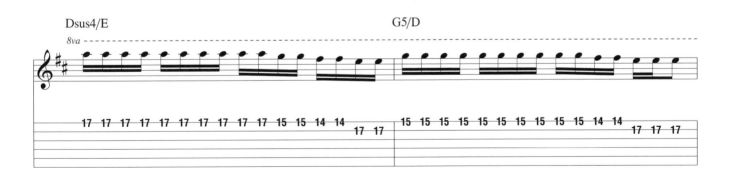

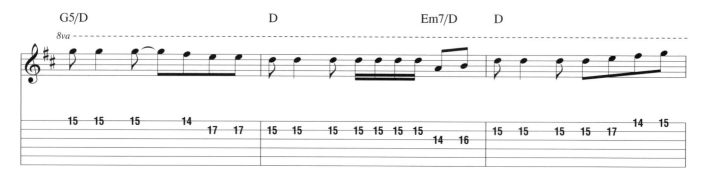

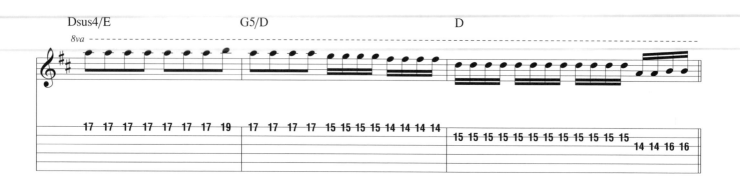

Outro

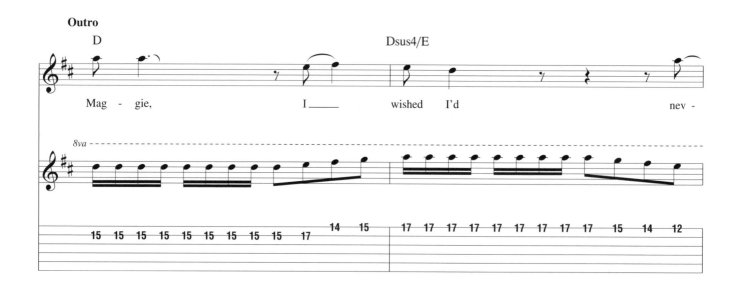

Mag - gie,   I ___ wished   I'd   nev -

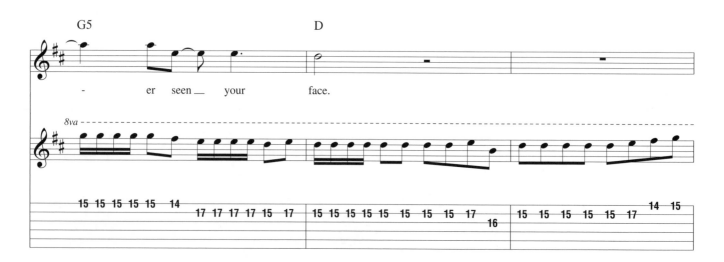

- er seen __ your   face.

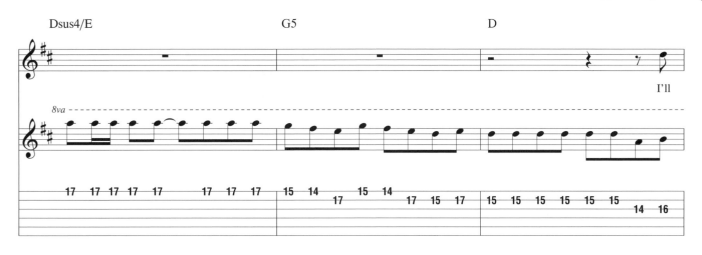

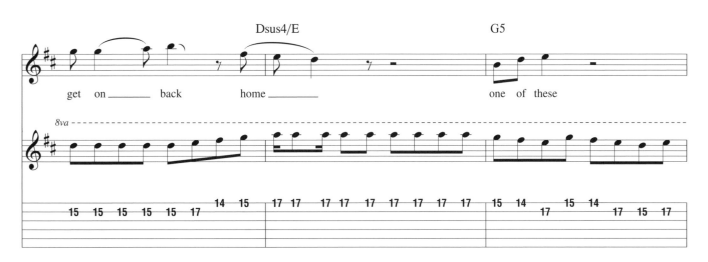

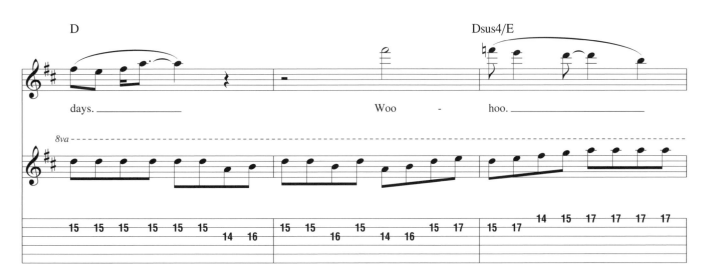

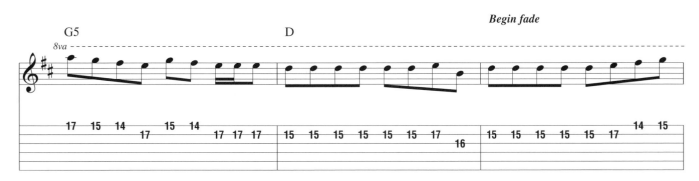

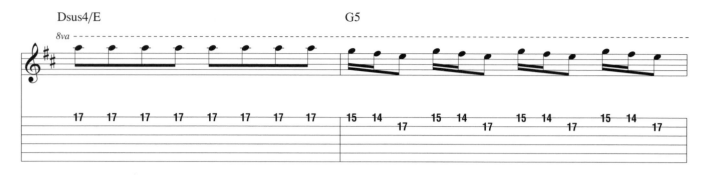

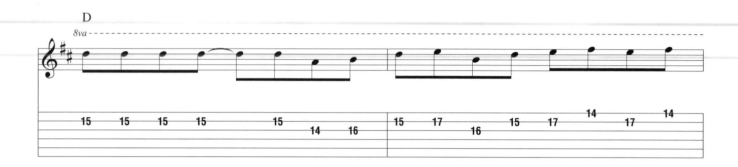

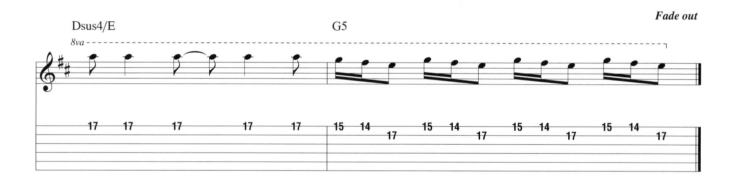

Additional Lyrics

2. The morning sun, when it's in your face, really shows your age.
   But that don't worry me none. In my eyes, you're everything.
   I laughed at all of your jokes.
   My love you didn't need to coax.
   Oh, Maggie, I couldn't have tried any more.
   You led me away from home
   Just to save you from being alone.
   You stole my soul, and that's a pain I can do without.

3. All I needed was a friend to lend a guiding hand.
   But you turned into a lover and, mother, what a lover! You wore me out.
   All you did was wreck my bed,
   And, in the morning, kick me in the head.
   Oh, Maggie, I couldn't have tried any more.
   You led me away from home
   'Cause you didn't want to be alone.
   You stole me heart; I couldn't leave you if I tried.

4. I suppose I could collect my books and get on back to school.
   Or steal my daddy's cue and make a living out of playing pool.
   Or find myself a rock 'n' roll band
   That needs a helping hand.
   Oh, Maggie, I wish I'd never seen your face.
   You made a first-class fool out of me.
   But I'm as blind as a fool can be.
   You stole me heart, but I love you anyway.

Night Moves

Words and Music by Bob Seger

Capo I

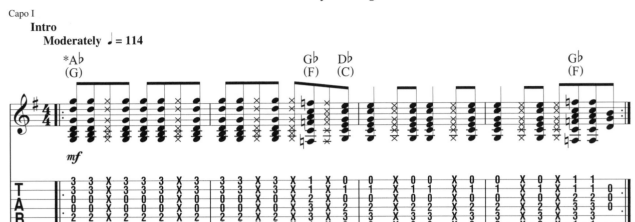

*Symbols in parentheses represent chord names respective to capoed guitar.
Symbols above reflect actual sounding chords.

Verse

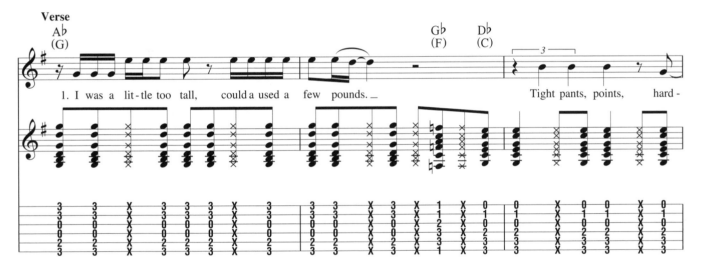

1. I was a lit-tle too tall, could a used a few pounds. _____ Tight pants, points, hard-

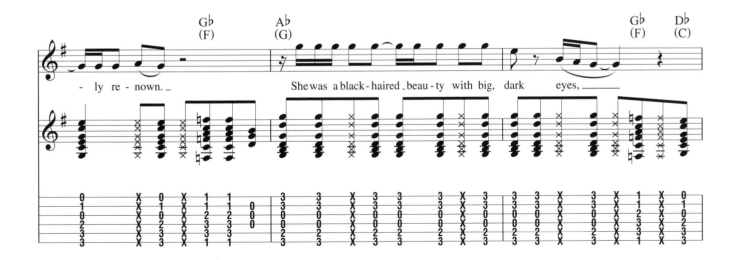

- ly re - nown. _____ She was a black-haired beau-ty with big, dark eyes, _____

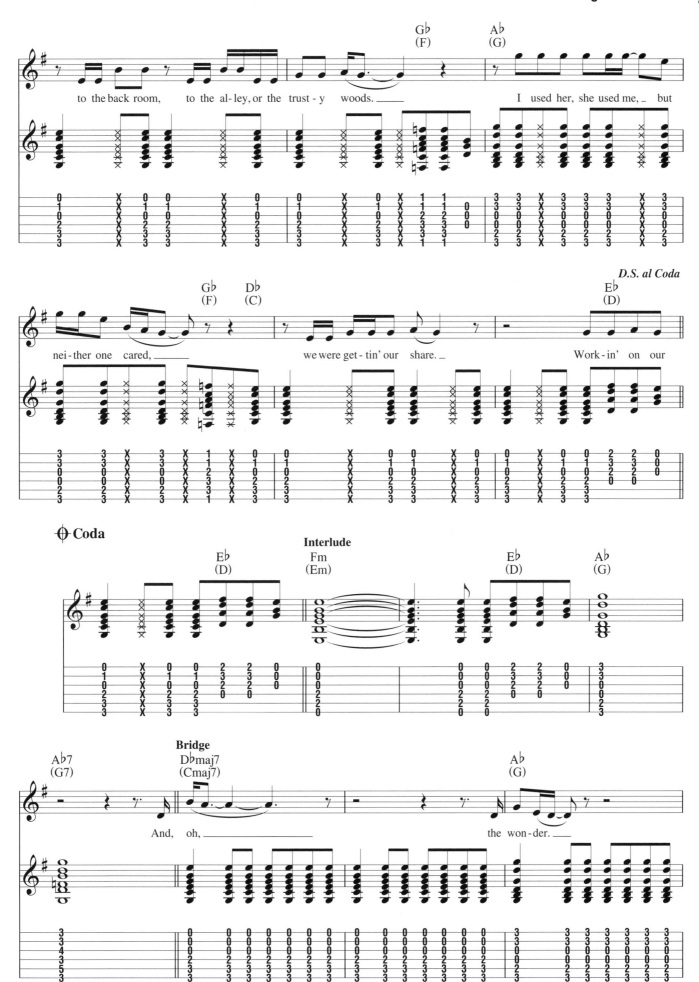

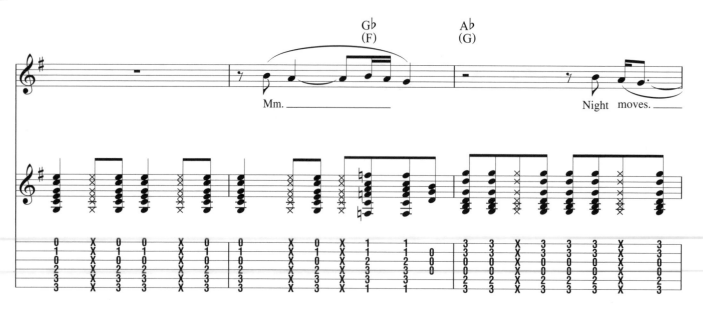

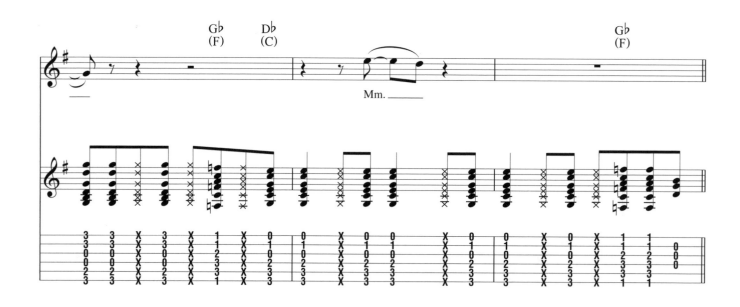

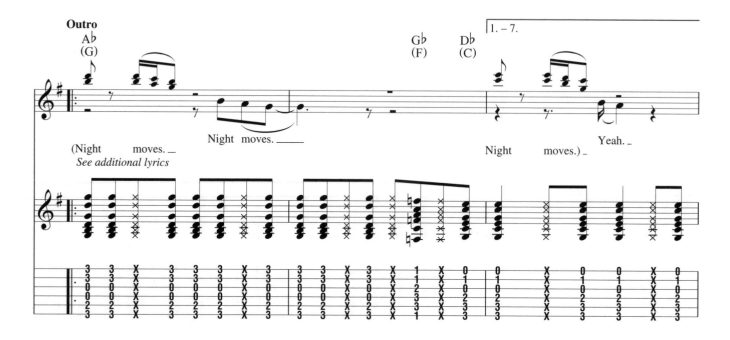

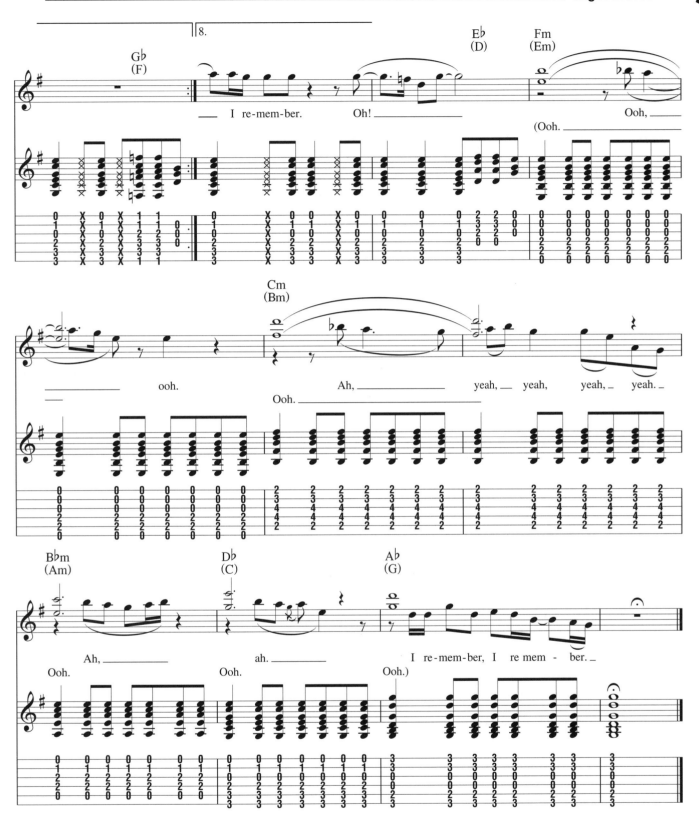

Additional Lyrics

Chorus Workin' on our night moves,
Tryin' to lose the awkward teenage blues.
Workin' on our night moves, mm,
And it was summertime, mm,
Sweet summertime, summertime.

Outro Moves, I sure remember the night moves.
In the morning, I remember.
Funny how you remember.
I remember, I remember, I remember, I remember.
Oh, oh, oh.
Keep it workin', workin' and practicin'.
Workin' and practicin' all of the night moves.
Night moves. Oh.
I remember, yeah, yeah, yeah, I remember.
Ooh. I remember, Lord, I remember, Lord, I remember.

Norwegian Wood (This Bird Has Flown)

Words and Music by John Lennon and Paul McCartney

Capo II

Intro

Moderately ♩. = 64

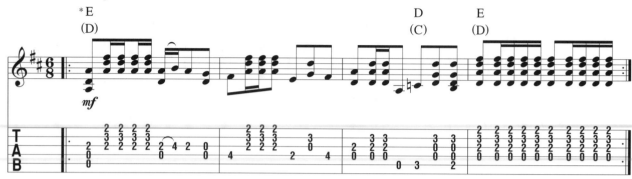

*Symbols in parentheses represent chord names respective to capoed guitar.
Symbols above reflect actual sounding chords. Capoed fret is "0" in tab.

Verse

1. I once ___ had a girl, or should I say she once had

me. She showed ___ me her room, is - n't it

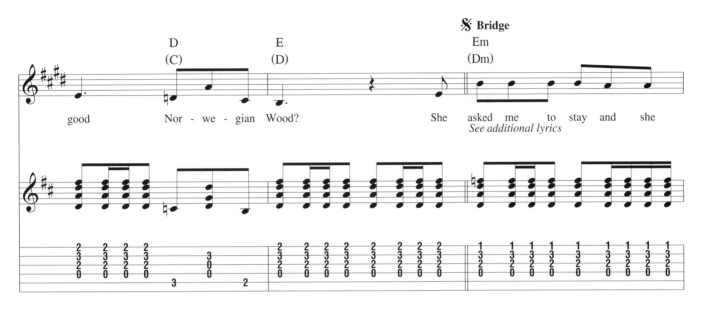

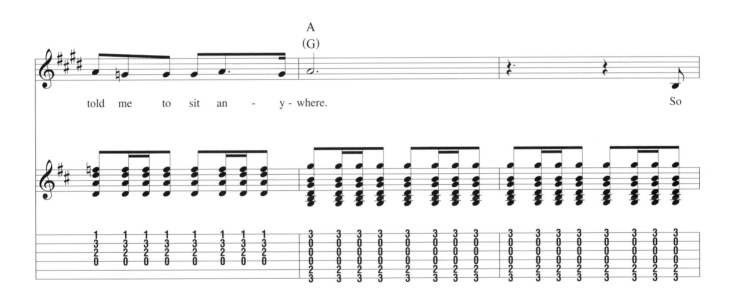

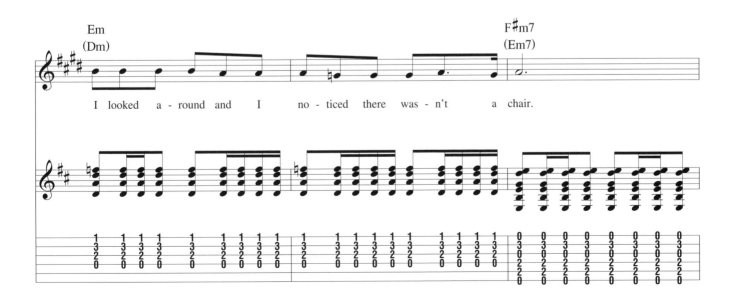

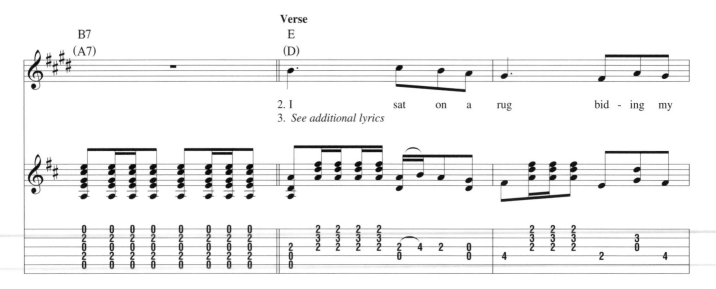

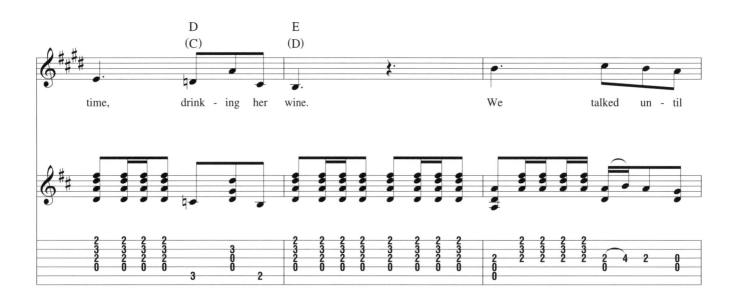

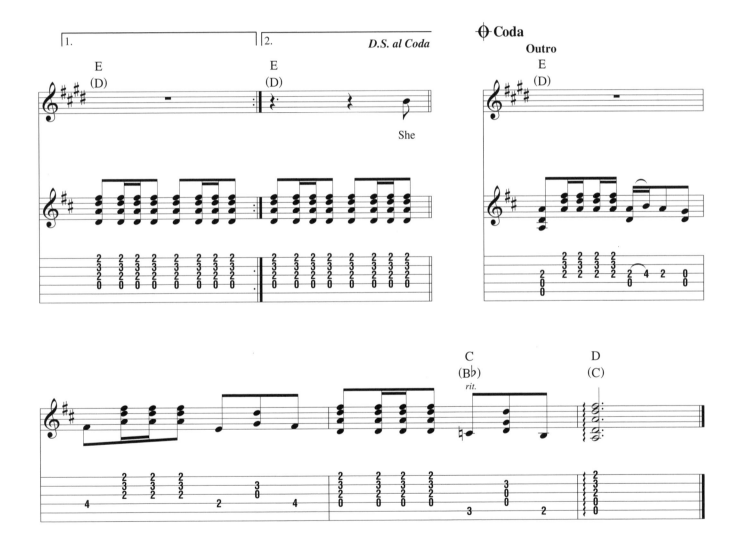

Additional Lyrics

Bridge   She told me she worked in the morning and started to laugh.
I told her I didn't and crawled off to sleep in the bath.

3.   And when I awoke I was alone; this bird had flown.
So, I lit a fire. Isn't it good Norwegian Wood?

Patience

Words and Music by W. Axl Rose, Slash, Izzy Stradlin', Duff McKagan and Steven Adler

Tune down 1/2 step:
(low to high) Eb-Ab-Db-Gb-Bb-Eb

Intro
Moderate Rock ♩ = 120
Half-time feel

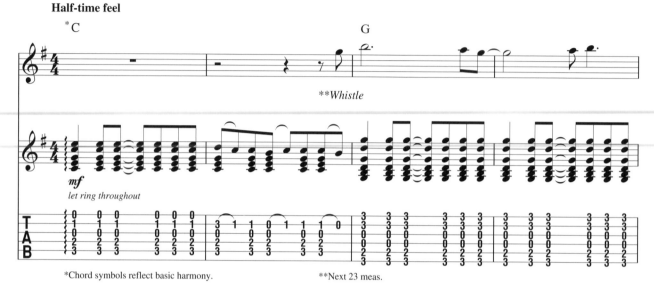

*Chord symbols reflect basic harmony.   **Next 23 meas.

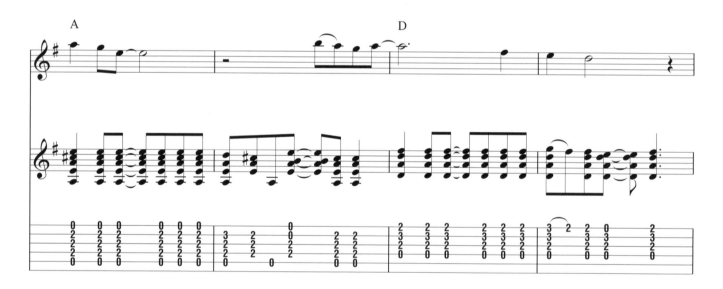

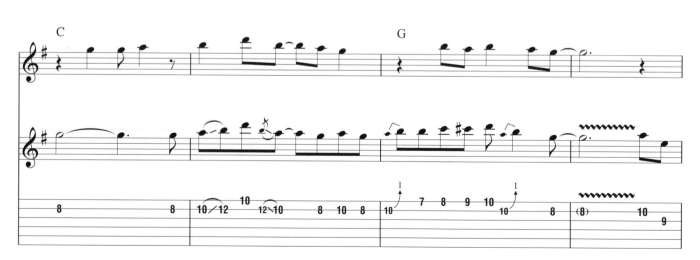

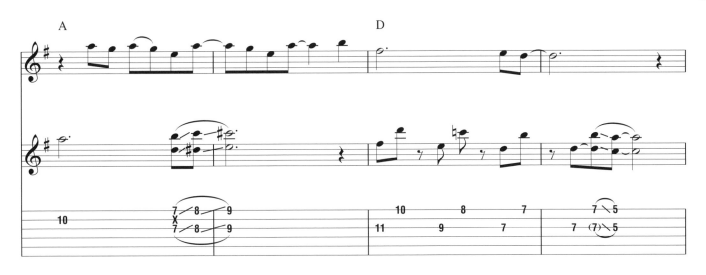

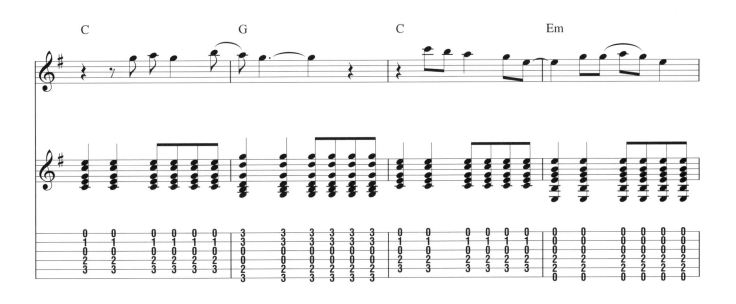

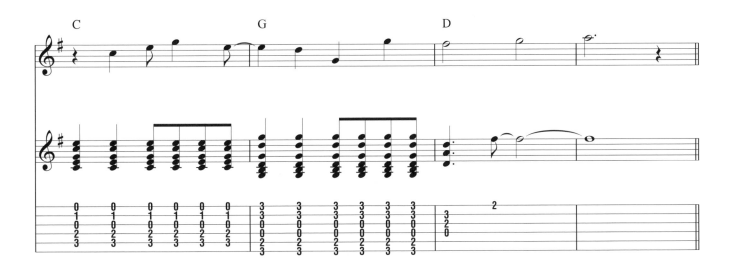

Verse

1. Shed a tear 'cause I'm miss-in' ___ you, ___ I'm still al - right ___ to smile. ___
2. *See additional lyrics*

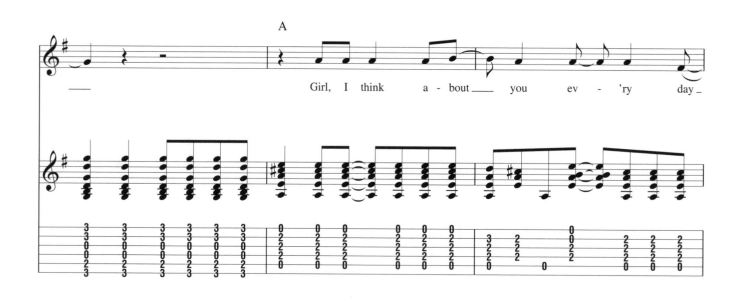

Girl, I think a - bout ___ you ev - 'ry day ___

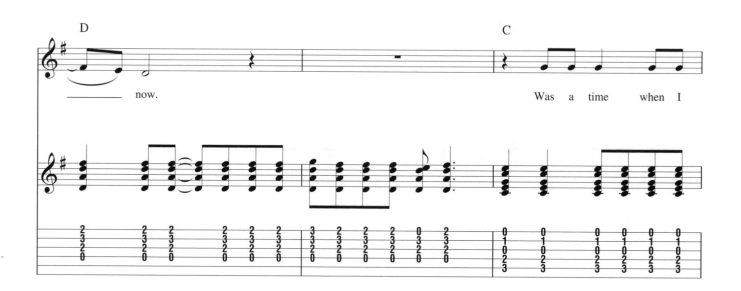

___ now. Was a time when I

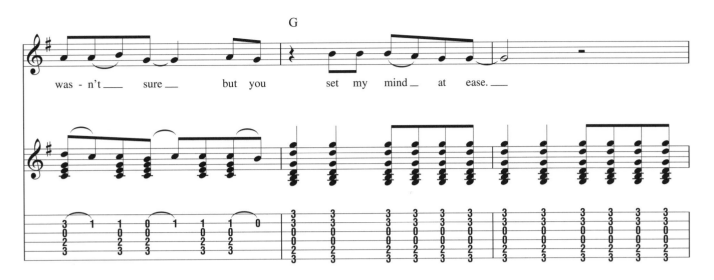

was-n't ___ sure ___ but you set my mind at ease. ___

There is no doubt ___ you're in ___ my heart ___ now.

Chorus

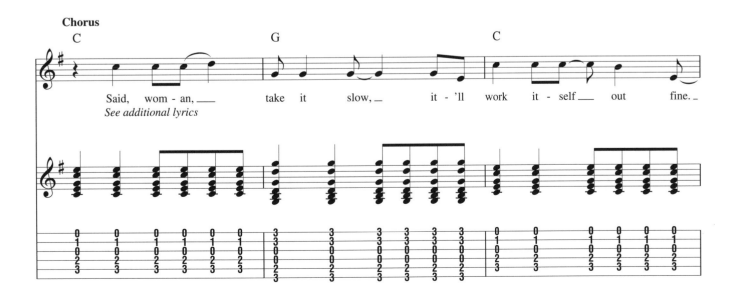

Said, wom - an, ___ take it slow, ___ it - 'll work it - self ___ out fine. ___
See additional lyrics

All we need ___ is just a lit - tle pa -

- tience. Said, Sug - ar, ___

make it slow ___ and we come to - geth - er fine. ___

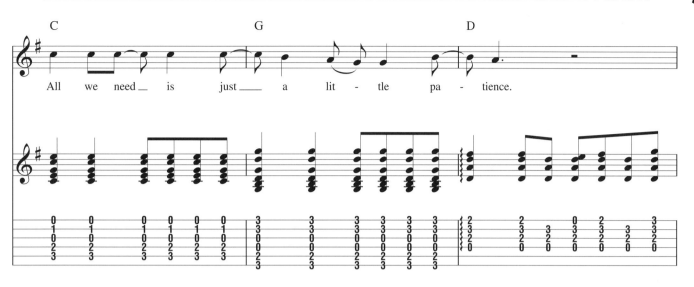

All we need __ is just __ a lit - tle pa - tience.

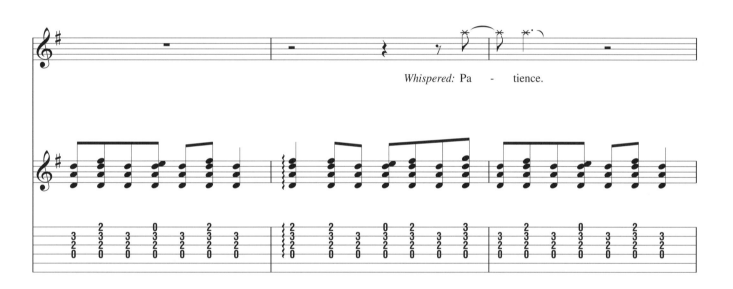

Whispered: Pa - tience.

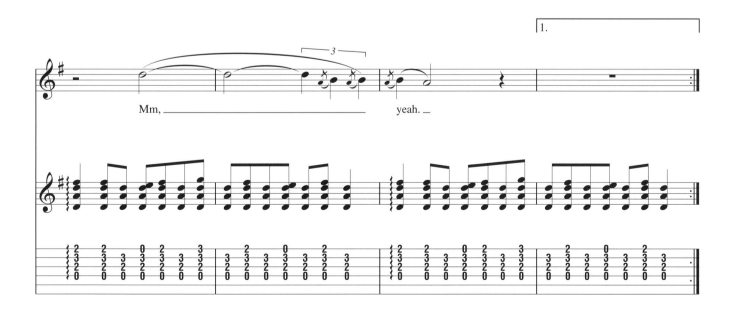

Mm, _____ yeah. __

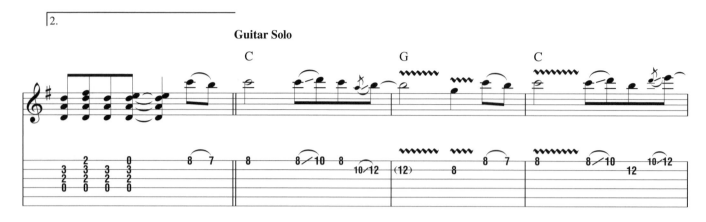

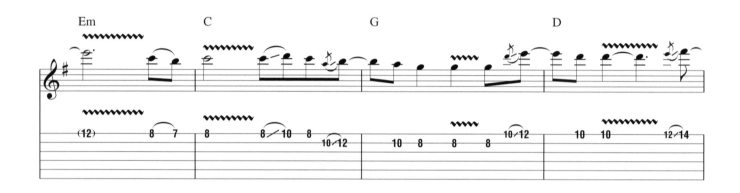

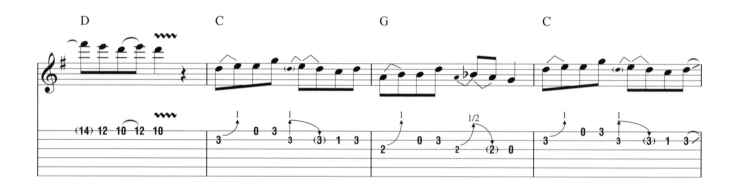

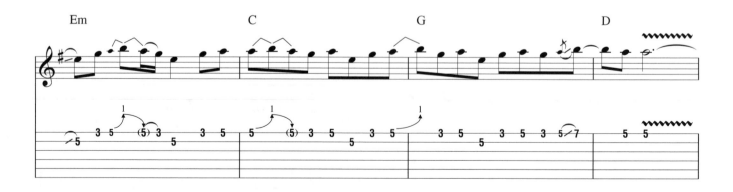

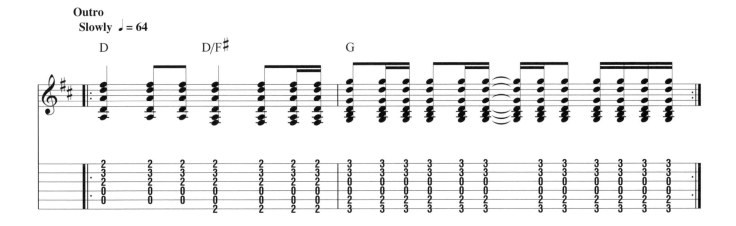

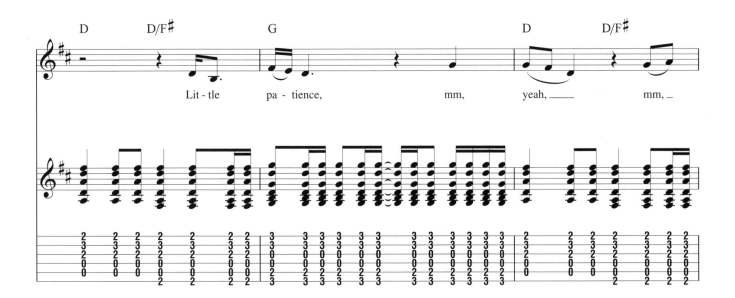

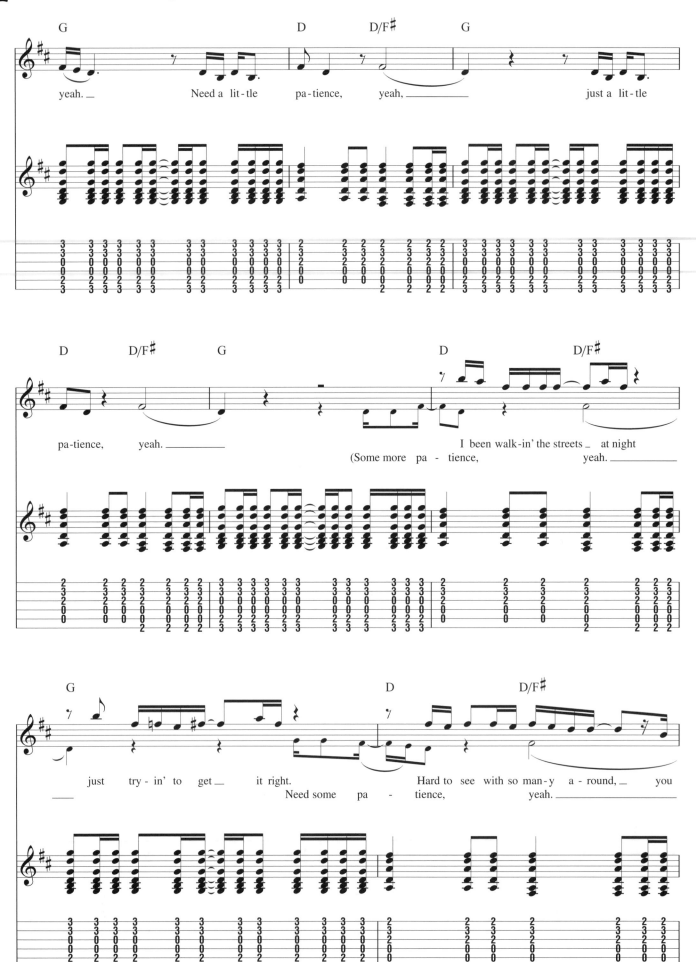

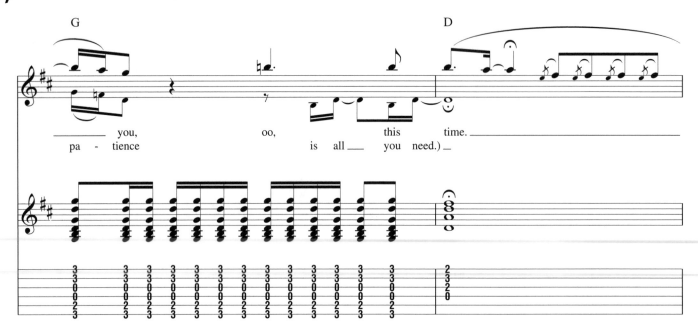

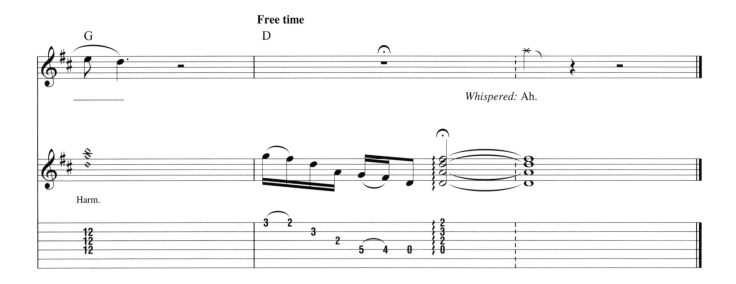

Additional Lyrics

2. I sit here on the stairs 'cause I'd rather be alone.
   If I can't have you right now I'll wait, dear.
   Sometimes I get so tense but I can't speed up the time.
   But you know, love, there's one more thing to consider.

Chorus Said, woman, take it slow and things will be just fine.
   You and I'll just use a little patience.
   Said, Sugar, take the time 'cause the lights are shining bright.
   You and I've got what it takes to make it.
   We won't fake it, ah, I'll never break it 'cause I can't take it.

Pink Houses

Words and Music by John Mellencamp

Open G tuning:
(low to high) D-G-D-G-B-D

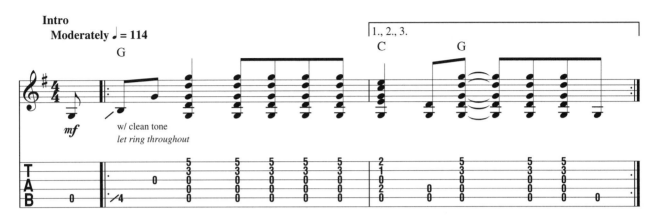

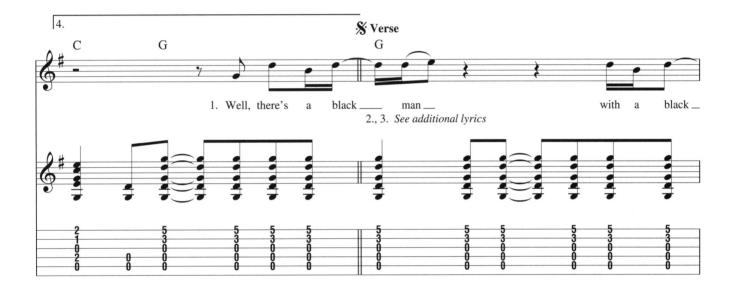

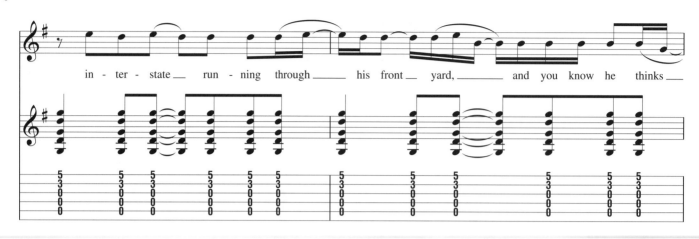

in - ter - state __ run - ning through _____ his front __ yard, _____ and you know he thinks __

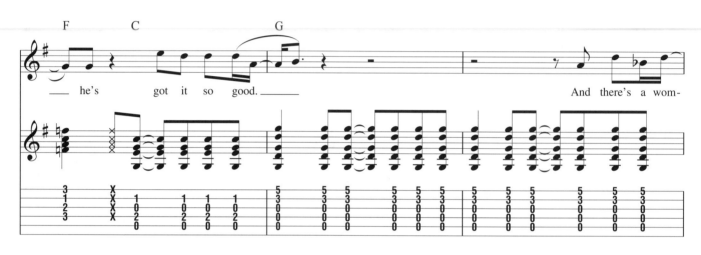

F   C   G

__ he's   got it so good. _____   And there's a wom-

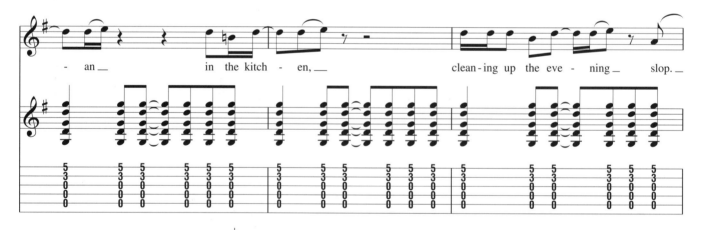

- an __   in the kitch - en, __   clean-ing up the eve - ning __ slop. __

To Coda 1 ⊕
To Coda 2 ⊕

F   C

__   And he looks __ at her and __ says, "Hey dar-lin',   I can re-mem-ber when __ you could __

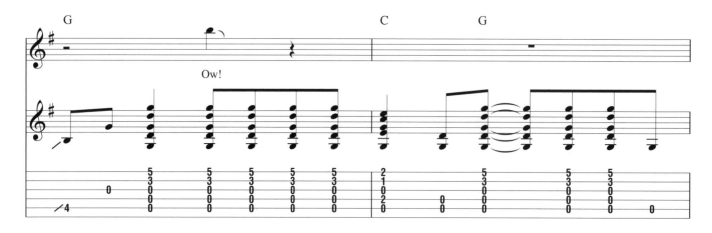

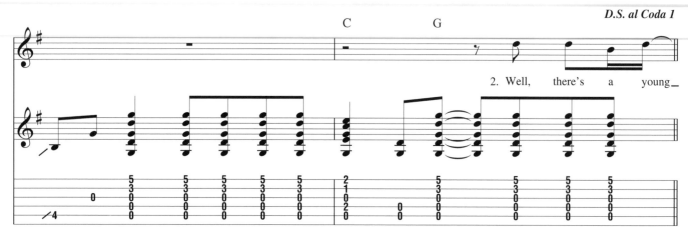

D.S. al Coda 1

Coda 1

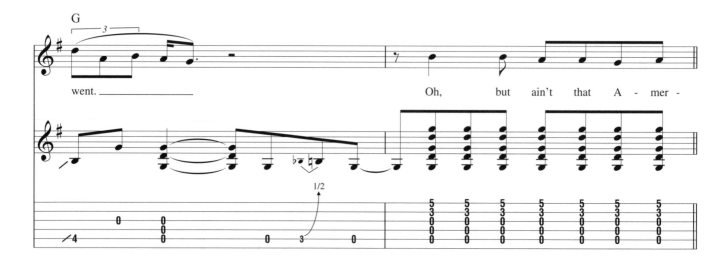

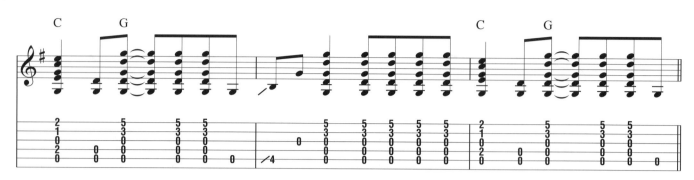

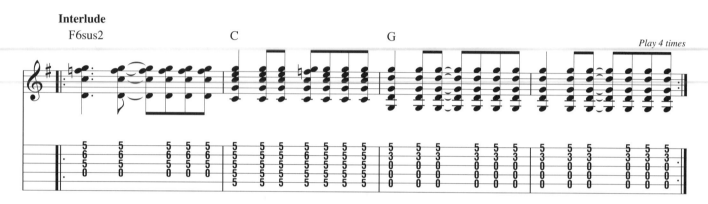

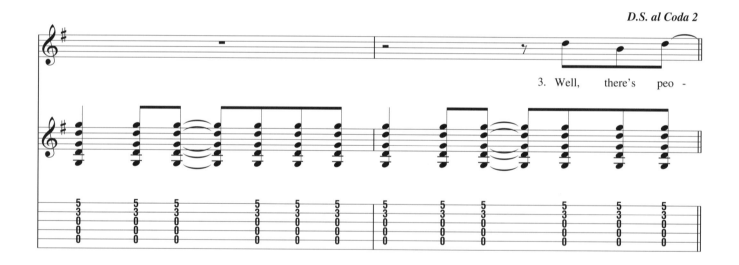

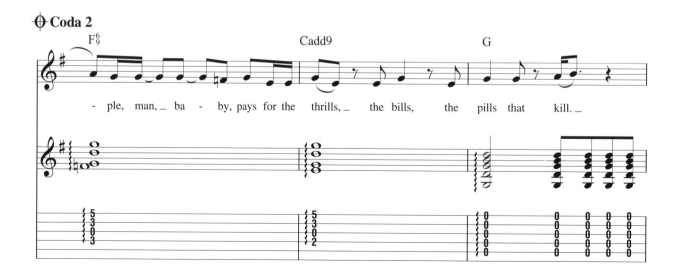

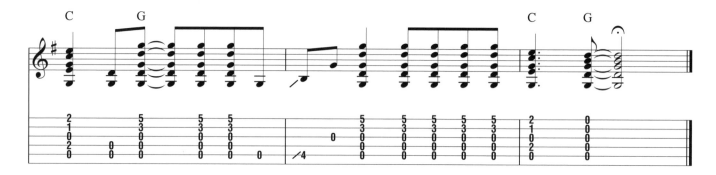

Additional Lyrics

2. Well, there's a young man in a tee-shirt,
   List'nin' to a rock 'n' roller station.
   He's got a greasy hair and a greasy smile.
   He says, "Lord, this must be my destination."
   'Cause they told me when I was younger,
   Sayin', "Boy, you're gonna be president."
   But just like ev'rything else, those old crazy dreams
   Just kinda came and went.

3. Well, there's people, and more people.
   What do they know, know, know?
   Go to work in some high rise
   And vacation down at the Gulf of Mexico, ooh, yeah.
   And there's winners and there's losers,
   But they ain't no big deal.
   'Cause the simple, man, baby, pays for the thrills,
   The bills, the pills that kill.

Signs

Words and Music by Les Emmerson

Intro
Moderately slow ♩ = 82

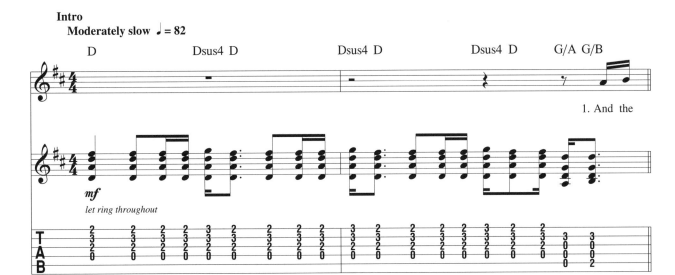

1. And the

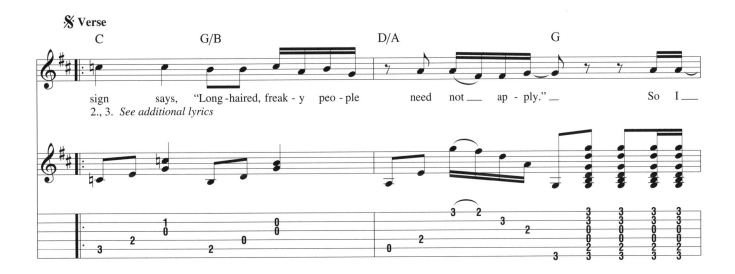

sign says, "Long-haired, freak-y peo-ple need not __ ap-ply." __ So I __
2., 3. *See additional lyrics*

__ tucked my hair up un-der my hat and I went in to ask him why. __

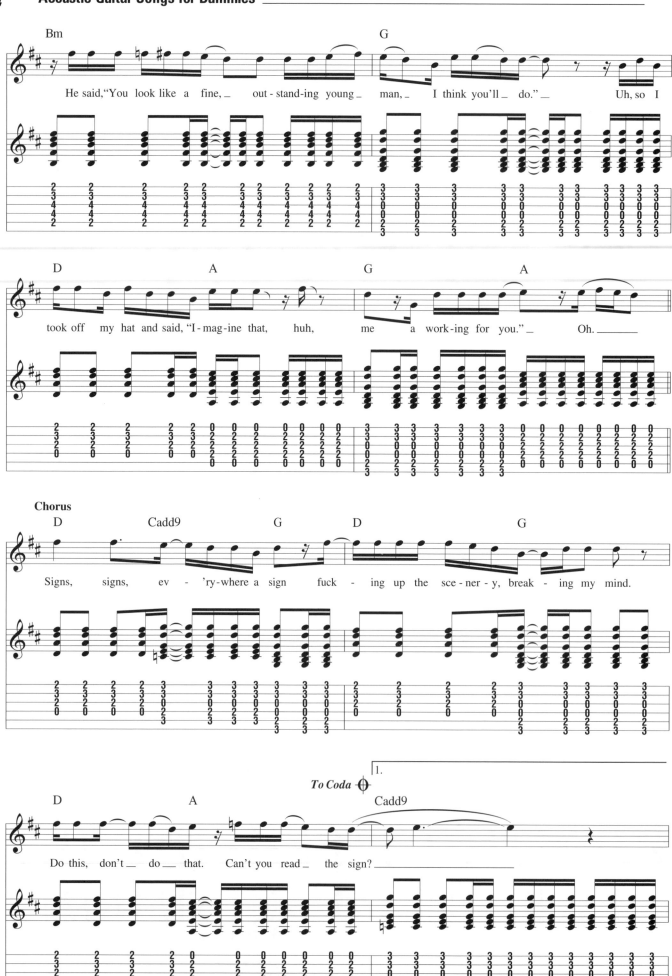

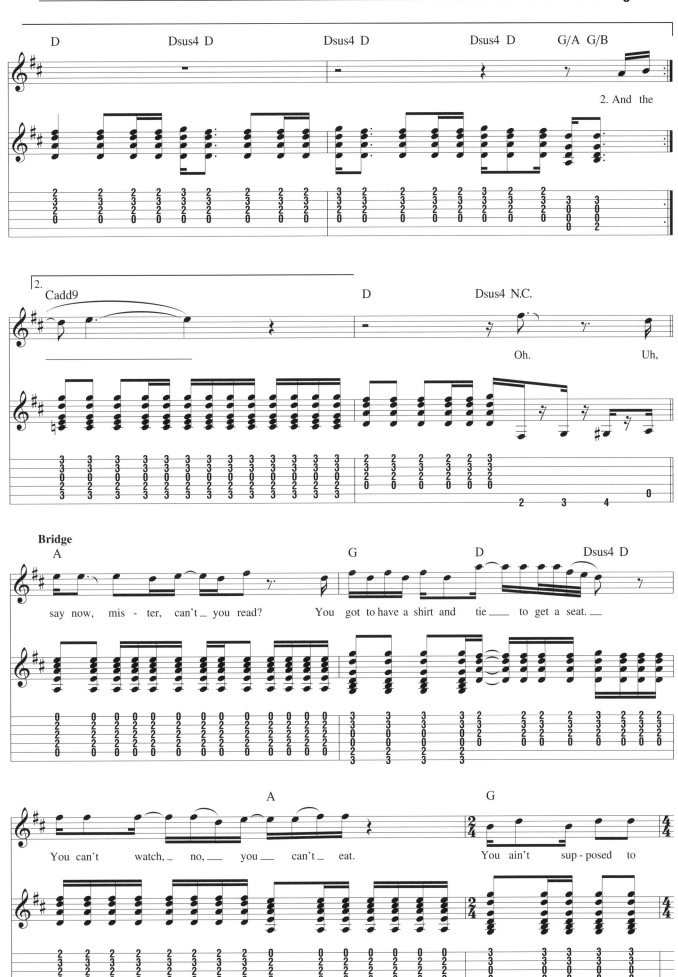

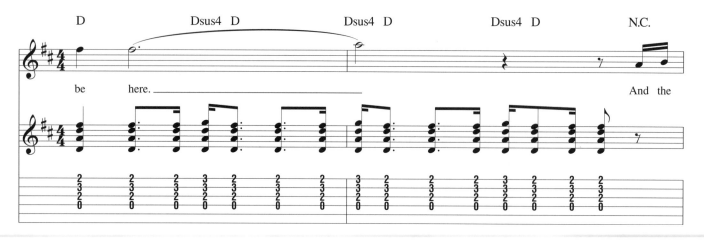

be here._____ And the

sign said, "You got to have a mem-ber-ship card to get in - side."_ Ooh!

Guitar Solo

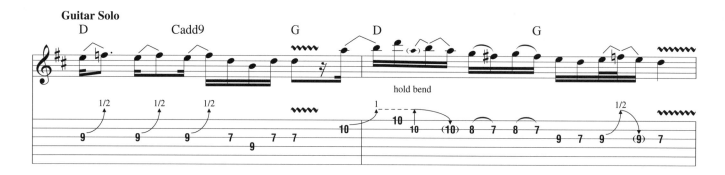

hold bend

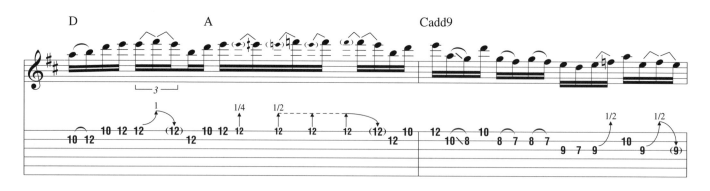

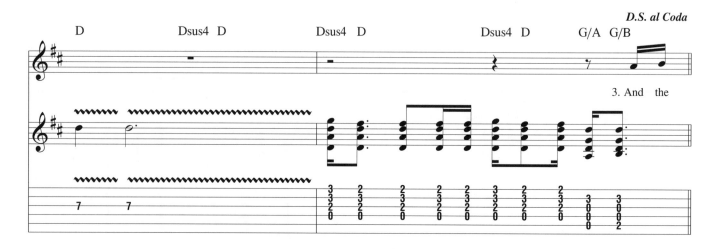

3. And the

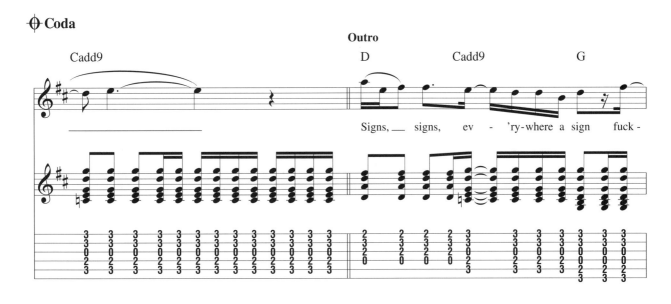

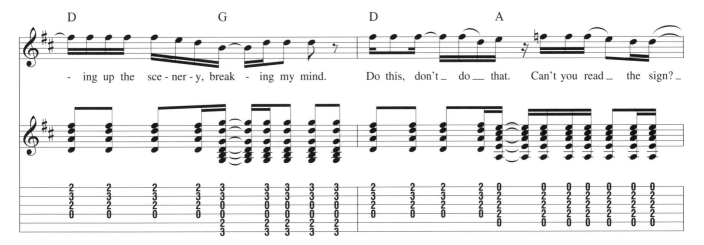

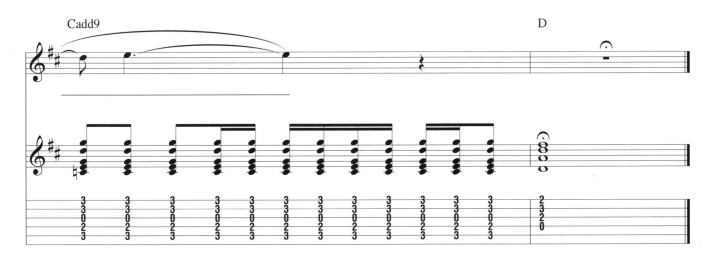

Additional Lyrics

2. And the sign says, "Anybody caught trespassing will be shot on sight."
   So I jumped the fence and yelled at the house, "Hey, what gives you the right
   To put up a fence to keep me out or to keep Mother Nature in?"
   If God was here he'd tell it to your face, "Man, you're some kinda sinner."

3. And the sign says, "Everybody welcome, come in and kneel down and pray."
   And then they pass around the plate at the end of it all, and I didn't have a penny to pay.
   So I got me a pen and paper, and I made up my own fuckin' sign.
   I said, "Thank you, Lord, for thinkin' about me, I'm alive and doing fine."

Space Oddity

Words and Music by David Bowie

Intro
Slowly ♩ = 68

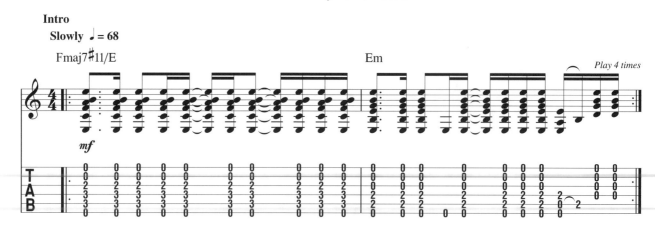

Verse

1. Ground Con-trol ___ to Ma - jor Tom. ___
2. *See additional lyrics*

Ground Con-trol ___ to Ma - jor Tom. ___

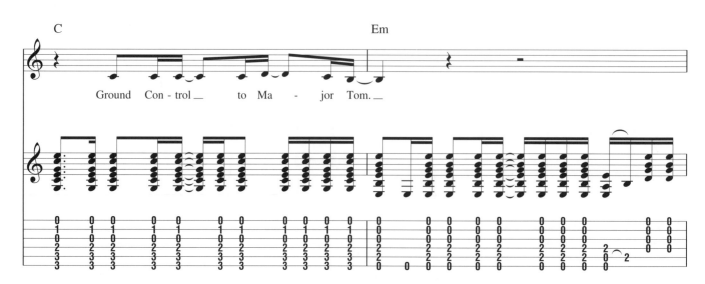

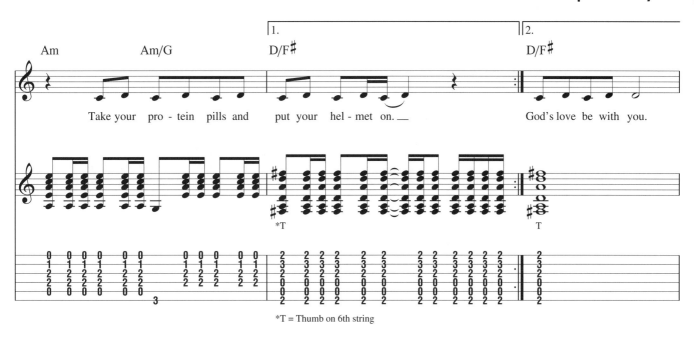

Take your pro - tein pills and put your hel - met on. ___ God's love be with you.

*T = Thumb on 6th string

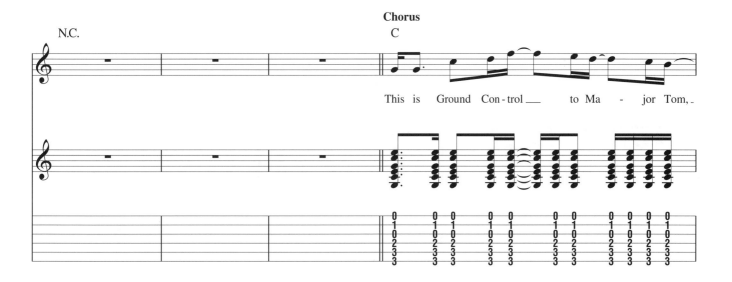

This is Ground Con - trol ___ to Ma - jor Tom, ___

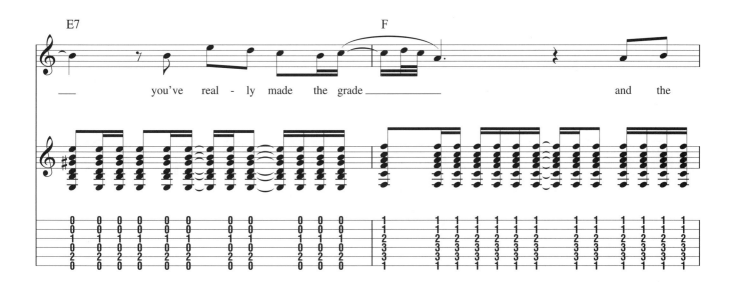

___ you've real - ly made the grade ___ and the

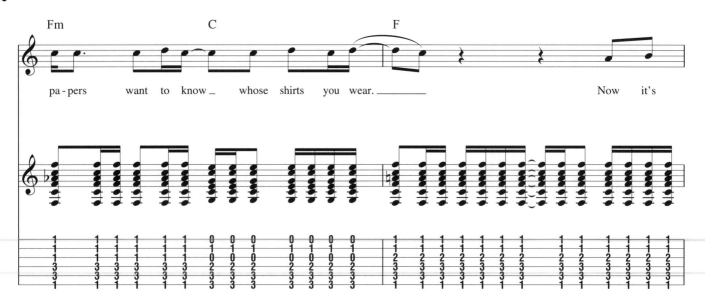

pa - pers   want   to   know _   whose   shirts   you   wear. _____   Now   it's

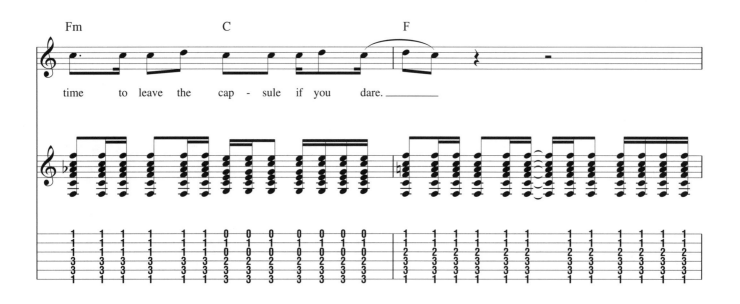

time   to   leave   the   cap - sule   if   you   dare. _____

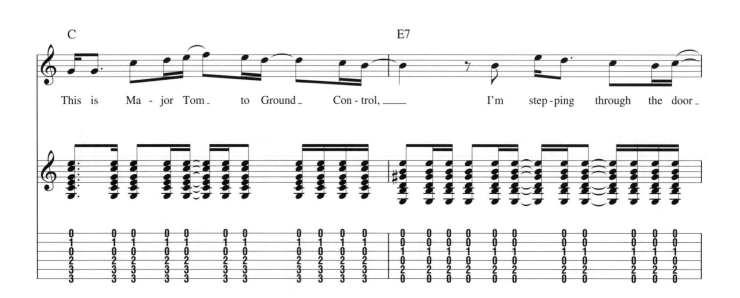

This   is   Ma - jor   Tom _   to   Ground _   Con - trol, _____   I'm   step - ping   through   the   door _

and I'm float - ing in a most a pe - cu - li - ar way_

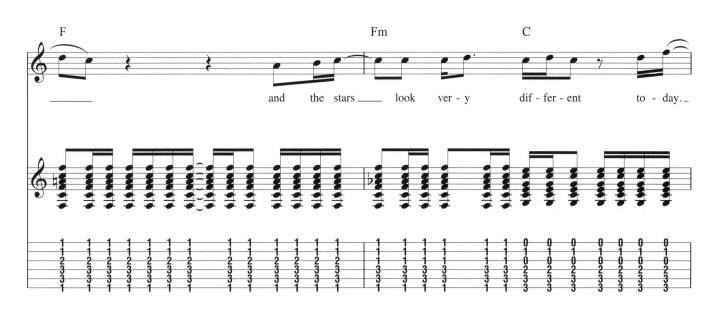

and the stars ___ look ver - y dif - fer - ent to - day._

𝄋 Bridge

Fmaj7#11

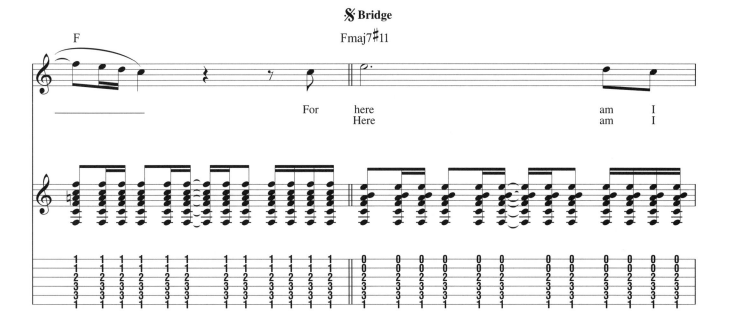

For here   am   I
Here   am   I

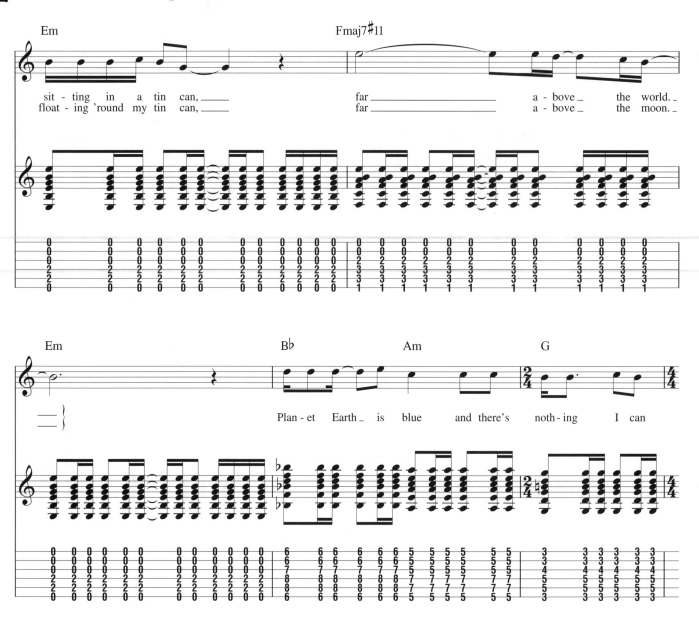

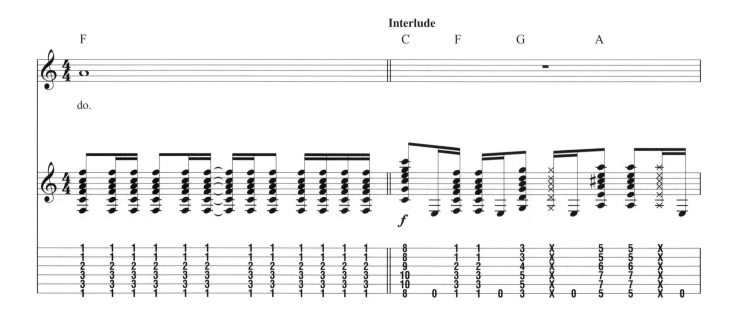

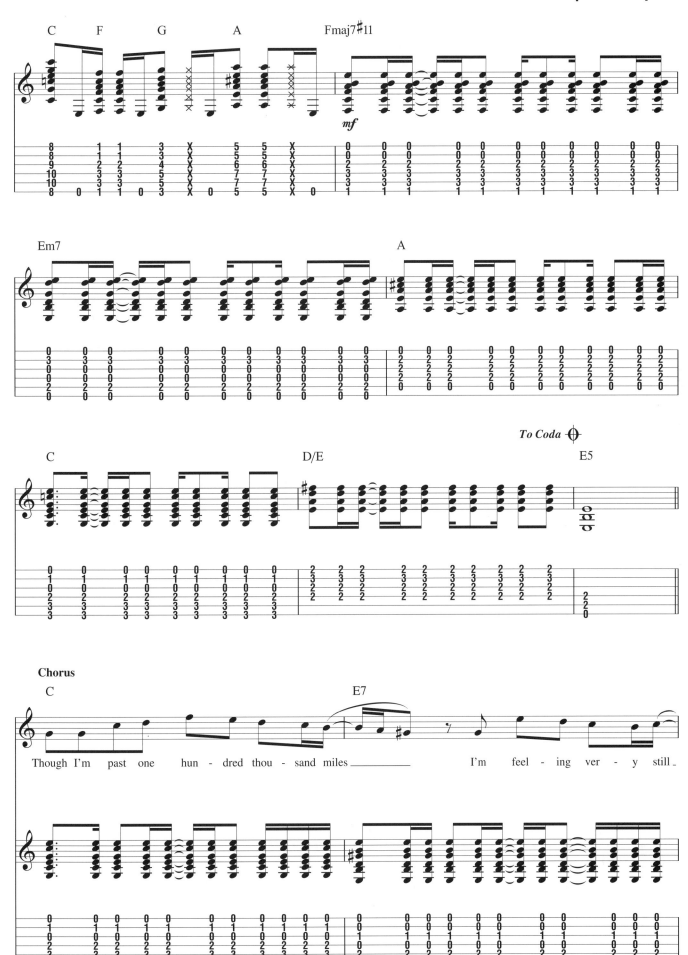

Chorus

Though I'm past one hun - dred thou - sand miles _____ I'm feel - ing ver - y still ___

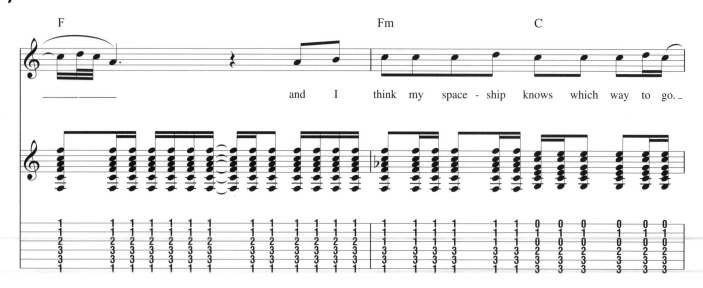

and I think my space - ship knows which way to go.

Tell my wife I love her ver - y much. She knows.

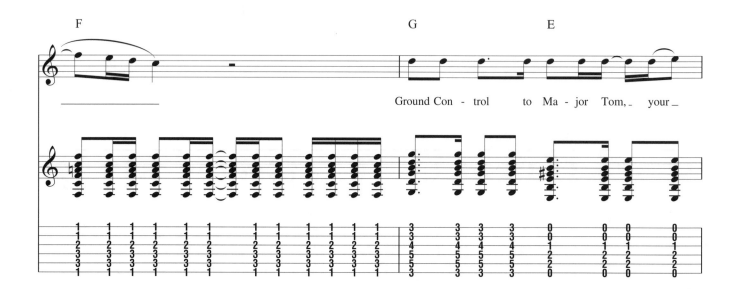

Ground Con - trol to Ma - jor Tom, your

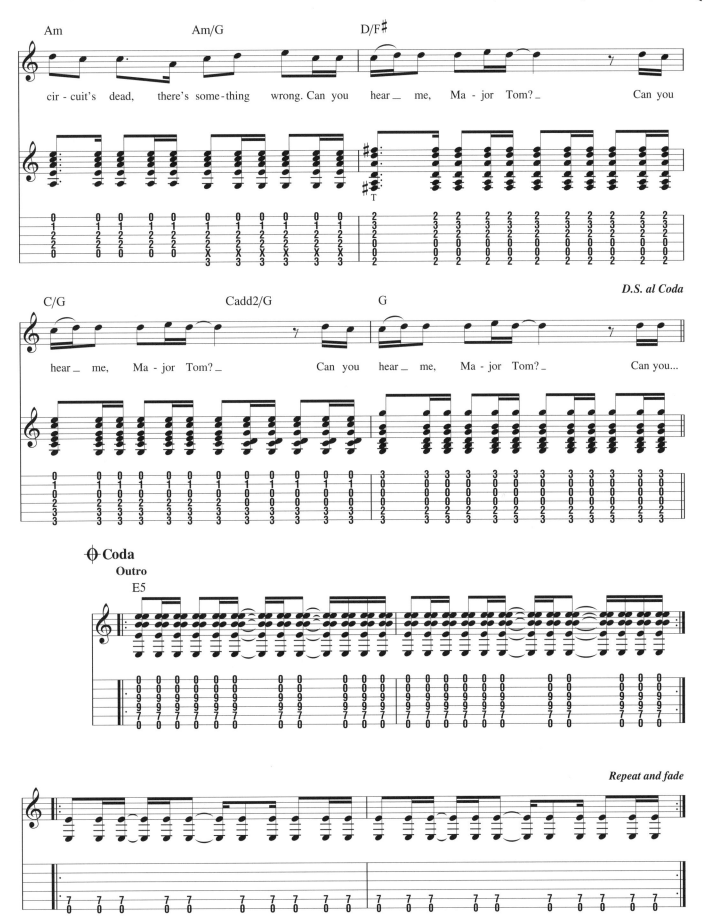

D.S. al Coda

Repeat and fade

Additional Lyrics

2. Ground Control to Major Tom,
   Commencing countdown; engines on.
   Check ignition and may God's love be with you.

Tangled Up in Blue

Words and Music by Bob Dylan

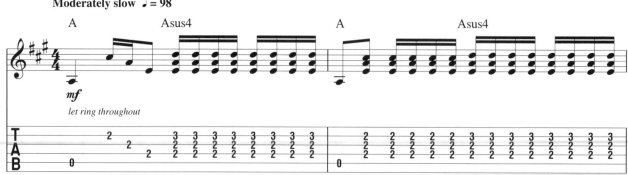

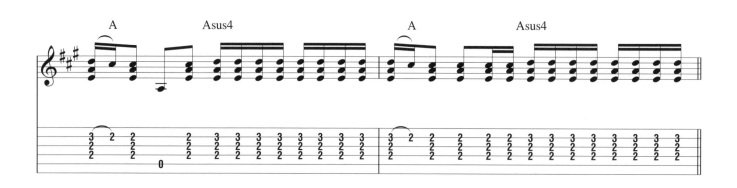

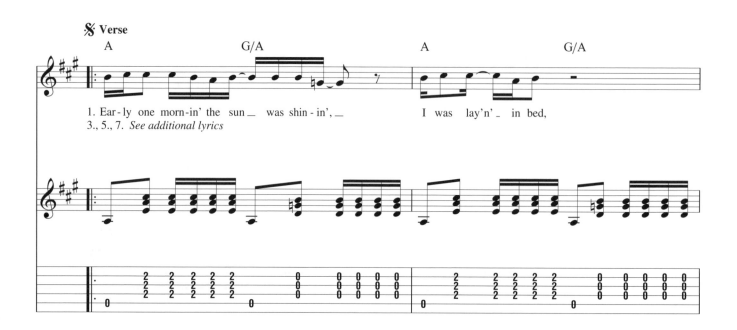

1. Ear-ly one morn-in' the sun __ was shin-in', __ I was lay'n' __ in bed,
3., 5., 7. *See additional lyrics*

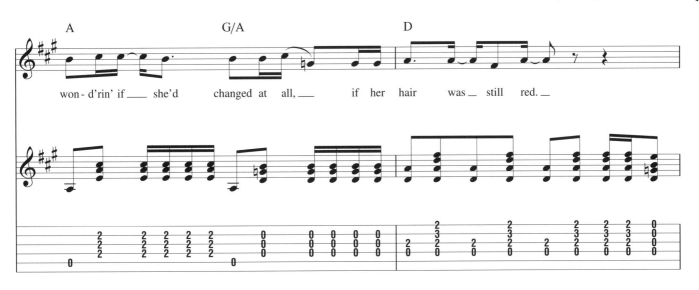

won-d'rin' if ___ she'd changed at all, ___ if her hair was ___ still red. ___

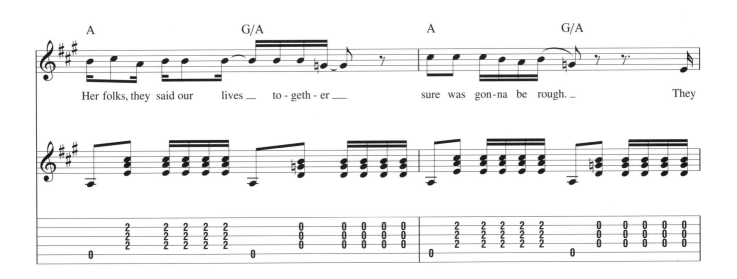

Her folks, they said our lives ___ to-geth-er ___ sure was gon-na be rough. ___ They

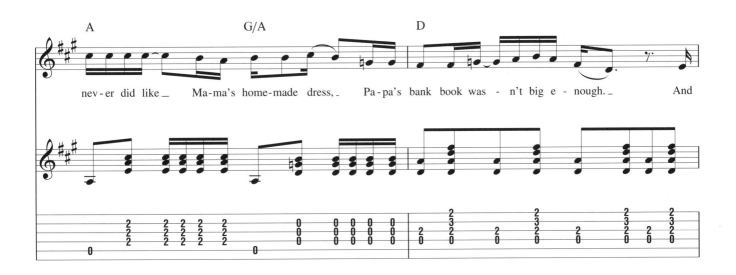

nev-er did like ___ Ma-ma's home-made dress, ___ Pa-pa's bank book was-n't big e-nough. ___ And

2. She was mar-ried when we ___ first met,
4., 6. *See additional lyrics*
8. *Instrumental*

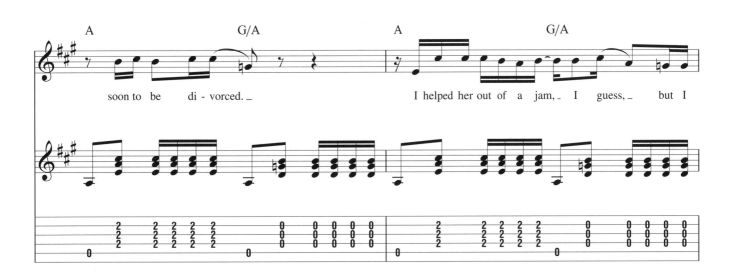

soon to be di-vorced. ___   I helped her out of a jam, ___ I guess, ___ but I

used a lit-tle too much force. _____   We drove that car as far as we could, ___ a-

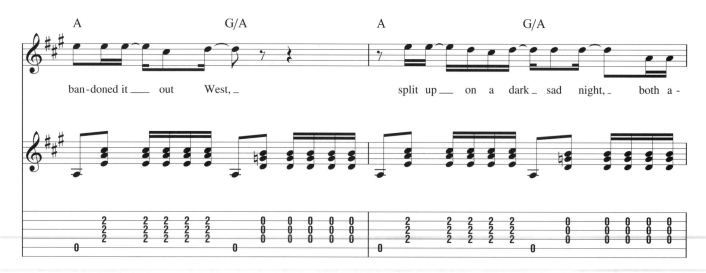

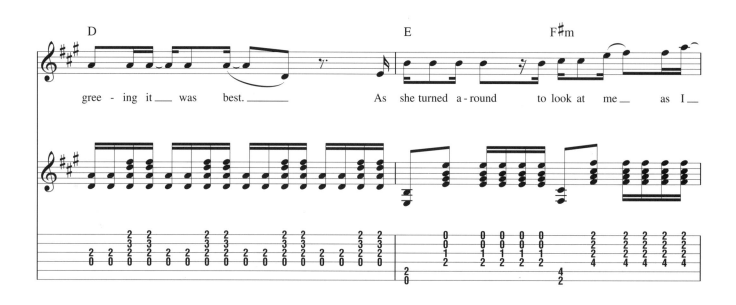

To Coda

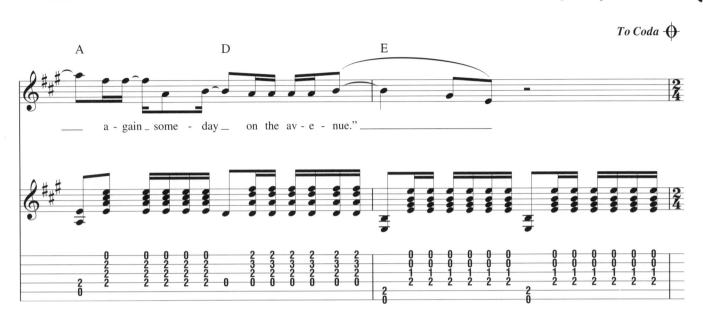

a - gain _ some - day _ on the av - e - nue."

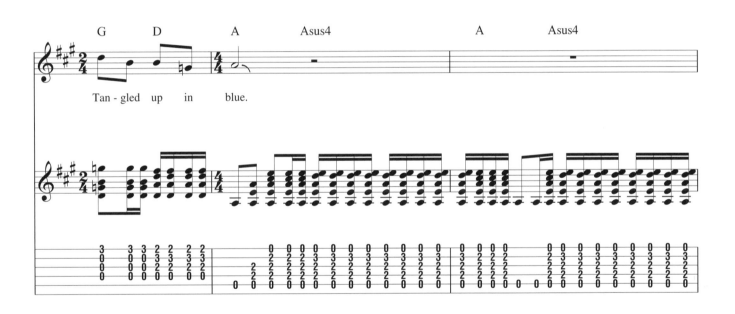

Tan - gled up in blue.

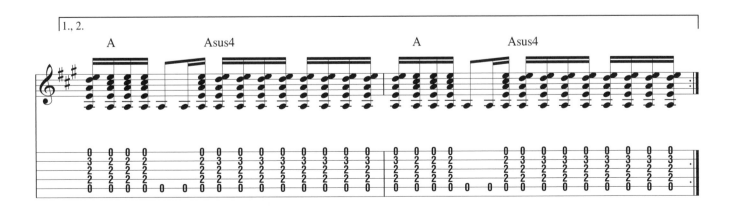

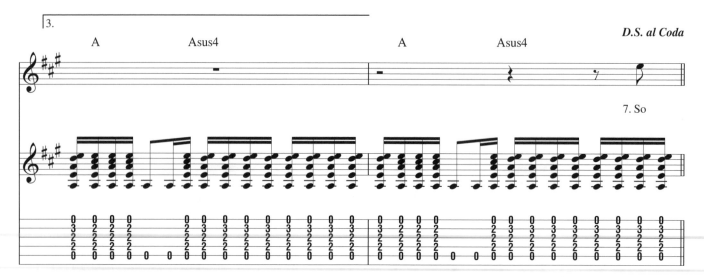

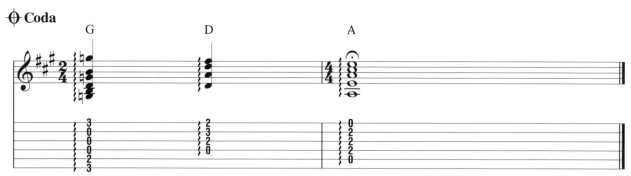

Additional Lyrics

3. I had a job in the great north woods,
   Working as a cook for a spell.
   But I never did like it all that much
   And one day the axe just fell.
   So I drifted down to New Orleans
   Where I lucky was to be employed.
   Workin' for a while on a fishin' boat
   Right outside of Delacroix.
   But all the while I was alone,
   The past was close behind.
   I seen a lot of women,
   But she never escaped my mind, and I just grew;
   Tangled up in blue.

4. She was workin' in a topless place
   And I stopped in for a beer.
   I just kept lookin' at the side of her face
   In the spotlight so clear.
   And later on when the crowd thinned out,
   I's just about to do the same.
   She was standin' there in back of my chair,
   Said to me, "Don't I know your name?"
   I muttered somethin' underneath my breath,
   She studied the lines on my face.
   I must admit I felt a little uneasy
   When she bent down to tie the laces of my shoe;
   Tangled up in blue.

5. She lit a burner on the stove and offered me a pipe.
   "I thought you'd never say hello," she said,
   "You look like the silent type."
   Then she opened up a book of poems
   And handed it to me,
   Written by an Italian poet
   From the thirteenth century.
   And ev'ry one of them words rang true
   And glowed like burnin' coal.
   Pourin' off of ev'ry page
   Like it was written in my soul from me to you;
   Tangled up in blue.

6. I lived with them on Montague Street
   In a basement down the stairs.
   There was music in the cafés at night
   And revolution in the air.
   Then he started into dealing with slaves
   And something inside of him died.
   She had to sell ev'rything she owned
   And froze up inside.
   And when it finally, the bottom fell out
   I became withdrawn.
   The only thing I knew how to do
   Was to keep on keepin' on like a bird that flew;
   Tangled up in blue.

7. So now I'm goin' back again,
   I got to get to her somehow.
   All the people we used to know,
   They're an illusion to me now.
   Some are mathematicians;
   Some are carpenter's wives.
   Don't know how it all got started,
   I don't know what they're doin' with their lives.
   But me, I'm still on the road,
   Headin' for another joint.
   We always did feel the same,
   We just saw it from a diff'rent point of view;
   Tangled up in blue.

Tears in Heaven

Words and Music by Eric Clapton and Will Jennings

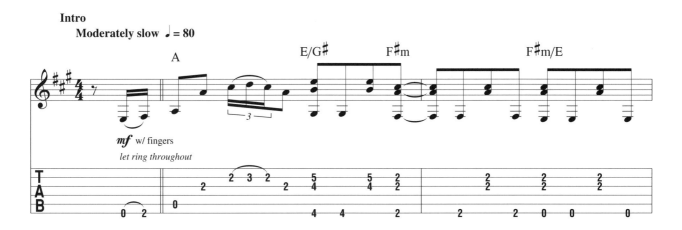

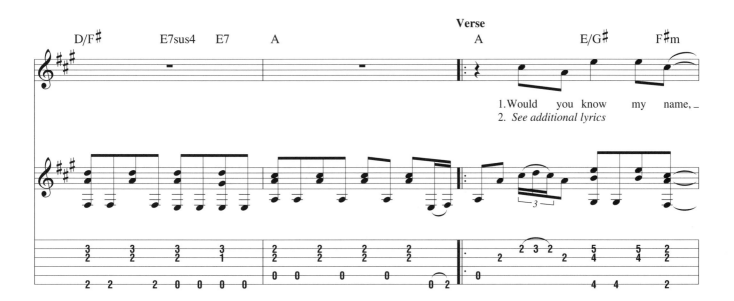

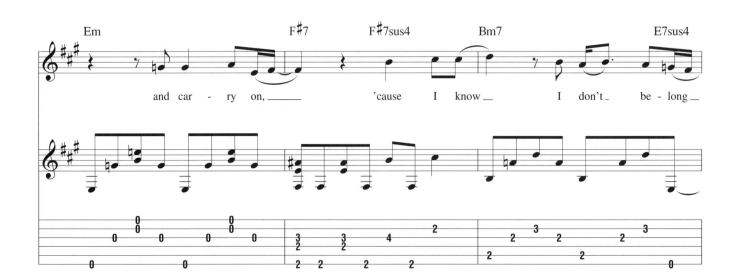

here in heav - en.

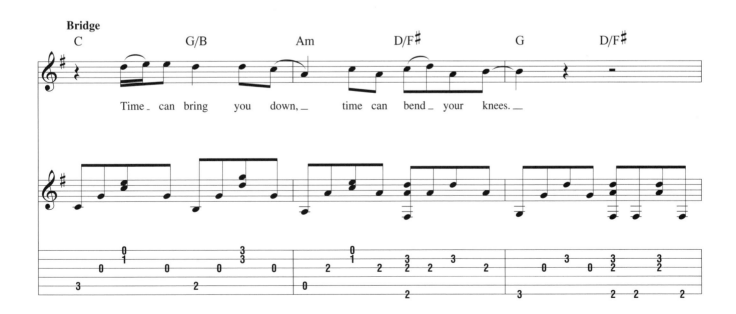

Time can bring you down, time can bend your knees.

Time _ can break your heart, __ have you beg - gin' please, __

Guitar Solo

beg - gin' please. _____

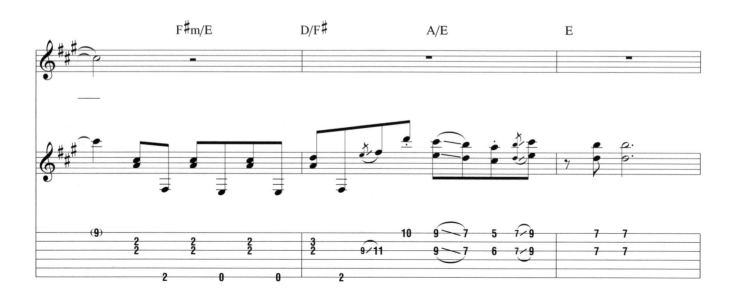

D.S. al Coda

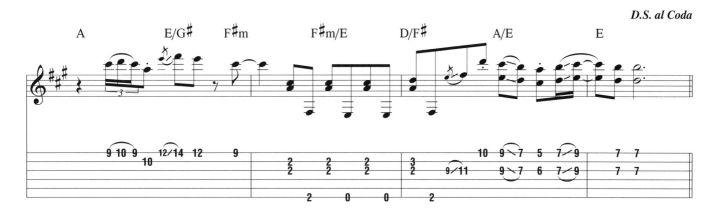

Coda

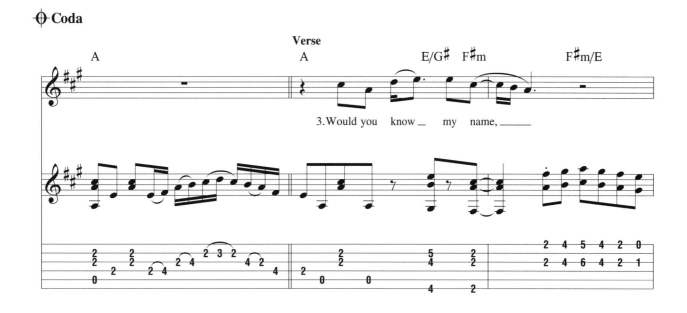

3.Would you know ___ my name, _____

if I saw you in heav - en?   Would it be ___ the same ___

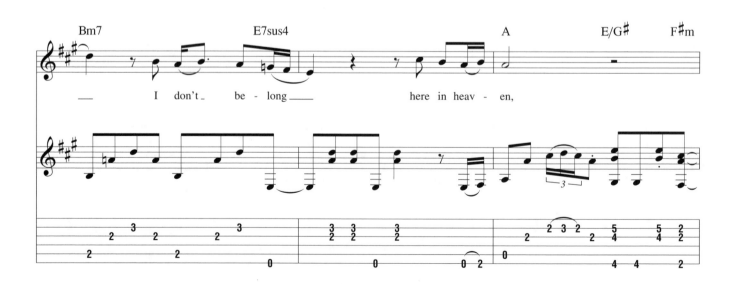

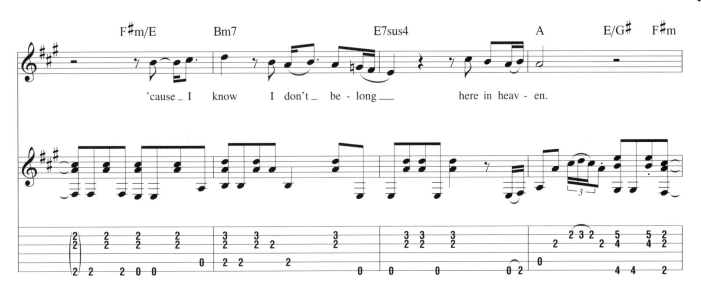

'cause _ I   know   I   don't _ be - long _   here in heav - en.

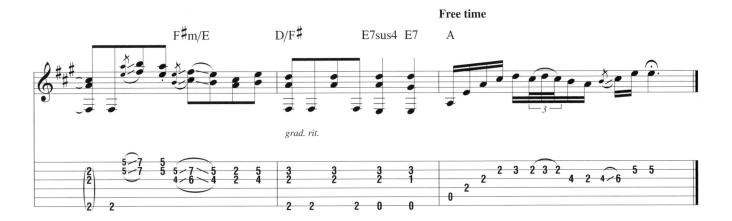

Additional Lyrics

2. Would you hold my hand
   If I saw you in heaven?
   Would ya help me stand
   If I saw you in heaven?

Chorus 2. I'll find my way
   Through night and day
   'Cause I know I just can't stay
   Here in heaven.

Chorus 3. Beyond the door
   There's peace, I'm sure,
   And I know there'll be no more
   Tears in heaven.

Thick As a Brick

Words and Music by Ian Anderson

Capo III

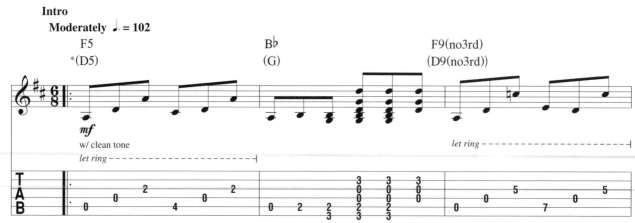

*Symbols in parentheses represent chord names respective to capoed guitar.
Symbols above reflect actual sounding chords. Capoed fret is "0" in tab.

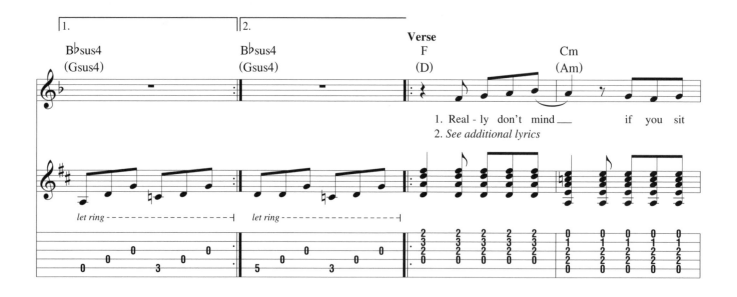

1. Real - ly don't mind ___ if you sit
2. See additional lyrics

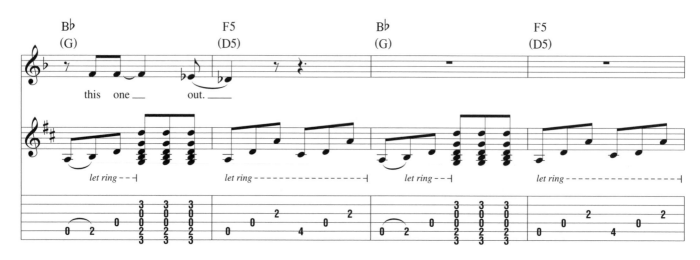

this one ___ out. ___

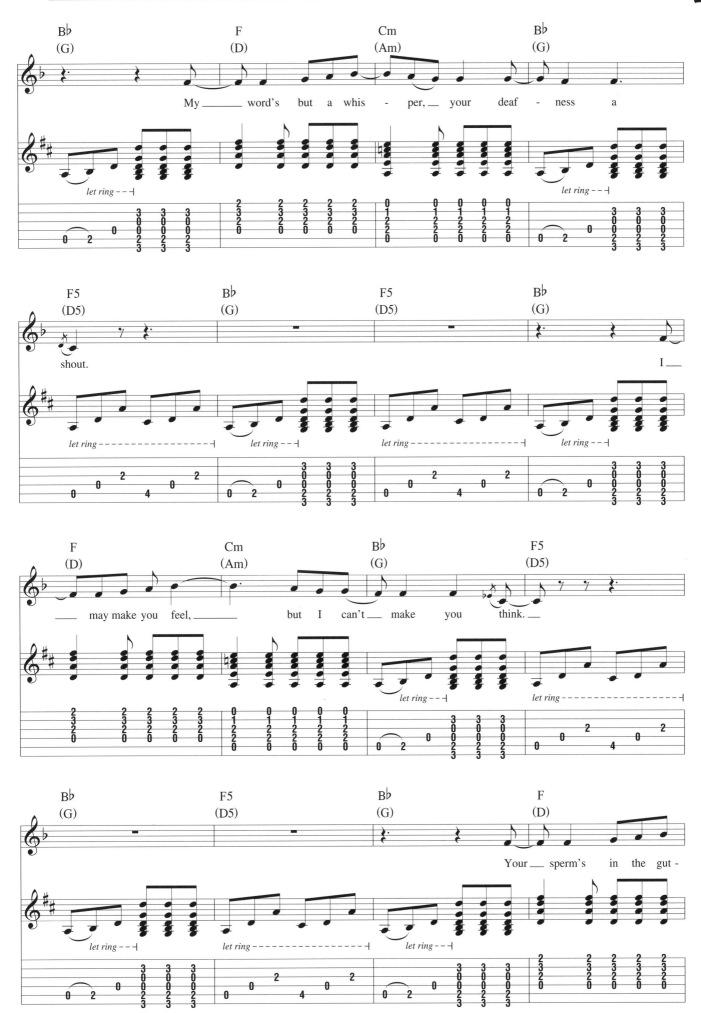

wise men __ don't __ know __ how it feels _____

to be thick __ as a brick. __

Interlude

2. And the __

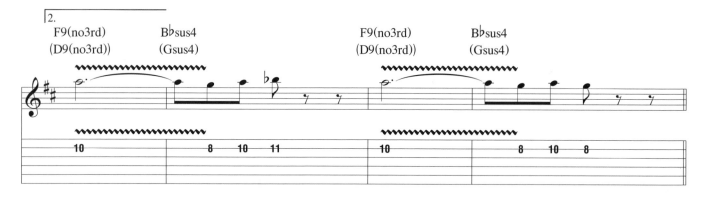

Bridge

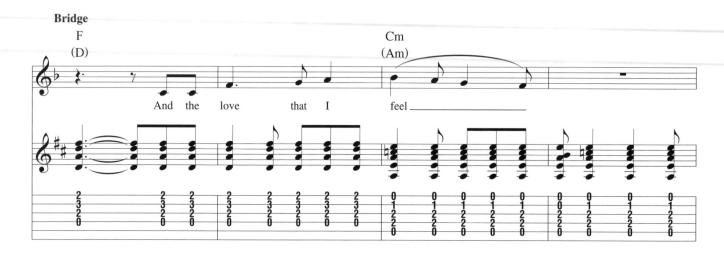

And the love that I feel ____

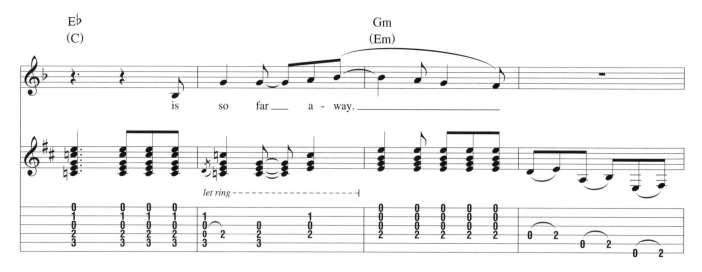

is so far ___ a - way. ____

I'm a bad dream ___ that I just had ____ to -

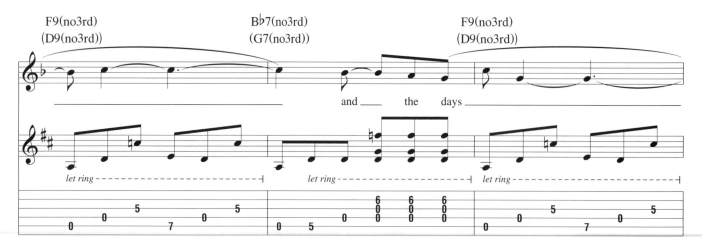

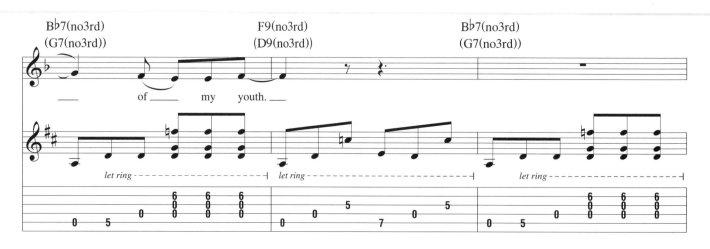

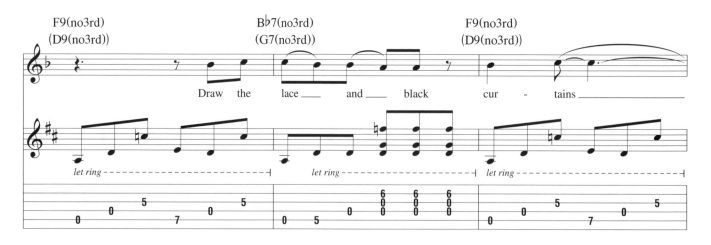

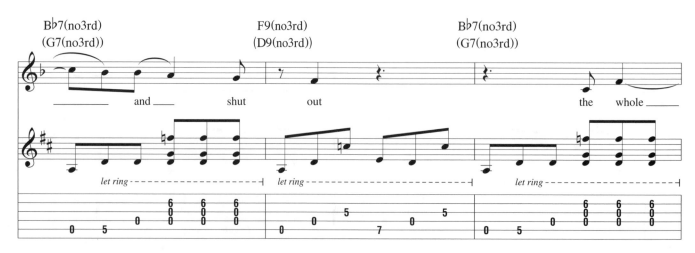

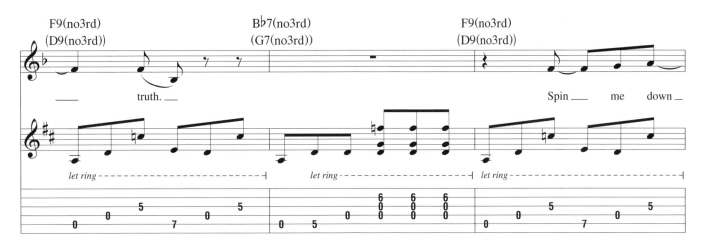

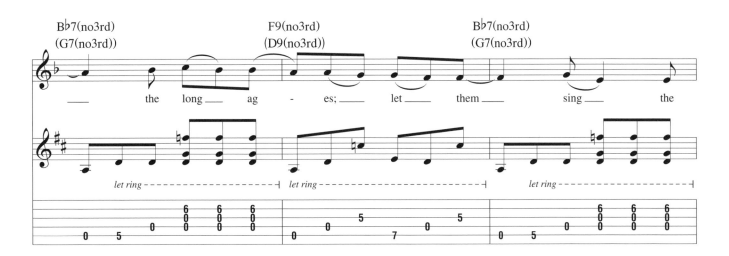

Repeat and fade

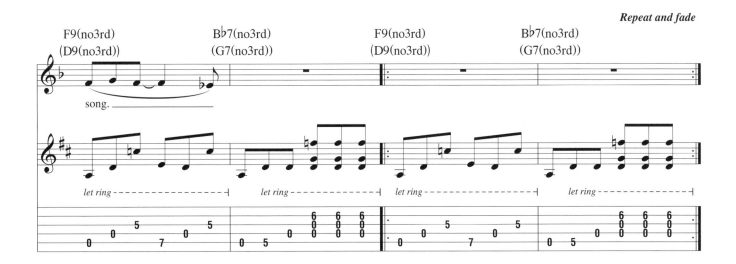

Additional Lyrics

2. And the sand castle virtues are all swept away
In the tidal destruction, the moral melee.
The elastic retreat rings the close of play
As the last wave uncovers the newfangled way.

Chorus But your new shoes are worn at the heels,
And your suntan does rapidly peel,
And your wise men don't know how it feels
To be thick as a brick.

3 AM

Lyrics by Rob Thomas
Music by Rob Thomas, Brian Yale, John Leslie Goff and John Joseph Stanley

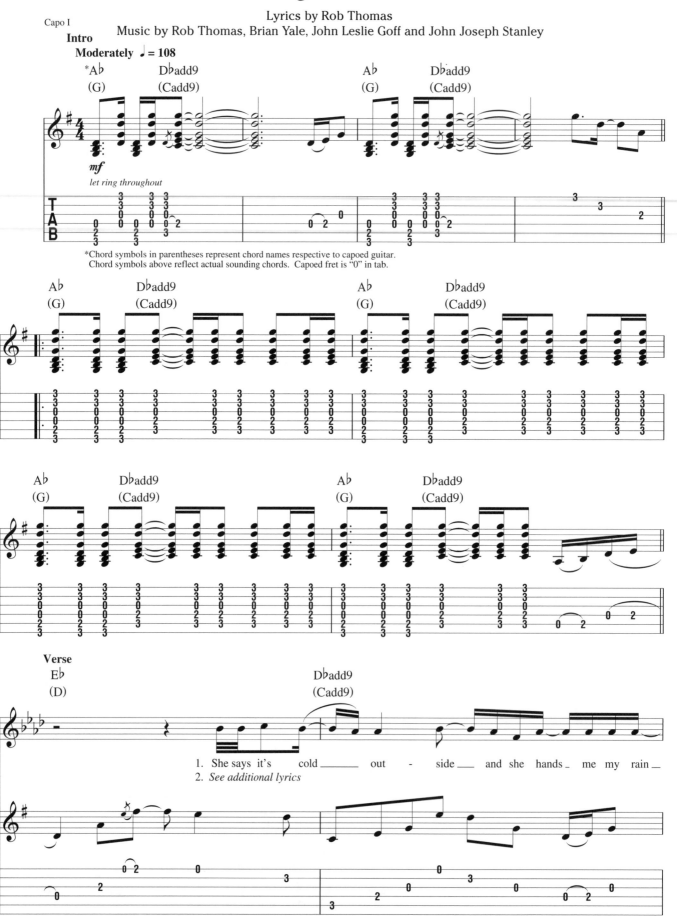

*Chord symbols in parentheses represent chord names respective to capoed guitar.
Chord symbols above reflect actual sounding chords. Capoed fret is "0" in tab.

1. She says it's   cold _____ out - side ___ and she hands ___ me my rain ___
2. *See additional lyrics*

rain's gon-na wash a-way,_ I be-lieve it.   rain's gon-na wash a-way,_ I be-lieve,_

_ yes. _

Interlude

A♭   D♭add9   A♭   D♭add9
(G)   (Cadd9)   (G)   (Cadd9)

A♭   D♭add9   A♭   D♭add9
(G)   (Cadd9)   (G)   (Cadd9)

Verse

3. Well, she be - lieves __ that life __ is made up of all __ that you're used __

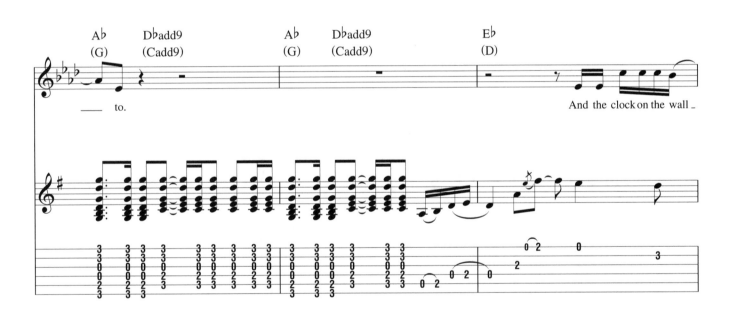

__ to. And the clock on the wall __

__ has __ been stuck at three __ for days __ and days. __

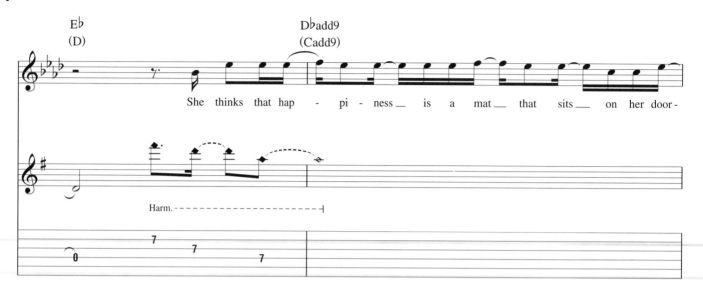

She thinks that hap - pi - ness _ is a mat _ that sits _ on her door -

- way, _ yeah.   But out - side _ it stopped

D.S. al Coda

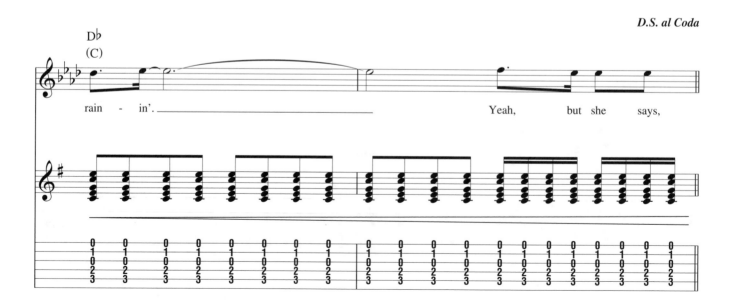

rain - in'. _   Yeah,   but she   says,

Coda

some - times." And the rain's gon-na wash a - way, I be - lieve

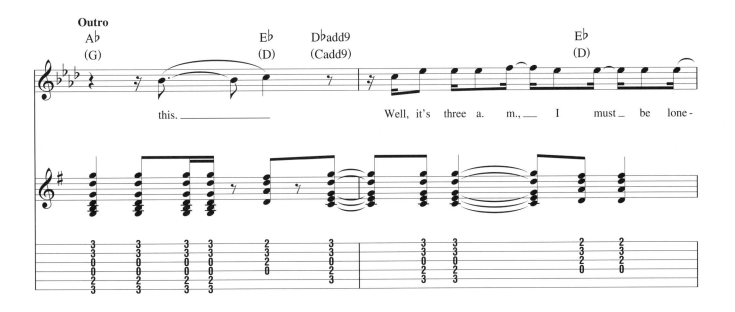

Outro

this. Well, it's three a. m., I must be lone-

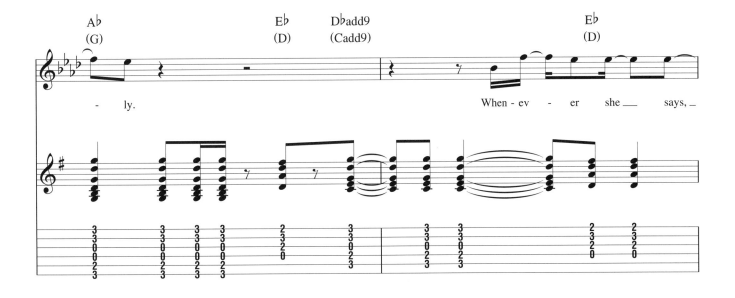

- ly. When - ev - er she says,

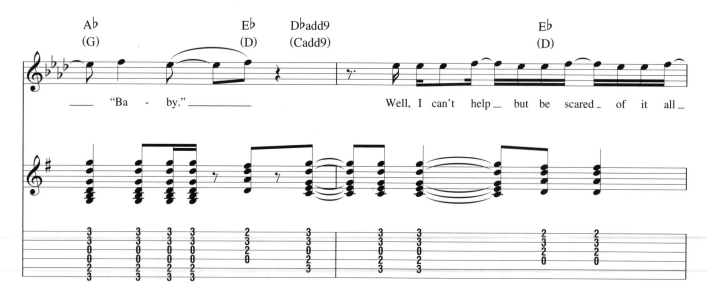

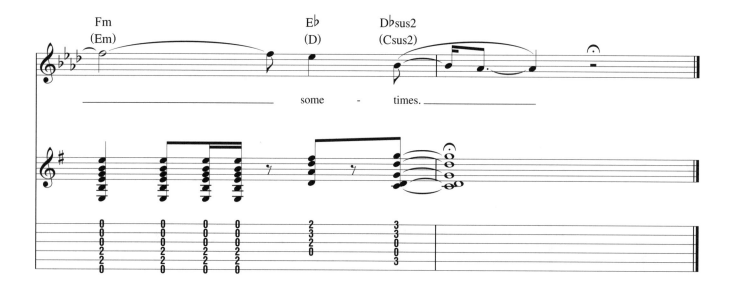

Additional Lyrics

2. But she's gotta little bit of somethin',
God, it's better than nothin'.
And in her color portrait world
She believes that she's got it all, all.
She swears the moon don't hang
Quite as high as it used to.
And she only sleeps when it's rainin'.
And she screams, and her voice is strainin'.

Time in a Bottle

Words and Music by Jim Croce

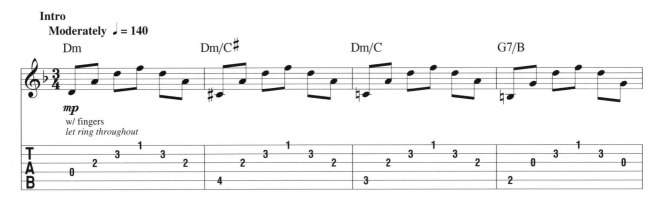

I could save ___ time in a bot - tle, _____ the

2., 3. *See additional lyrics*

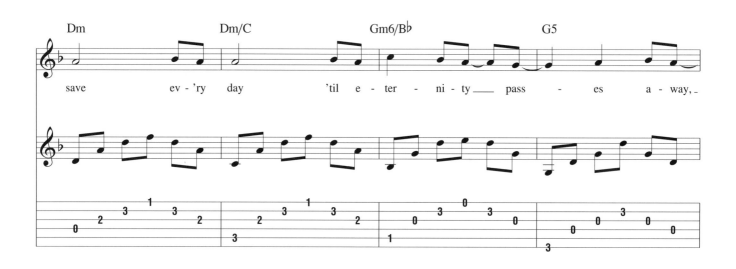

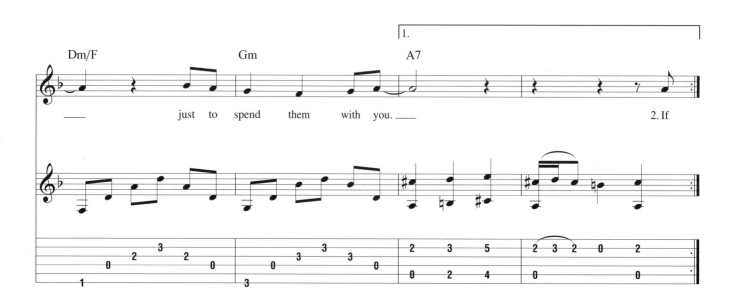

But there nev-er seems ___ to be e-nough time ___ to

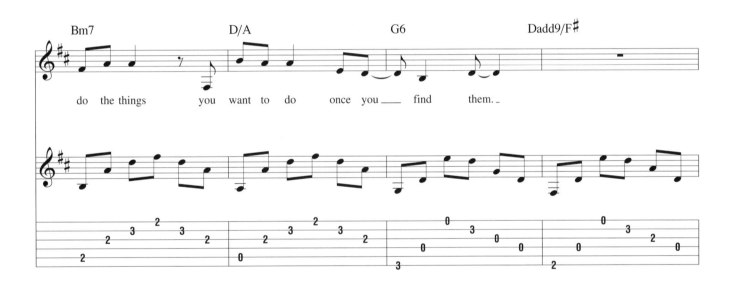

do the things you want to do once you ___ find them. _

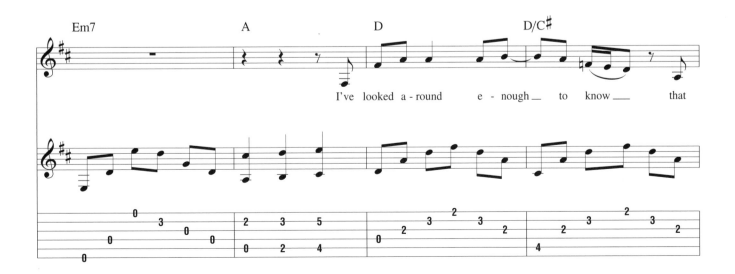

I've looked a-round e-nough ___ to know ___ that

To Coda ⊕

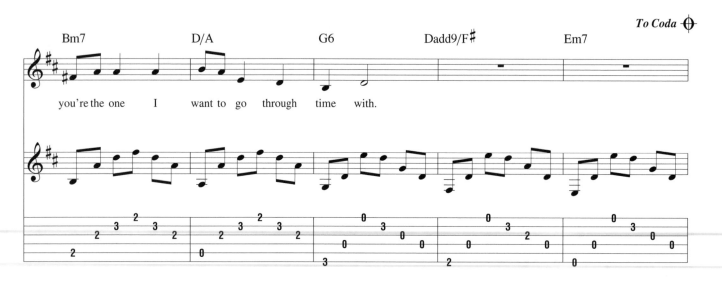

you're the one   I   want to go   through   time   with.

D.C. al Coda
(take 2nd ending)

⊕ **Coda**

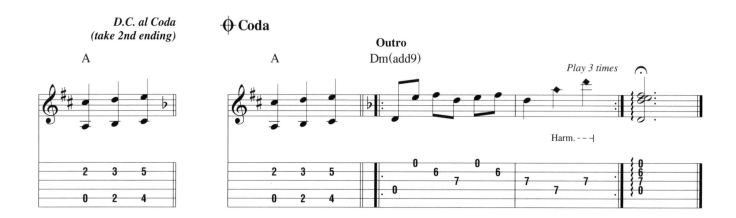

Additional Lyrics

2. If I could make days last forever,
   If words could make wishes come true,
   I'd save ev'ry day like a treasure, and then
   Again I would spend them with you.

3. If I had a box just for wishes,
   And dreams that had never come true,
   The box would be empty except for the mem'ry
   Of how they were answered by you.

To Be With You

Words and Music by Eric Martin and David Grahame

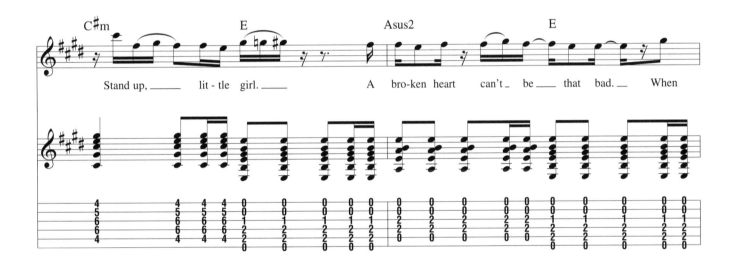

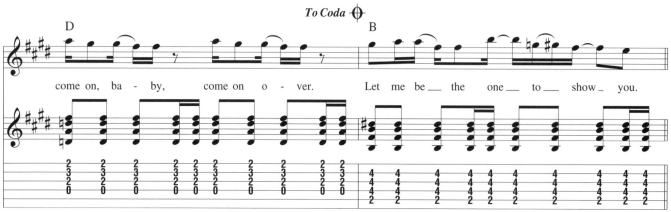

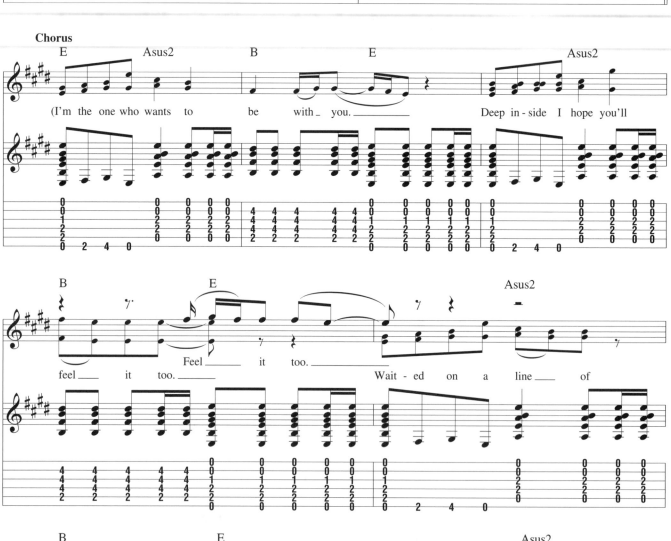

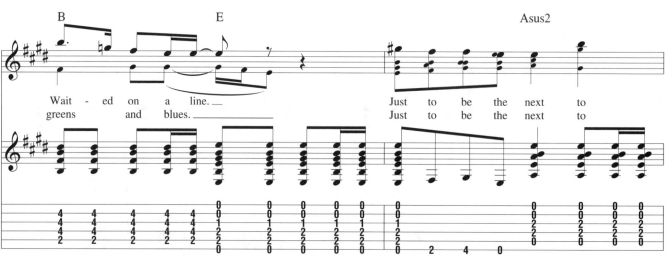

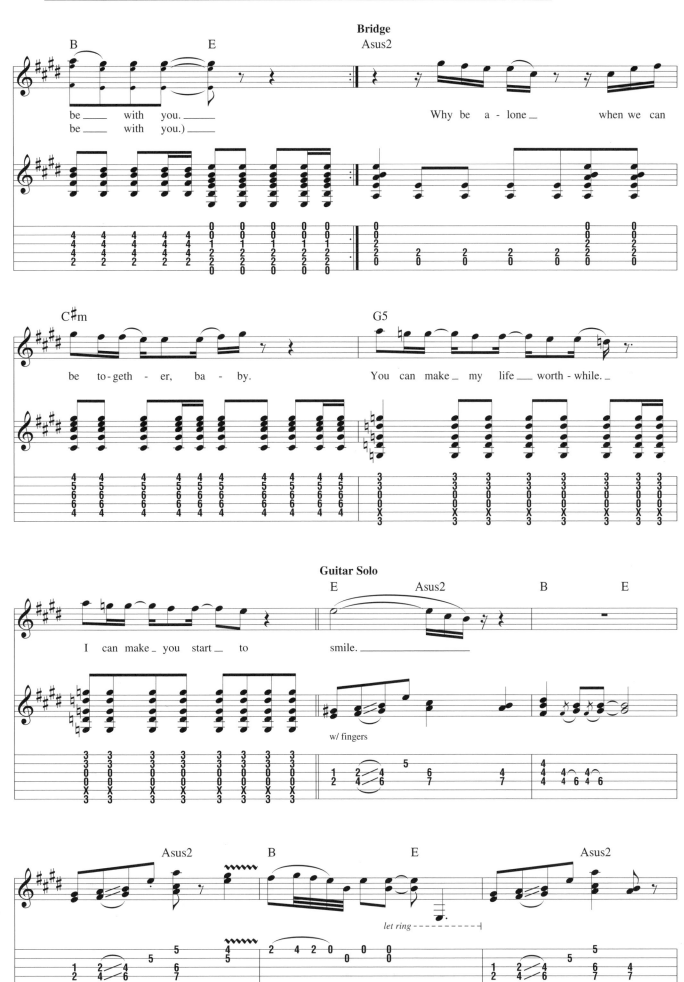

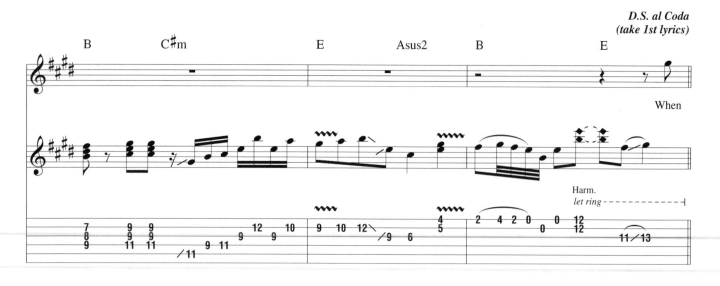

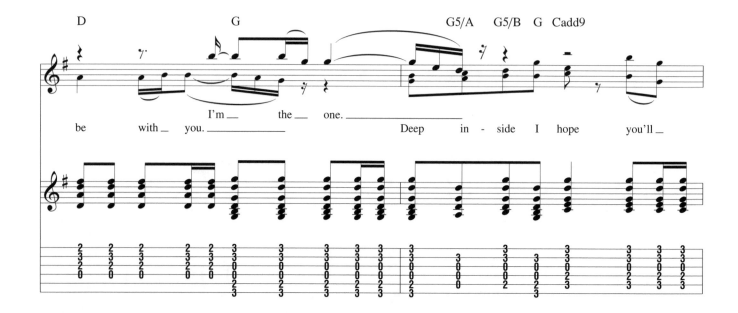

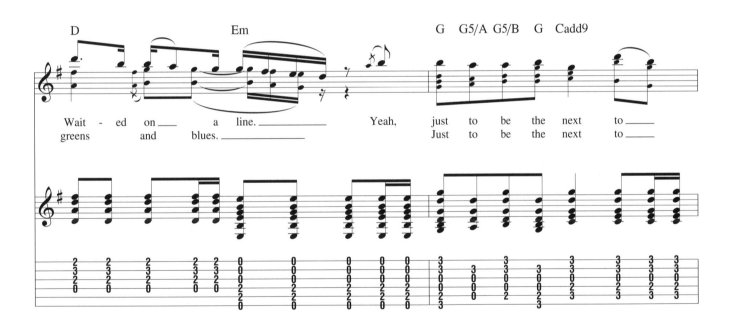

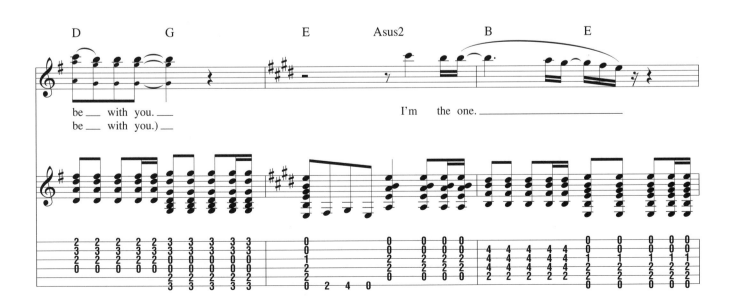

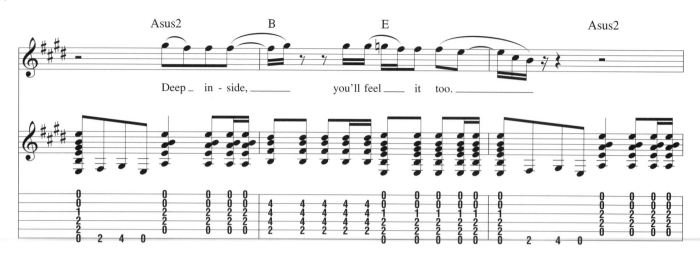

Outro

Additional Lyrics

2. Build up your confidence
   So you can be on top for once.
   Wake up. Who cares about
   Little boys that talk too much?
   I've seen it all go down.
   Your game of love was all rained out.
   So come on, baby, come on over.
   Let me be the one to hold you.

Wanted Dead or Alive

Words and Music by Jon Bon Jovi and Richie Sambora

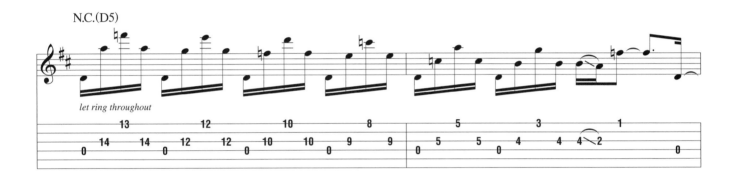

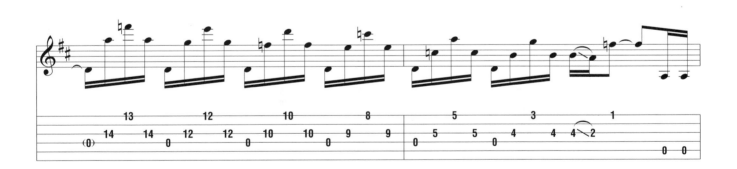

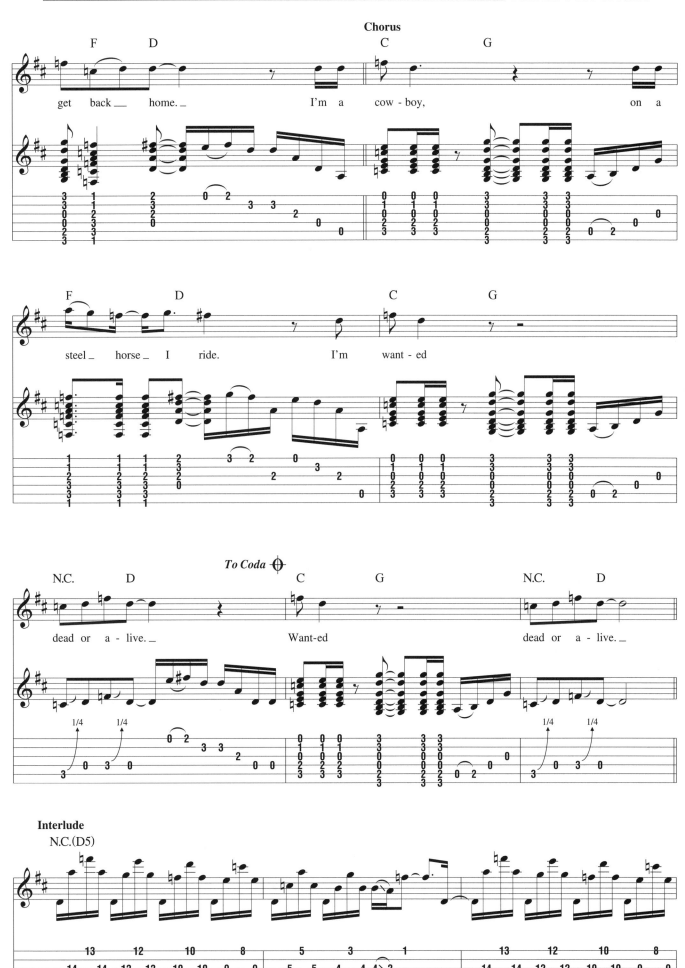

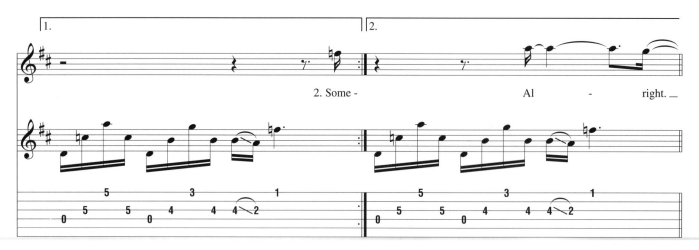

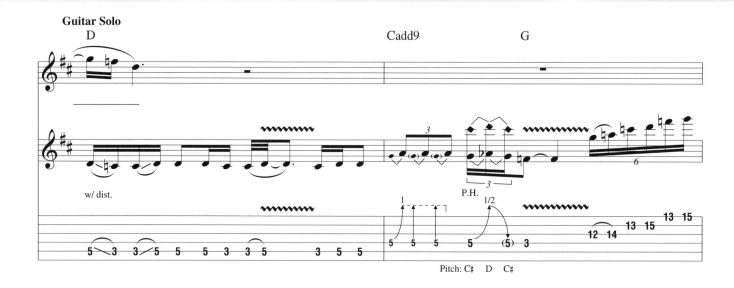

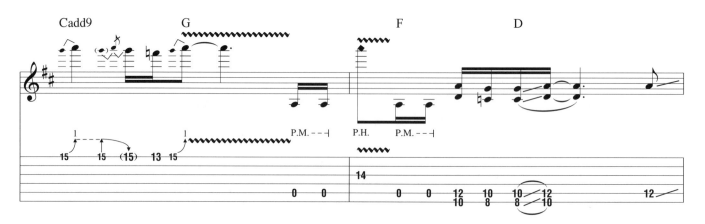

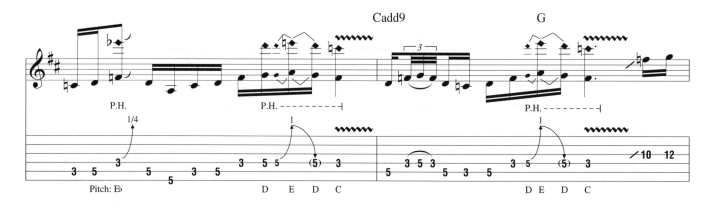

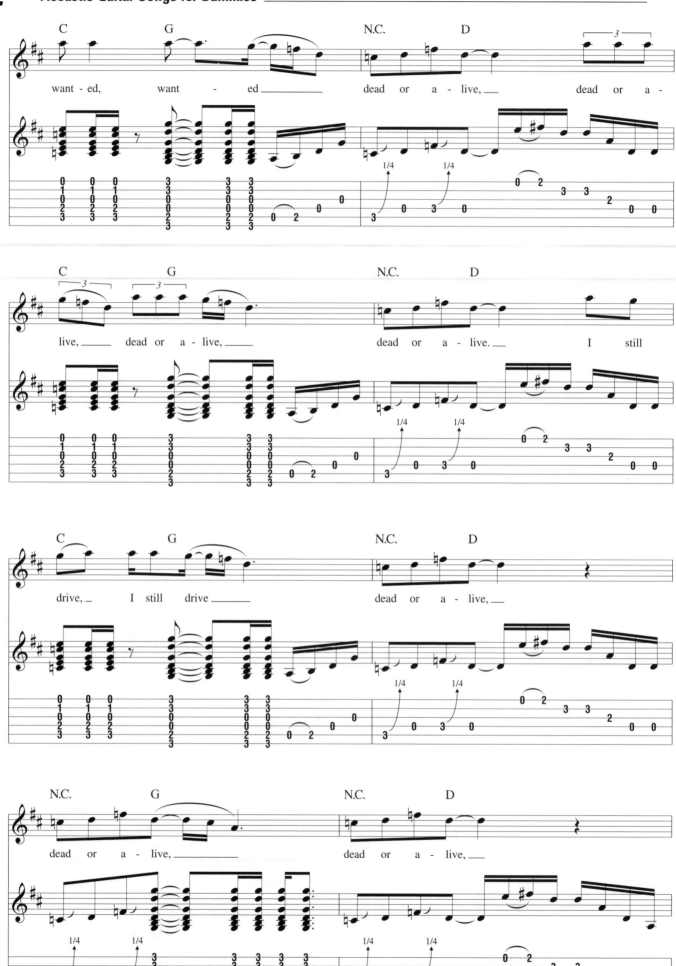

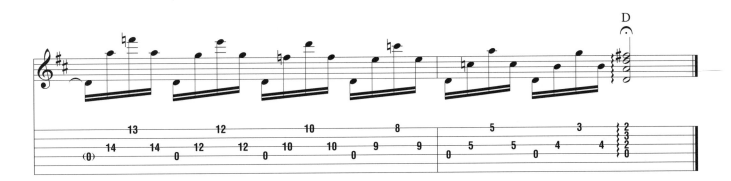

Additional Lyrics

2. Sometimes I sleep, sometimes it's not for days.
   The people I meet always go their sep'rate ways.
   Sometimes you tell the day by the bottle that you drink.
   And times when you're alone, all you do is think.

3. And I walk these streets, a loaded six-string on my back.
   I play for keeps, 'cause I might not make it back.
   I been ev'rywhere, still I'm standing tall.
   I've seen a million faces, and I've rocked them all.

When the Children Cry

Words and Music by Mike Tramp and Vito Bratta

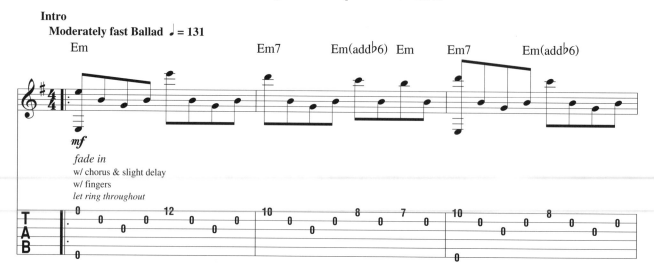

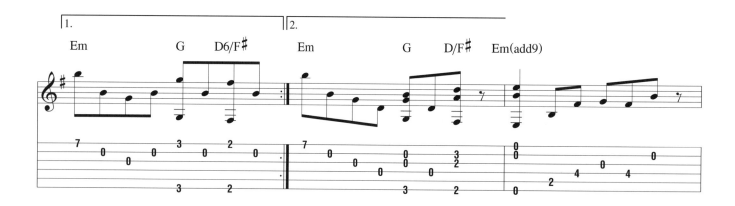

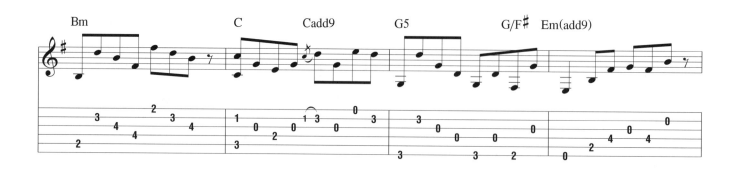

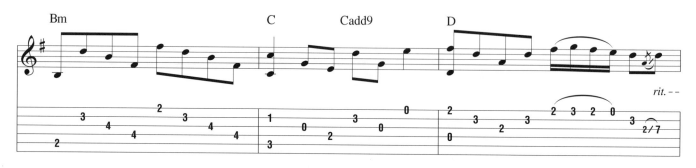

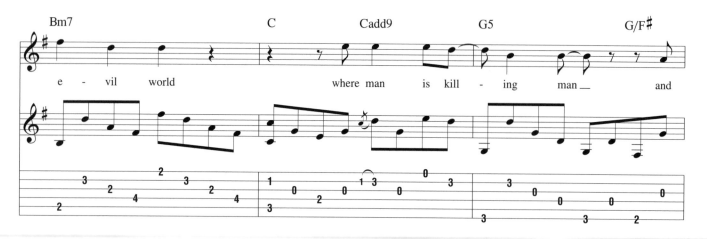

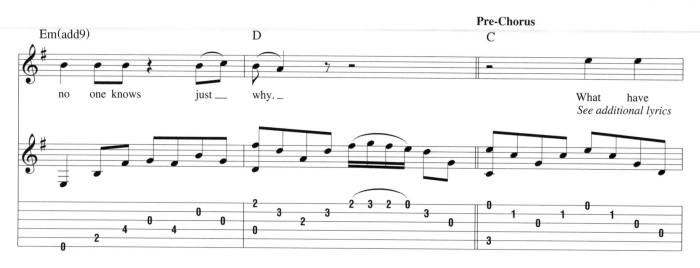

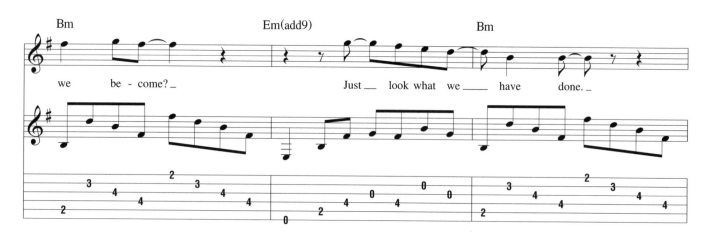

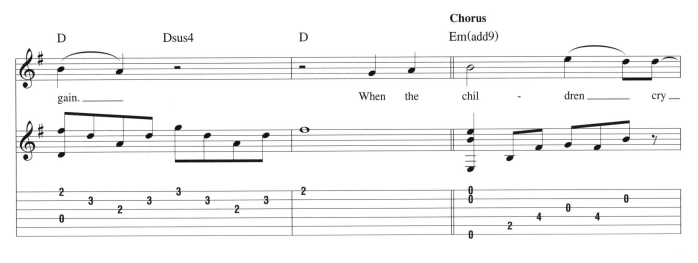

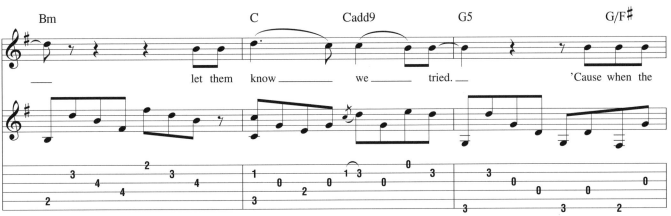

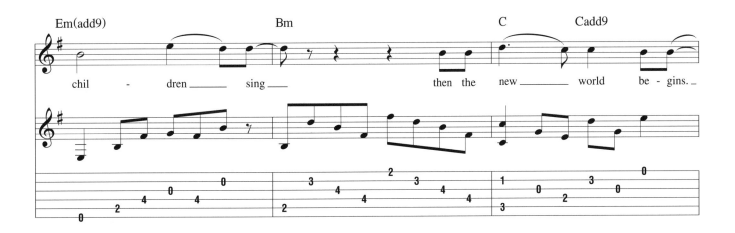

Guitar Solo

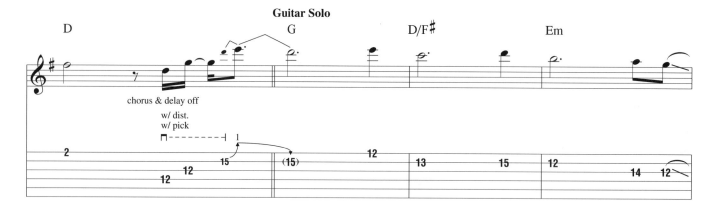

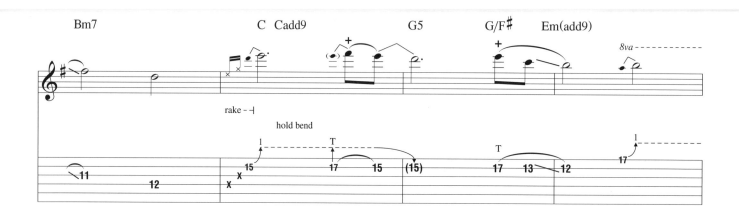

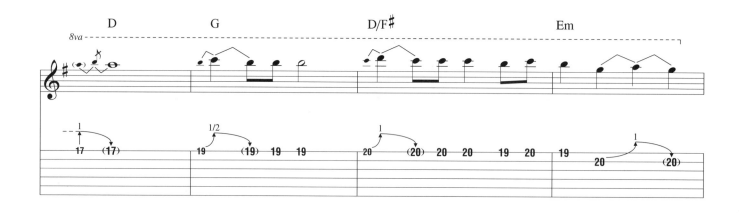

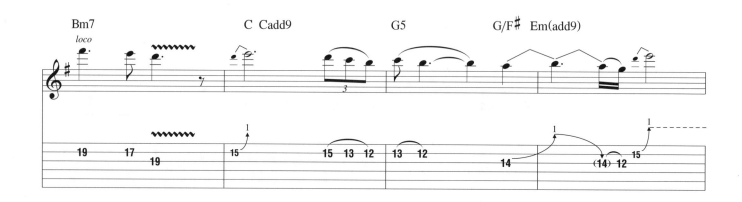

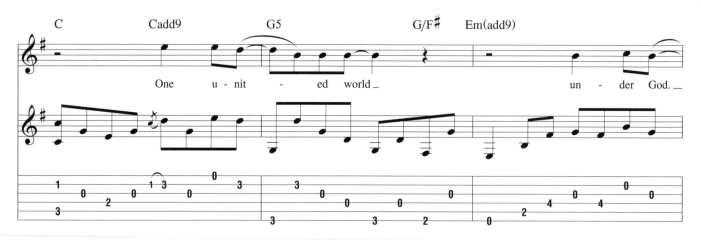

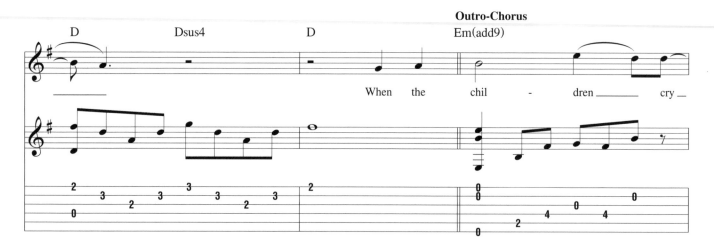

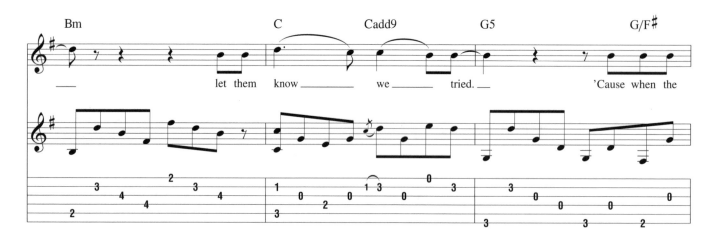

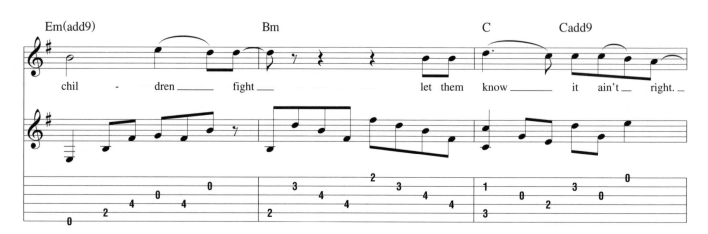

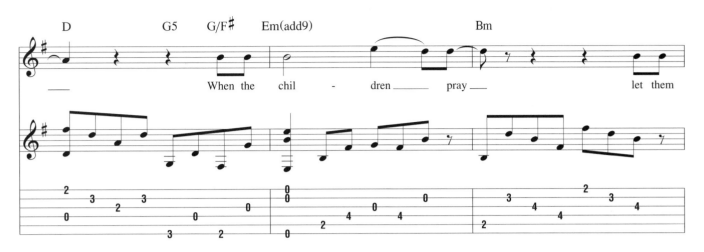

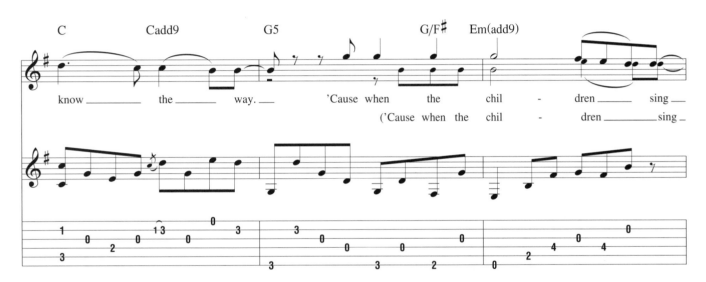

Additional Lyrics

2. Little child, you must show the way
To a better day for all the young.
'Cause you were born for all the world to see
That we all can live with love and peace.

Pre-Chorus   No more presidents.
And all the wars will end.
One united world under God.

You've Got a Friend

Words and Music by Carole King

Capo II

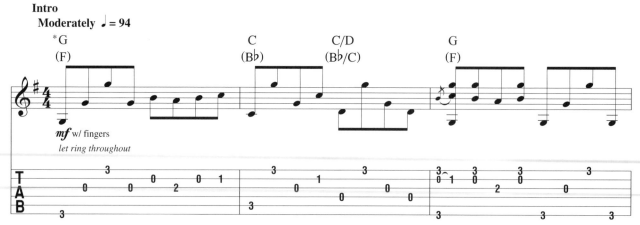

*Symbols in parentheses represent chord names respective to capoed guitar.
Symbols above reflect actual sounding chords. Capoed fret is "0" in tab.

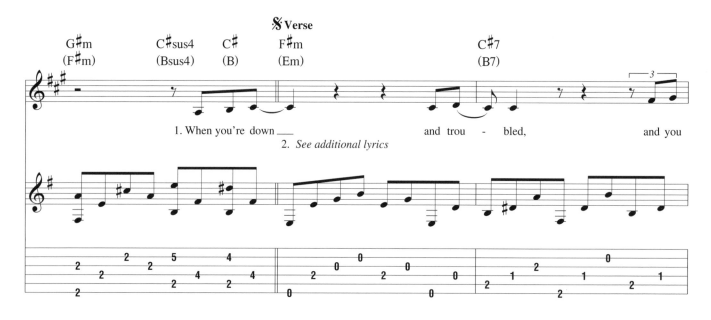

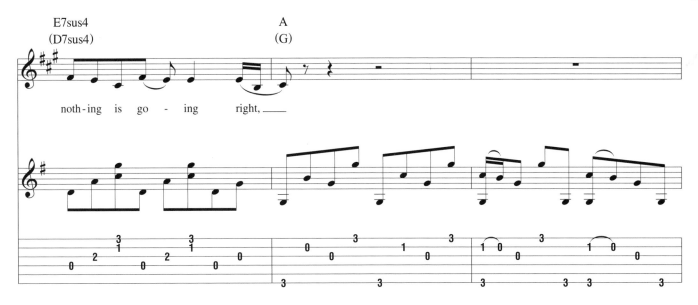

nothing is going right, ____

close your eyes ___ and think of me, and soon I will ___ be there ___

To Coda ⊕

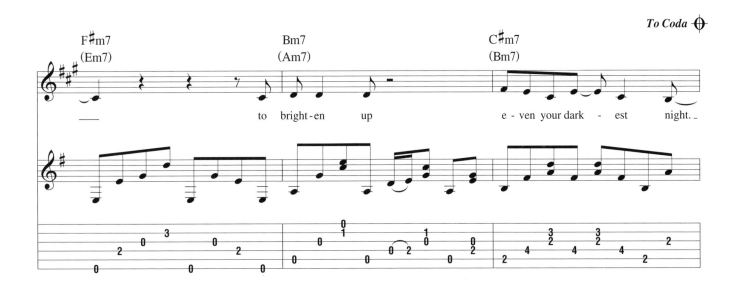

____ to brighten up even your darkest night. ___

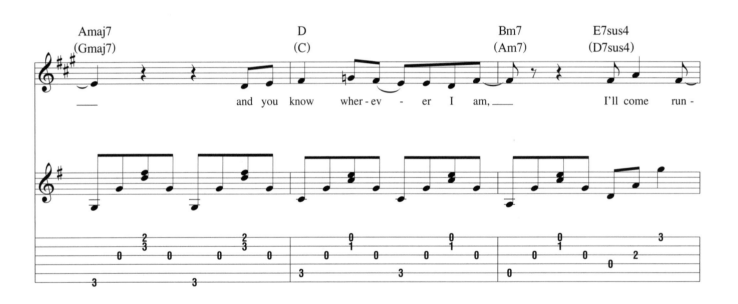

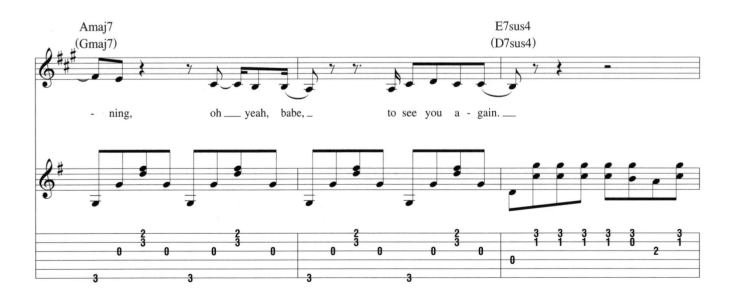

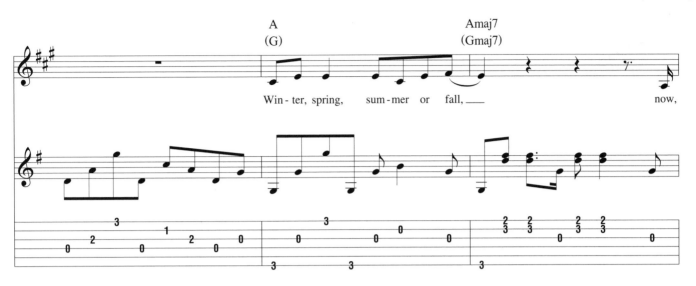

Winter, spring, sum-mer or fall, ___ now,

all you got to do_ is___ call, ___ and I'll be there, _____ yeah,_ yeah, yeah._

You've got a friend._

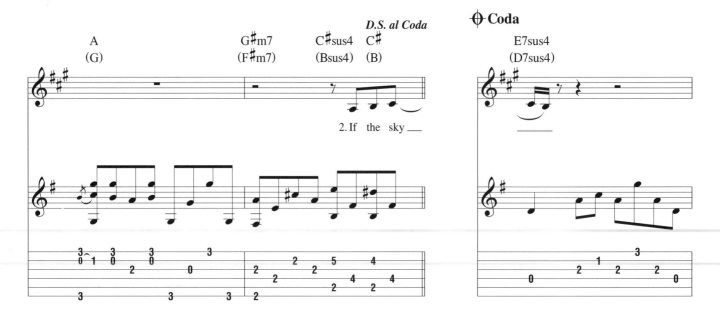

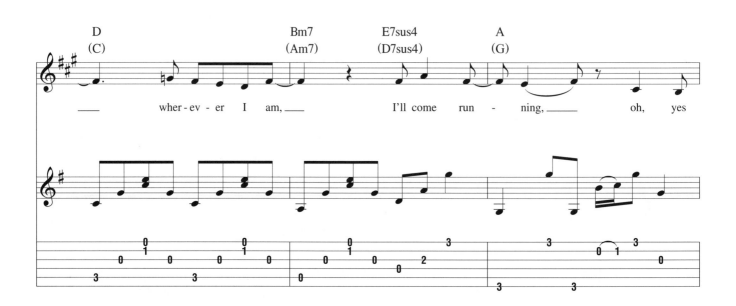

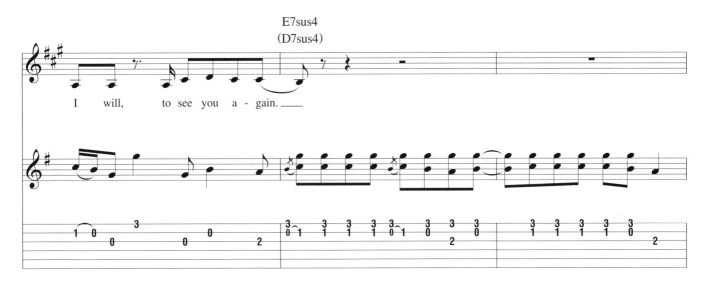

I will, to see you a-gain.____

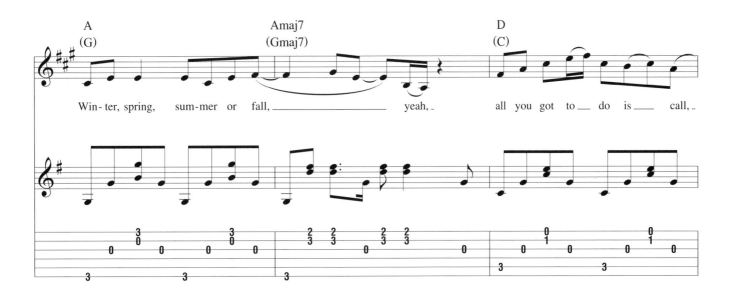

Win-ter, spring, sum-mer or fall,_____ yeah,_ all you got to __ do is __ call,_

____ and I'll be there, yeah,_ yeah, yeah.____ Hey, ain't_

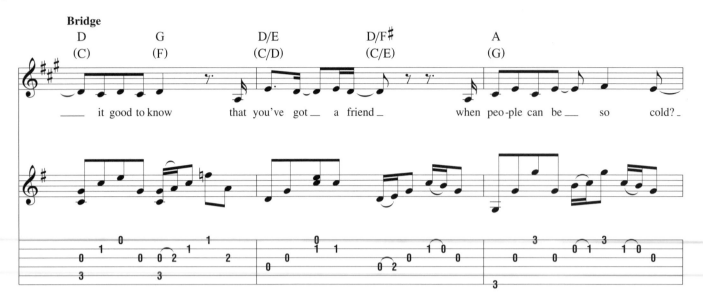

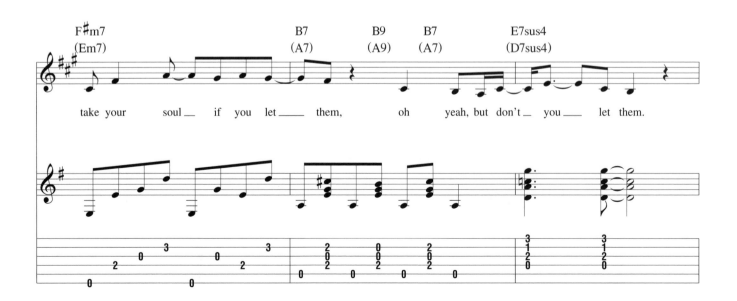

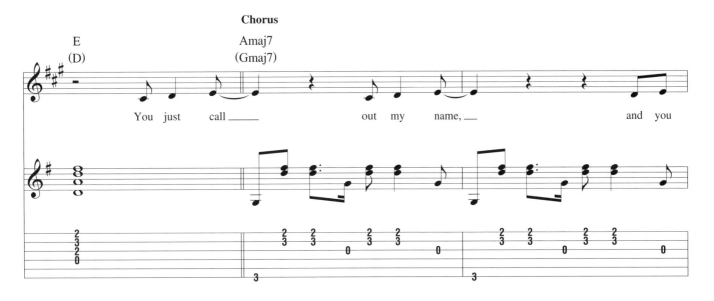

Chorus

You just call ____ out my name, ____ and you

know wher-ev - er I am, ____ I'll come run - ning ____

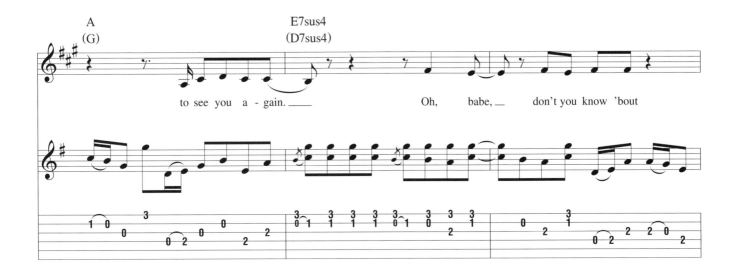

to see you a - gain. ____ Oh, babe, ____ don't you know 'bout

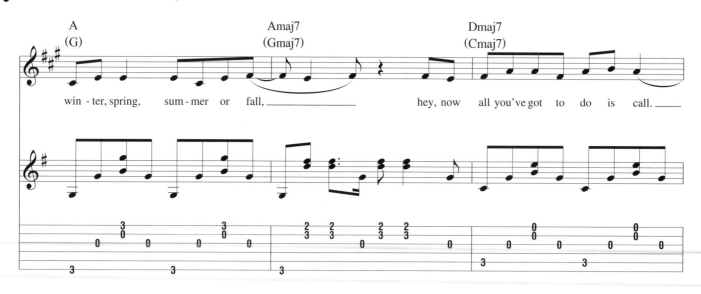

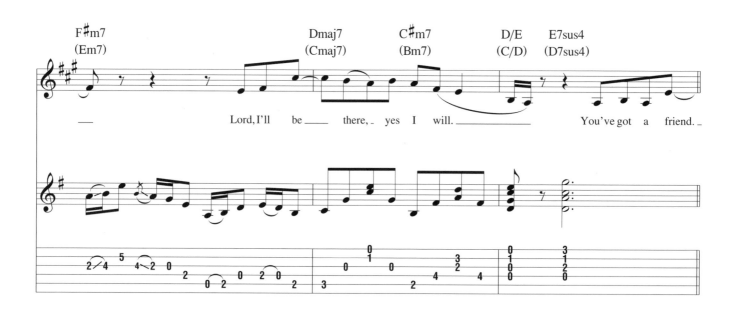

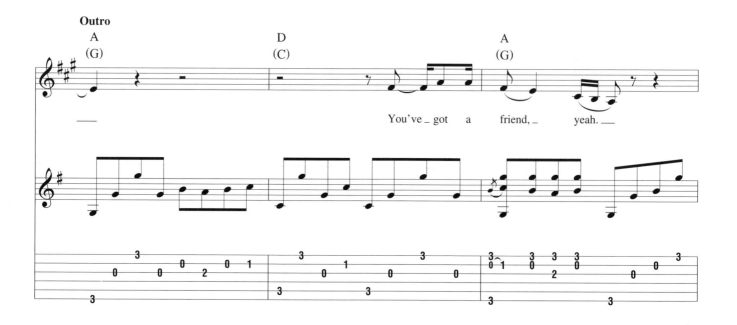

Ain't it good _ to know you've got _____ a friend? _   Ain't it good _ to know you've got a friend? _

Oh, yeah, _ yeah. ___ You've got a friend. ___

Additional Lyrics

2. If the sky above you grows dark and full of clouds,
   And that ol' North wind begins to blow;
   Keep your head together and call my name out loud.
   Soon you'll hear me knockin' at your door.

Guitar Notation Legend

Guitar Music can be notated three different ways: on a *musical staff*, in *tablature*, and in *rhythm slashes*.

RHYTHM SLASHES are written above the staff. Strum chords in the rhythm indicated. Use the chord diagrams found at the top of the first page of the transcription for the appropriate chord voicings. Round noteheads indicate single notes.

THE MUSICAL STAFF shows pitches and rhythms and is divided by bar lines into measures. Pitches are named after the first seven letters of the alphabet.

TABLATURE graphically represents the guitar fingerboard. Each horizontal line represents a a string, and each number represents a fret.

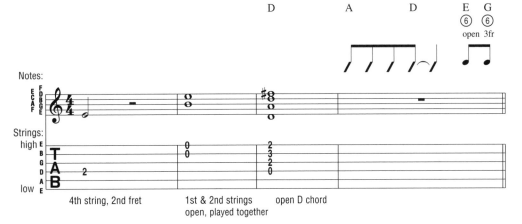

4th string, 2nd fret

1st & 2nd strings open, played together

open D chord

Definitions for Special Guitar Notation

HALF-STEP BEND: Strike the note and bend up 1/2 step.

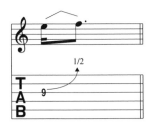

WHOLE-STEP BEND: Strike the note and bend up one step.

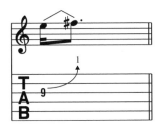

GRACE NOTE BEND: Strike the note and immediately bend up as indicated.

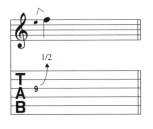

SLIGHT (MICROTONE) BEND: Strike the note and bend up 1/4 step.

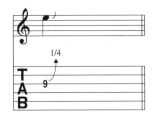

BEND AND RELEASE: Strike the note and bend up as indicated, then release back to the original note. Only the first note is struck.

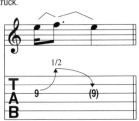

PRE-BEND: Bend the note as indicated, then strike it.

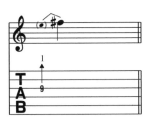

PRE-BEND AND RELEASE: Bend the note as indicated. Strike it and release the bend back to the original note.

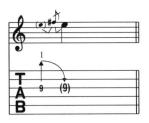

UNISON BEND: Strike the two notes simultaneously and bend the lower note up to the pitch of the higher.

VIBRATO: The string is vibrated by rapidly bending and releasing the note with the fretting hand.

WIDE VIBRATO: The pitch is varied to a greater degree by vibrating with the fretting hand.

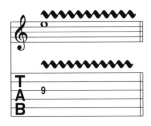

HAMMER-ON: Strike the first (lower) note with one finger, then sound the higher note (on the same string) with another finger by fretting it without picking.

PULL-OFF: Place both fingers on the notes to be sounded. Strike the first note and without picking, pull the finger off to sound the second (lower) note.

LEGATO SLIDE: Strike the first note and then slide the same fret-hand finger up or down to the second note. The second note is not struck.

SHIFT SLIDE: Same as legato slide, except the second note is struck.

TRILL: Very rapidly alternate between the notes indicated by continuously hammering on and pulling off.

TAPPING: Hammer ("tap") the fret indicated with the pick-hand index or middle finger and pull off to the note fretted by the fret hand.

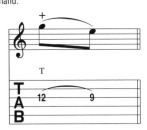

NATURAL HARMONIC: Strike the note while the fret-hand lightly touches the string directly over the fret indicated.

Harm.

12

PINCH HARMONIC: The note is fretted normally and a harmonic is produced by adding the edge of the thumb or the tip of the index finger of the pick hand to the normal pick attack.

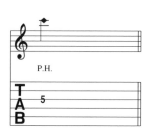

P.H.

5

HARP HARMONIC: The note is fretted normally and a harmonic is produced by gently resting the pick hand's index finger directly above the indicated fret (in parentheses) while the pick hand's thumb or pick assists by plucking the appropriate string.

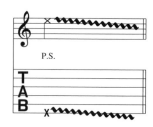

H.H.

7(19)

PICK SCRAPE: The edge of the pick is rubbed down (or up) the string, producing a scratchy sound.

P.S.

MUFFLED STRINGS: A percussive sound is produced by laying the fret hand across the string(s) without depressing, and striking them with the pick hand.

PALM MUTING: The note is partially muted by the pick hand lightly touching the string(s) just before the bridge.

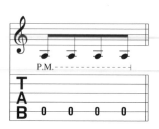

P.M.

0   0   0   0

RAKE: Drag the pick across the strings indicated with a single motion.

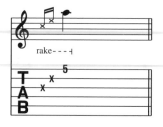

rake - - - -

5

TREMOLO PICKING: The note is picked as rapidly and continuously as possible.

5   7

ARPEGGIATE: Play the notes of the chord indicated by quickly rolling them from bottom to top.

5
5
5
5

VIBRATO BAR DIVE AND RETURN: The pitch of the note or chord is dropped a specified number of steps (in rhythm) then returned to the original pitch.

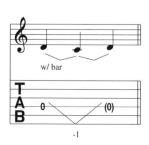

w/ bar

0   (0)

-1

VIBRATO BAR SCOOP: Depress the bar just before striking the note, then quickly release the bar.

w/ bar - - - - - - - -|

4   5   7

VIBRATO BAR DIP: Strike the note and then immediately drop a specified number of steps, then release back to the original pitch.

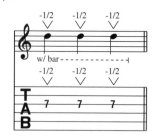

-1/2 -1/2 -1/2

w/ bar - - - - - - - - - - - -|

-1/2 -1/2 -1/2

7   7   7

Additional Musical Definitions

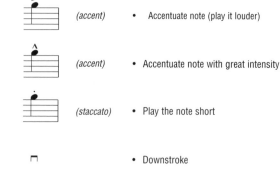

(accent) • Accentuate note (play it louder)

(accent) • Accentuate note with great intensity

(staccato) • Play the note short

• Downstroke

∨ • Upstroke

D.S. al Coda • Go back to the sign (𝄋), then play until the measure marked "*To Coda*," then skip to the section labelled "*Coda*."

D.C. al Fine • Go back to the beginning of the song and play until the measure marked "*Fine*" (end).

Rhy. Fig. • Label used to recall a recurring accompaniment pattern (usually chordal).

Riff • Label used to recall composed, melodic lines (usually single notes) which recur.

Fill • Label used to identify a brief melodic figure which is to be inserted into the arrangement.

Rhy. Fill • A chordal version of a Fill.

tacet • Instrument is silent (drops out).

 • Repeat measures between signs.

1.   2.

• When a repeated section has different endings, play the first ending only the first time and the second ending only the second time.

NOTE: Tablature numbers in parentheses mean:
1. The note is being sustained over a system (note in standard notation is tied), or
2. The note is sustained, but a new articulation (such as a hammer-on, pull-off, slide or vibrato begins), or
3. The note is a barely audible "ghost" note (note in standard notation is also in parentheses).

Chord Chart

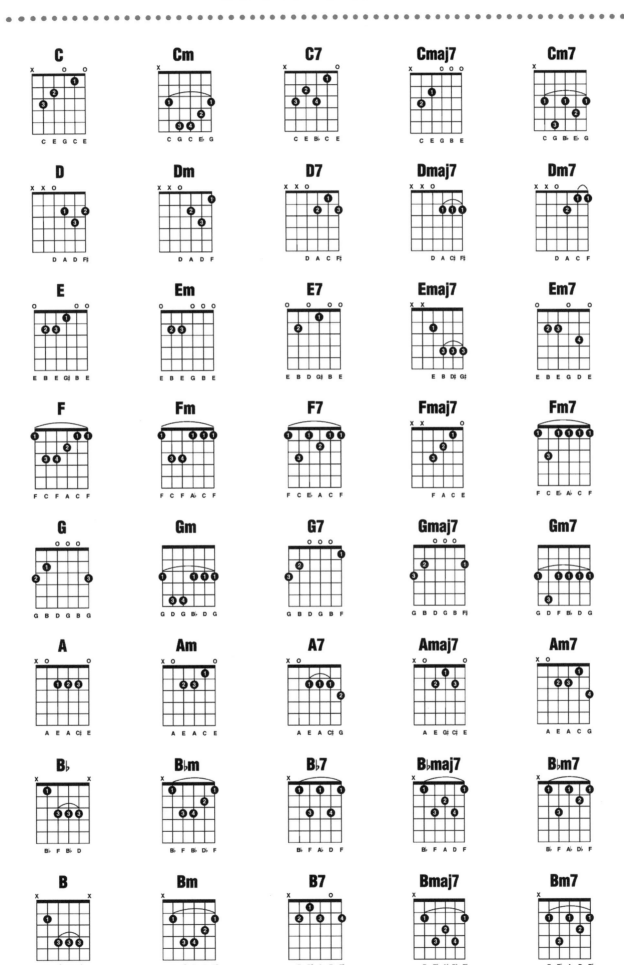

HAL·LEONARD GUITAR PLAY·ALONG

This series will help you play your favorite songs quickly and easily. Just follow the tab and listen to the CD to hear how the guitar should sound, and then play along using the separate backing tracks. Mac or PC users can also slow down the tempo without changing pitch by using the CD in their computer. The melody and lyrics are included in the book so that you can sing or simply follow along.

INCLUDES TAB

VOL. 1 – ROCK GUITAR   00699570 / $14.95
Day Tripper • Message in a Bottle • Refugee • Shattered • Sunshine of Your Love • Takin' Care of Business • Tush • Walk This Way.

VOL. 2 – ACOUSTIC   00699569 / $14.95
Angie • Behind Blue Eyes • Best of My Love • Blackbird • Dust in the Wind • Layla • Night Moves • Yesterday.

VOL. 3 – HARD ROCK   00699573 / $14.95
Crazy Train • Iron Man • Living After Midnight • Rock You like a Hurricane • Round and Round • Smoke on the Water • Sweet Child O' Mine • You Really Got Me.

VOL. 4 – POP/ROCK   00699571 / $14.95
Breakdown • Crazy Little Thing Called Love • Hit Me with Your Best Shot • I Want You to Want Me • Lights • R.O.C.K. in the U.S.A. • Summer of '69 • What I Like About You.

VOL. 5 – MODERN ROCK   00699574 / $14.95
Aerials • Alive • Bother • Chop Suey! • Control • Last Resort • Take a Look Around (Theme from *M:I-2*) • Wish You Were Here.

VOL. 6 – '90S ROCK   00699572 / $14.95
Are You Gonna Go My Way • Come Out and Play • I'll Stick Around • Know Your Enemy • Man in the Box • Outshined • Smells Like Teen Spirit • Under the Bridge.

VOL. 7 – BLUES GUITAR   00699575 / $14.95
All Your Love (I Miss Loving) • Born Under a Bad Sign • Hide Away • I'm Tore Down • I'm Your Hoochie Coochie Man • Pride and Joy • Sweet Home Chicago • The Thrill Is Gone.

VOL. 8 – ROCK   00699585 / $14.95
All Right Now • Black Magic Woman • Get Back • Hey Joe • Layla • Love Me Two Times • Won't Get Fooled Again • You Really Got Me.

VOL. 9 – PUNK ROCK   00699576 / $14.95
All the Small Things • Fat Lip • Flavor of the Weak • I Feel So • Lifestyles of the Rich and Famous • Say It Ain't So • Self Esteem • (So) Tired of Waiting for You.

VOL. 10 – ACOUSTIC   00699586 / $14.95
Here Comes the Sun • Landslide • The Magic Bus • Norwegian Wood (This Bird Has Flown) • Pink Houses • Space Oddity • Tangled Up in Blue • Tears in Heaven.

VOL. 11 – EARLY ROCK   00699579 / $14.95
Fun, Fun, Fun • Hound Dog • Louie, Louie • No Particular Place to Go • Oh, Pretty Woman • Rock Around the Clock • Under the Boardwalk • Wild Thing.

VOL. 12 – POP/ROCK   00699587 / $14.95
867-5309/Jenny • Every Breath You Take • Money for Nothing • Rebel, Rebel • Run to You • Ticket to Ride • Wonderful Tonight • You Give Love a Bad Name.

VOL. 13 – FOLK ROCK   00699581 / $14.95
Annie's Song • Leaving on a Jet Plane • Suite: Judy Blue Eyes • This Land Is Your Land • Time in a Bottle • Turn! Turn! Turn! • You've Got a Friend • You've Got to Hide Your Love Away.

VOL. 14 – BLUES ROCK   00699582 / $14.95
Blue on Black • Crossfire • Cross Road Blues (Crossroads) • The House Is Rockin' • La Grange • Move It on Over • Roadhouse Blues • Statesboro Blues.

VOL. 15 – R&B   00699583 / $14.95
Ain't Too Proud to Beg • Brick House • Get Ready • I Can't Help Myself • I Got You (I Feel Good) • I Heard It Through the Grapevine • My Girl • Shining Star.

VOL. 16 – JAZZ   00699584 / $14.95
All Blues • Bluesette • Footprints • How Insensitive • Misty • Satin Doll • Stella by Starlight • Tenor Madness.

VOL. 17 – COUNTRY   00699588 / $14.95
Amie • Boot Scootin' Boogie • Chattahoochee • Folsom Prison Blues • Friends in Low Places • Forever and Ever, Amen • T-R-O-U-B-L-E • Workin' Man Blues.

VOL. 18 – ACOUSTIC ROCK   00699577 / $14.95
About a Girl • Breaking the Girl • Drive • Iris • More Than Words • Patience • Silent Lucidity • 3 AM.

VOL. 19 – SOUL   00699578 / $14.95
Get Up (I Feel Like Being) a Sex Machine • Green Onions • In the Midnight Hour • Knock on Wood • Mustang Sally • Respect • (Sittin' On) The Dock of the Bay • Soul Man.

VOL. 20 – ROCKABILLY   00699580 / $14.95
Be-Bop-A-Lula • Blue Suede Shoes • Hello Mary Lou • Little Sister • Mystery Train • Rock This Town • Stray Cat Strut • That'll Be the Day.

VOL. 21 – YULETIDE   00699602 / $14.95
Angels We Have Heard on High • Away in a Manger • Deck the Hall • The First Noel • Go, Tell It on the Mountain • Jingle Bells • Joy to the World • O Little Town of Bethlehem.

VOL. 22 – CHRISTMAS   00699600 / $14.95
The Christmas Song • Frosty the Snow Man • Happy Xmas • Here Comes Santa Claus • Jingle-Bell Rock • Merry Christmas, Darling • Rudolph the Red-Nosed Reindeer • Silver Bells.

VOL. 23 – SURF   00699635 / $14.95
Let's Go Trippin' • Out of Limits • Penetration • Pipeline • Surf City • Surfin' U.S.A. • Walk Don't Run • The Wedge.

VOL. 24 – ERIC CLAPTON   00699649 / $14.95
Badge • Bell Bottom Blues • Change the World • Cocaine • Key to the Highway • Lay Down Sally • White Room • Wonderful Tonight.

VOL. 25 – LENNON & McCARTNEY   00699642 / $14.95
Back in the U.S.S.R. • Drive My Car • Get Back • A Hard Day's Night • I Feel Fine • Paperback Writer • Revolution • Ticket to Ride.

VOL. 26 – ELVIS PRESLEY   00699643 / $14.95
All Shook Up • Blue Suede Shoes • Don't Be Cruel • Heartbreak Hotel • Hound Dog • Jailhouse Rock • Little Sister • Mystery Train.

VOL. 27 – DAVID LEE ROTH   00699645 / $14.95
Ain't Talkin' 'Bout Love • Dance the Night Away • Hot for Teacher • Just Like Paradise • A Lil' Ain't Enough • Runnin' with the Devil • Unchained • Yankee Rose.

VOL. 28 – GREG KOCH   00699646 / $14.95
Chief's Blues • Death of a Bassman • Dylan the Villain • The Grip • Holy Grail • Spank It • Tonus Diabolicus • Zoiks.

VOL. 29 – BOB SEGER   00699647 / $14.95
Against the Wind • Betty Lou's Gettin' Out Tonight • Hollywood Nights • Mainstreet • Night Moves • Old Time Rock & Roll • Rock and Roll Never Forgets • Still the Same.

VOL. 30 – KISS   00699644 / $14.95
Cold Gin • Detroit Rock City • Deuce • Firehouse • Heaven's on Fire • Love Gun • Rock and Roll All Nite • Shock Me.

VOL. 31 – CHRISTMAS HITS   00699652 / $14.95
Blue Christmas • Do You Hear What I Hear • Happy Holiday • I Saw Mommy Kissing Santa Claus • I'll Be Home for Christmas • Let It Snow! Let It Snow! Let It Snow! • Little Saint Nick • Snowfall.

VOL. 32 – THE OFFSPRING   00699653 / $14.95
Bad Habit • Come Out and Play • Gone Away • Gotta Get Away • Hit That • The Kids Aren't Alright • Pretty Fly (For a White Guy) • Self Esteem.

VOL. 33 – ACOUSTIC CLASSICS   00699656 / $14.95
Across the Universe • Babe, I'm Gonna Leave You • Crazy on You • Heart of Gold • Hotel California • I'd Love to Change the World • Thick As a Brick • Wanted Dead or Alive.

VOL. 34 – CLASSIC ROCK   00699658 / $14.95
Aqualung • Born to Be Wild • The Boys Are Back in Town • Brown Eyed Girl • Reeling in the Years • Rock'n Me • Rocky Mountain Way • Sweet Emotion.

VOL. 35 – HAIR METAL   00699660 / $14.95
Decadence Dance • Don't Treat Me Bad • Down Boys • Seventeen • Shake Me • Up All Night • Wait • Talk Dirty to Me.

VOL. 36 – SOUTHERN ROCK   00699661 / $14.95
Can't You See • Flirtin' with Disaster • Hold on Loosely • Jessica • Mississippi Queen • Ramblin' Man • Sweet Home Alabama • What's Your Name.

VOL. 37 – ACOUSTIC METAL   00699662 / $14.95
Every Rose Has Its Thorn • Fly to the Angels • Hole Hearted • Love Is on the Way • Love of a Lifetime • Signs • To Be with You • When the Children Cry.

VOL. 38 – BLUES   00699663 / $14.95
Boom Boom • Cold Shot • Crosscut Saw • Everyday I Have the Blues • Frosty • Further On up the Road • Killing Floor • Texas Flood.

VOL. 39 – '80S METAL   00699664 / $14.95
Bark at the Moon • Big City Nights • Breaking the Chains • Cult of Personality • Lay It Down • Living on a Prayer • Panama • Smokin' in the Boys Room.

VOL. 40 – INCUBUS   00699668 / $14.95
Are You In? • Drive • Megalomaniac • Nice to Know You • Pardon Me • Stellar • Talk Shows on Mute • Wish You Were Here.

VOL. 41 – ERIC CLAPTON   00699669 / $14.95
After Midnight • Can't Find My Way Home • Forever Man • I Shot the Sheriff • I'm Tore Down • Pretending • Running on Faith • Tears in Heaven.

VOL. 42 – CHART HITS   00699670 / $14.95
Are You Gonna Be My Girl • Heaven • Here Without You • I Believe in a Thing Called Love • Just Like You • Last Train Home • This Love • Until the Day I Die.

VOL. 43 – LYNYRD SKYNYRD   00699681 / $14.95
Don't Ask Me No Questions • Free Bird • Gimme Three Steps • I Know a Little • Saturday Night Special • Sweet Home Alabama • That Smell • You Got That Right.

VOL. 44 – JAZZ   00699689 / $14.95
I Remember You • I'll Remember April • Impressions • In a Mellow Tone • Moonlight in Vermont • On a Slow Boat to China • Things Ain't What They Used to Be • Yesterdays.

VOL. 46 – MAINSTREAM ROCK   00699722 / $14.95
Just a Girl • Keep Away • Kryptonite • Lightning Crashes • 1979 • One Step Closer • Scar Tissue • Torn.

VOL. 47 – HENDRIX SMASH HITS   00699723/ $16.95
All Along the Watchtower • Can You See Me? • Crosstown Traffic • Fire • Foxey Lady • Hey Joe • Manic Depression • Purple Haze • Red House • Remember • Stone Free • The Wind Cries Mary.

VOL. 48 – AEROSMITH CLASSICS   00699724 / $14.95
Back in the Saddle • Draw the Line • Dream On • Last Child • Mama Kin • Same Old Song & Dance • Sweet Emotion • Walk This Way.

VOL. 50 – NÜ METAL   00699726 / $14.95
Duality • Here to Stay • In the End • Judith • Nookie • So Cold • Toxicity • Whatever.

VOL. 51 – ALTERNATIVE '90S   00699727 / $14.95
Alive • Cherub Rock • Come As You Are • Give It Away • Jane Says • No Excuses • No Rain • Santeria.

VOL. 56 – FOO FIGHTERS   00699749 / $14.95
All My Life • Best of You • DOA • I'll Stick Around • Learn to Fly • Monkey Wrench • My Hero • This Is a Call.

VOL. 57 – SYSTEM OF A DOWN   00699751 / $14.95
Aerials • B.Y.O.B. • Chop Suey! • Innervision • Question! • Spiders • Sugar • Toxicity.

Prices, contents, and availability subject to change without notice.